D0463753

ELISHA

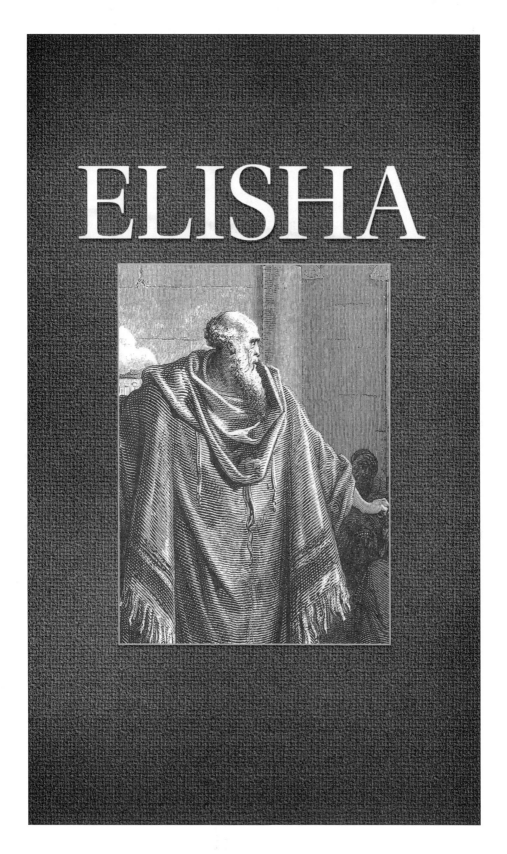

CHARACTERS OF THE BIBLE SERIES
BY JIMMY SWAGGART:

Abraham

David

Elijah

Elisha

Great Women of the Bible, New Testament

Great Women of the Bible, Old Testament

Joseph

Noah

Paul, The Apostle

ELISHA

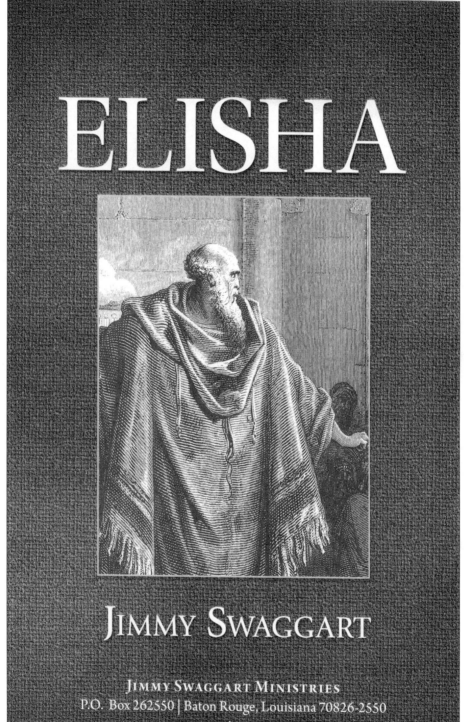

JIMMY SWAGGART

JIMMY SWAGGART MINISTRIES
P.O. Box 262550 | Baton Rouge, Louisiana 70826-2550
www.jsm.org

ISBN 978-1-941403-30-3

09-134 | COPYRIGHT © 2016 Jimmy Swaggart Ministries®

16 17 18 19 20 21 22 23 24 25 / EBM / 10 9 8 7 6 5 4 3 2 1

All rights reserved. Printed and bound in U.S.A.

No part of this publication may be reproduced in any form or
by any means without the publisher's prior written permission.

TABLE OF CONTENTS

ELISHA

INTRODUCTION

INTRODUCTION

IT IS AMAZING THAT two of the greatest prophets who ever lived were sent to the northern kingdom of Israel, which was an ungodly kingdom. Of course, I speak of Elijah and his protégé, Elisha. No human beings in history, other than our Lord, saw miracles as did Elijah and Elisha.

It was His way of trying to pull Israel back to the Cross, one might say. In other words, the Lord did everything that could be done but, sadly and regrettably, to no avail.

We will find that the Lord chose both men, with man having nothing to do with that choice. That has always been God's method and is His method presently. Unfortunately, the modern church is filled with individuals who are man-called and not God-called. As such, nothing but harm is brought about for the kingdom of God.

THE PROPHETS

If we date the ministry of Elisha from his call, it extended through the reigns of Ahab, Ahaziah, Jehoram, Jehu, Jehoaz, and Jehoash, a period, incidentally, of more than 50 years.

ELIJAH'S PROPHETIC MANTLE

The ministry of Elisha was not so much an anointing (I Ki. 19:16) as an ordination by investiture with Elijah's prophetic mantle. Until Elijah's translation, Elisha, one might say, remained the servant of Elijah (I Ki. 19:21; II Ki. 3:11).

THE DOUBLE PORTION

It was not until Elisha, at his request, received the double portion of the anointing of the Holy Spirit from his master, Elijah, that his work as a prophet actually began. In some ways, his experience is reminiscent of the replacement of Moses by Joshua as leader of Israel.

Until the Spirit of God came upon him, which it did at the translation of Elijah, Elisha served, as already stated, as little more than a servant to Elijah. However, no doubt, the Holy Spirit was helping to train him those years for the ministry that lay ahead.

As we study the account of this man that is given in the Bible, we will see, I think, the power of God in operation as seldom experienced on this earth. Truly, Elisha received a double portion of that which his master Elijah had. The Lord greatly and grandly honored his faith, and He did it in a way that glorified the Lord of heaven.

As we study this prophet, hopefully, we will see ourselves, but most of all, hopefully, we will see our Lord and our Saviour, the Lord Jesus Christ.

There are people, almost everywhere,
Whose hearts are all aflame,
With the fire that fell at Pentecost,
Which made them all acclaim;
It is burning now within my heart,
All glory to His name!

Though these people may not learned be,
Nor boast of worldly fame,
They have all received their Pentecost,
Through faith in Jesus' name;
And are telling now both far and wide,
His power is yet the same.

They were gathered in the temple place,
All praying in His name,
They were baptized with the Holy Spirit,
And power for service came;
Now what He did for them that day,
He'll do for you the same.

Come, my brother, receive this blessing,
That will cleanse your heart from sin,
That will start the joy bells ringing,
And will keep the soul aflame ;
It is burning now within my heart,
Oh glory to His name!

ELISHA

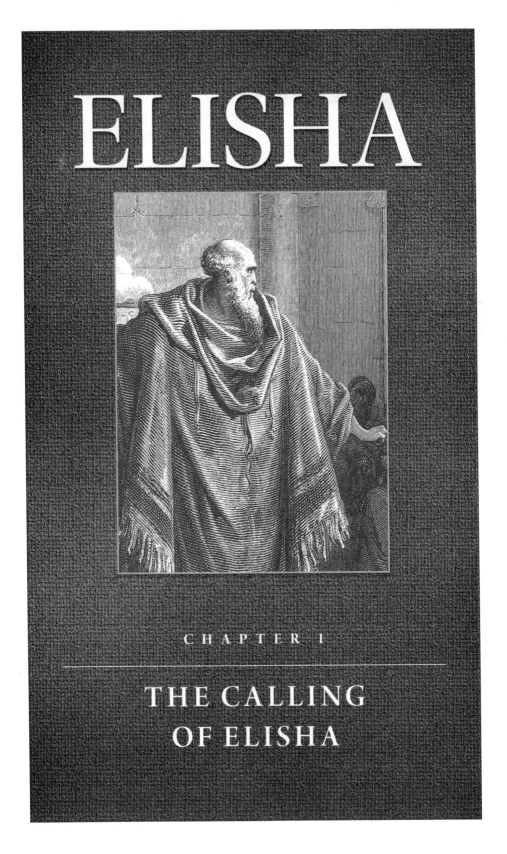

CHAPTER 1

THE CALLING
OF ELISHA

THE CALLING OF ELISHA

"SO HE DEPARTED THENCE, and found Elisha the son of Shaphat, who was plowing with twelve yoke of oxen before him, and he with the twelfth: and Elijah passed by him, and cast his mantle upon him. And he left the oxen, and ran after Elijah, and said, Let me, I pray you, kiss my father and my mother, and then I will follow you. And he said unto him, Go back again: for what have I done to you? And he returned back from him, and took a yoke of oxen, and killed them, and boiled their flesh with the instruments of the oxen, and gave unto the people, and they did eat. Then he arose, and went after Elijah, and ministered unto him" (I Ki. 19:19-21).

ELISHA

Now we are introduced to Elisha, but in a most unusual way.

Nearby was a school of the prophets, but upon none of these did Elijah cast his mantle; however, guided by the Holy Spirit, he cast it upon a plowboy. How different are God's thoughts from man's! The Lord chose Amos, who was a gatherer of sycamore fruit; Paul, who was not one of the Twelve; and Moody, who was uneducated. Through men like these, He rebukes and refreshes the "official ministry."

A greater readiness to obey the prophetic summons, Elisha could not well have shown. He only asked that he be allowed to go bid his parents farewell, which was the right thing for him to do, and to which Elijah readily acquiesced.

Verse 21 presents a symbolic act that was expressive of Elisha's entire renunciation of his secular calling. This was a farewell, not a religious feast. He was, in essence, saying that he would not be back. He was obeying the call of God to the fullest, even as he should have done.

THE CALLING OF ELISHA

Elijah left Horeb and found one of the 7,000 mentioned by the Lord, i.e., Elisha.

As is obvious, the Lord chose Elisha to take the place of Elijah, at least when Elijah would be translated. Of course, it is very doubtful that the great prophet then knew or understood that he, in fact, would not die but would be translated. Actually, it would be some 10 years before this great occasion.

From the words *"found Elisha,"* it is implied that Elijah didn't really even know this young man and had to search him out. That should not have been difficult as the Lord had told him, *"And Elisha the son of Shaphat of Abel-meholah shall you anoint to be prophet in your room"* (I Ki. 19:16).

So, the prophet found Elisha and *"cast his mantle upon him,"* even though he was then plowing with a yoke of oxen.

What we're seeing here is God's way as it regards His call upon the hearts and lives of those whom He chooses. Too many individuals are in the ministry at the present time who have called themselves. As a result, there is no anointing upon their ministry, as should be obvious.

THE ANOINTING OF THE HOLY SPIRIT

The Lord anoints only those whom He has called, and that anointing is very, very special.

As well, it should be understood that no individual can give his anointing—at least should he have such—to someone else. That is strictly and totally the prerogative of the Lord (I Cor. 12:11).

It is unfortunate that at the present time, we have preachers who claim they can give their anointing to others. Irrespective of the manner in which it is suggested, it amounts to money every time. In other words, "If you give me money, I will give you my anointing."

I think it can be said scripturally without any fear of exaggeration or contradiction that any preacher who would attempt such has no anointing. Whatever he might have had in the past, if anything, he no longer has it presently. Prophets and preachers were and are used of God to recognize those whom God has already called; however, all that they can do is recognize the calling. It is the Lord, and only the Lord, who does the anointing.

I heard a preacher recently over television say, "If you will come and join my group," or words to that effect, "you will come under my anointing." As well, there was a certain sum of money that they had to give.

No, they won't come under his anointing!

I'll say it again: if that preacher did have the anointing at one time, it is doubtful that it is still possessed.

PREACHERS AND PEOPLE

The truth is that every believer is going to follow some preacher.

In fact, the Scripture says:

And He gave (our Lord does the calling) *some, apostles* (has reference to the fact that not all who are called to be ministers will be called to be apostles; this applies to the other designations as well; 'apostles' serve as the de facto leaders of the church, and do so through the particular message given to them by the Lord for the church); *and some, prophets* (who stand in the office of the prophet, thereby, foretelling and forthtelling); *and some, evangelists* (to gather the harvest); *and some, pastors* (shepherds) *and teachers* (those with a special ministry to teach the Word to the body of Christ; 'apostles' can and do function in all of the callings); *For the perfecting of the saints* (to 'equip for service'), *for the work of the ministry* (to proclaim the message of redemption to the entirety of the world), *for the edifying of the body of Christ* (for the spiritual building up of the church):

THE FULLNESS OF CHRIST

Till we all come in the unity of the faith (to bring all believers to a proper knowledge of Christ and the Cross), *and of the knowledge of the Son of God* (which again refers to what He did for us at the Cross), *unto a perfect man* (the believer who functions in maturity), *unto the measure of the stature of the fulness of Christ* (the 'measure' is the 'fullness of Christ,' which can only be attained by a proper faith in the Cross): *That we henceforth be no more children* (presents the opposite of maturity and speaks of those whose faith is in that other than the Cross), *tossed to and fro, and carried about with every wind of doctrine, by the sleight of men* (Satan uses preachers), *and cunning craftiness* (they make a way other than the Cross, which seems to be right), *whereby they lie in wait to deceive* (refers to a deliberate planning or system) (Eph. 4:11-14) (The Expositor's Study Bible).

SATAN USES PREACHERS

As is obvious from this text, not all are called of God. Sadly, some who definitely have been called of God leave the true path of righteousness and go astray.

Satan uses many preachers to deceive Christians, and many are successful at what they do.

So, every person must choose carefully the preacher whom they follow. Is he truly preaching the gospel? To be blunt, if he's not preaching the Cross of Christ, then whatever it is he is preaching is not the gospel.

If a person follows a preacher who is a deceiver, that person will not only be deceived, but he will also become a deceiver. If he's following one who is promoting false doctrine in any fashion, he will be deceived by that false doctrine. Conversely, if he is following a preacher who is preaching the truth, the truth will have its positive effect within his life.

So, we'll say it again: every believer should be very careful as to the church he attends and the preacher to whom he listens, and it's because of all the obvious reasons.

Our very souls are at stake!

Elisha would become one of the greatest prophets who ever lived. As we shall see, he didn't fail the Lord at all. He learned from Elijah and was given that for which he asked, "the double portion," which we will ultimately see.

Rock of Ages cleft for me,
Let me hide myself in Thee;
Let the water and the blood,
From Your wounded side which flowed,

Be of sin the double cure,
Save from wrath and make me pure.
Could my tears forever flow,
Could my zeal no languor know,

These for sin could not atone;
You must save, and You alone:
In my hand no price I bring,
Simply to the Cross I cling.

While I draw this fleeting breath,
When my eyes shall close in death,
When I rise to worlds unknown,
And behold You on Your throne.

Rock of Ages, cleft for me,
Let me hide myself in Thee.

ELISHA

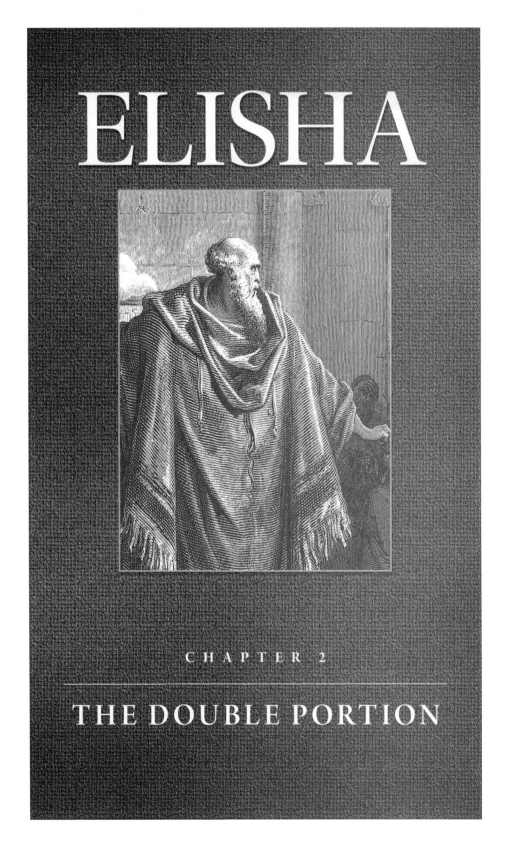

CHAPTER 2

THE DOUBLE PORTION

THE DOUBLE PORTION

"AND IT CAME TO PASS, when the LORD *would take up Elijah into heaven by a whirlwind, that Elijah went with Elisha from Gilgal. And Elijah said unto Elisha, Tarry here, I pray you; for the* LORD *has sent me to Beth-el. And Elisha said unto him, As the* LORD *lives, and as your soul lives, I will not leave you. So they went down to Beth-el. And the sons of the prophets who were at Beth-el came forth to Elisha, and said unto him, Know you that the* LORD *will take away your master from your head today? And he said, Yes, I know it; hold you your peace. And Elijah said unto him, Elisha, tarry here, I pray you; for the* LORD *has sent me to Jericho. And he said, As the* LORD *lives, and as your soul lives, I will not leave you. So they came to Jericho. And the sons of the prophets who were at Jericho came to Elisha, and said unto him, Know you that the* LORD *will take away your master from your head today? And he answered, Yes, I know it; hold you your peace. And Elijah said unto him, Tarry, I pray you, here; for the* LORD *has sent me to Jordan.*

And he said, As the LORD lives, and as your soul lives, I will not leave you. And they two went on" (II Ki. 2:1-6).

THE TRAINING OF ELISHA

Since called of God, Elisha had now been with Elijah for approximately 10 years. His training had been by firsthand observation. It most definitely would prove to be sufficient, which would result in a tremendous visitation for Israel.

Elisha knew that Elijah was about to be taken, but at this stage, he did not know how he would be taken; consequently, he would not let the great prophet out of his sight. Also, how these sons of the prophets knew that Elijah would be taken, we aren't told. It is the persistent soul who reaps the benefits of what Christ has done for us at Calvary, and only the persistent soul (Lk. 11:5-13).

THE PERSISTENCE OF ELISHA

There is a tremendous lesson to be learned here as it regards the last days of the prophet Elijah and the persistence that Elisha evidenced as it regarded what he desired. We must take note of that persistence.

The things of God are not come by easily. We cannot merit them, and neither can we earn them. They are freely given. Yet, the Lord does not hand out His gifts indiscriminately. In other words, they aren't easily possessed.

We must know and understand that whatever it is we receive from God, and I mean whatever, it is received by grace. What do we mean by "received by grace?"

THE GRACE OF GOD

The grace of God is simply the goodness of God extended to undeserving saints. In a sense, that could be said of the entirety of mankind. In fact, God can deal with mankind only from the premise of grace.

However, we must understand that grace is made possible entirely by the Cross of Christ. In other words, our Lord is the source of grace, while the Cross is the means by which such is given unto us.

God did not have any less grace 3,000 years ago than He does now. It's the Cross that has made grace available to us in an unlimited quantity, and it's the Cross alone.

This unequivocally means that the believer must place his faith exclusively in Christ and the Cross, which, in essence, is placing it in the Word of God. Faith placed in the Cross and maintained in the Cross will give the Holy Spirit latitude and liberty to work within our hearts and lives.

Concerning this, Jesus said:

Howbeit when He, the Spirit of truth, is come (which He did on the day of Pentecost), *He will guide you into all truth* (if our faith is properly placed in Christ and the Cross, the Holy Spirit can then bring forth truth to us;

He doesn't guide into some truth, but rather 'all truth'): *for He shall not speak of Himself* (tells us not only what He does, but whom He represents); *but whatsoever He shall hear, that shall He speak* (doesn't refer to lack of knowledge, for the Holy Spirit is God, but rather He will proclaim the work of Christ only): *and He will show you things to come* (pertains to the new covenant, which would shortly be given).

THE HOLY SPIRIT

He shall glorify Me (will portray Christ and what Christ did at the Cross for dying humanity): *for He shall receive of Mine* (the benefits of the Cross), *and shall show it unto you* (which He did when He gave these great truths to the apostle Paul [Rom., Chpts. 6-8, etc.]). *All things that the Father has are Mine* (has always been the case; however, due to the Cross, all these things can now be given to the believer as well): *therefore said I, that He shall take of Mine, and shall show it unto you* (the foundation of all the Holy Spirit reveals to the church is what Christ did at the Cross) (Jn. 16:13-15) (The Expositor's Study Bible).

GILGAL

Elijah and Elisha began this odyssey, one might say, at a place called Gilgal. It has been argued as to whether this was the Gilgal next to Jericho where the children of Israel under

Joshua came into the Promised Land approximately 700 years before, or the other Gilgal up north. Scholars have debated it both ways. However, even though I once thought it was near Jericho, upon further investigation, I personally think it was the Gilgal up north. They would have begun there and then come south, where the great prophet would be translated.

Incidentally, the word *Gilgal* means "rolled away." Some of you reading these words are presently standing, spiritually speaking, at your Gilgal. Irrespective of the past, it can be, and, in fact, the Lord intends for it to be, a new beginning for you. In a sense, it was to be a new beginning for Elisha, and it can be for anyone who will trust the Lord.

This is what is so beautifully amazing about the Lord. Irrespective as to what has been done in the past, if a person will dare to believe God and will consecrate fully to Him and do what He desires, and only what He desires, such a person can have a new beginning. It cannot be done anywhere else or by anything else, but it can be done with the Lord.

You see, the Lord does not function from a three strikes and you are out syndrome, but He is ready and willing, irrespective of the past, to do great things for you if you will only believe Him, trust Him, and consecrate wholly to Him. The past can roll away. So, they started at Gilgal and would now go to Beth-el.

BETH-EL

The word means "house of God." So, Elijah and Elisha

came from the place of "rolled away," signifying that the past can be rolled away, to the "house of God," which was quite a proper place to go.

And yet, all of this is symbolism, but I personally feel it spoke volumes to Elisha. Wherever Elijah went at this time, no doubt, was ordered by the Lord, and all for the benefit, it seems, of Elisha.

Beth-el was the place where Jacob had his encounter with the Lord as it regards the ladder to heaven, which was right after he left home due to problems concerning Esau. So now, as it refers to Elisha, it would in some way speak to him as well. The next stop would be Jericho.

JERICHO

Jericho was the first obstacle encountered by the children of Israel when they came into the Promised Land after crossing the Jordan. It was one of the greatest cities in the land of Canaan. However, its walls would fall beneath the power of God, and the city would be taken with virtually no casualties whatsoever as it regarded God's people.

What had been so formidable now became a symbol of great victory. Once again, this symbolism, I am sure, was not lost on Elisha.

We begin at Gilgal, the place of "rolled away," referring to the fact that the past can be rolled away. It speaks of Israel, but sadly, Israel would not heed the Word of the Lord from Elisha any more than they did Elijah. But yet, the opportunity was given to them by the Lord if they had so desired.

Elijah then went to Beth-el, meaning the "house of God," which is where God once spoke, and I refer to Jacob. Then the two prophets went to Jericho, the scene of the great victory of the children of Israel so many, many years before.

All of this time, the great prophet was telling Elisha, "Tarry here." The answer always from Elisha was, *"As the* LORD *lives, and as your soul lives, I will not leave you."*

AND THEY TWO WENT ON

Undoubtedly, Elisha knew that the days of Elijah were numbered. How much he knew, we aren't told, but there was something there that pressed him—the significance of these last days. Irrespective of what Elijah told him, at least as it regarded his place and position, he let the great prophet know that he would not leave him, no matter what. This is the persistence that God desires.

So, the narrative states, *"And they two went on."*

The anointing of the Holy Spirit was upon Elijah. Elisha knew this, so he would not let the great prophet out of his sight.

THE ANOINTING

Let the reader understand the following: This is the key and the criterion for the place and position of the saint of God. Find out who the Lord is anointing with the Holy Spirit and make doubly certain that it, in fact, is the Holy Spirit, and then take up your place beside that person. The anointing is the key!

However, even as we have already alluded, there is much fake anointing in the land, but if the believer will earnestly seek the Lord, asking for leading and guidance, to be sure, he will be led to the right preacher and the right place.

THE SONS OF THE PROPHETS

"And fifty men of the sons of the prophets went, and stood to view afar off: and they two stood by Jordan. And Elijah took his mantle, and wrapped it together, and smote the waters, and they were divided hither and thither, so that they two went over on dry ground" (II Ki. 2:7-8).

The sons of the prophets could have had, at least somewhat, the blessing as received by Elisha; however, their thoughts and interests were elsewhere.

The last miracle of the great prophet Elijah would be the opening of the Jordan, through which he and Elisha walked to the other side. Once again, the Scripture emphasizes that *"they two went over on dry ground."*

While it would not have been proper for the sons of the prophets to have placed themselves in the same position as Elisha, still, they should have been closer than merely to *"view afar off."* This is all too often the condition of the church. At best, it views the anointing from afar off. There is no record in the Scriptures that the sons of the prophets had the anointing; consequently, there was very little good they did in Israel or Judah.

THE CROSSING OF THE JORDAN

This would be the last miracle, it seems, performed by Elijah. He would take his mantle, which was a robe-like affair, smite the Jordan, and the waters would open. He and Elisha would go to the eastern side of the river. This would be at the foot of Mount Pisgah, from which Moses viewed the Promised Land but was not allowed to enter.

In a sense, Elijah and Elisha were similar to Moses and Joshua; consequently, the Lord would translate Elijah very near where he personally conducted the funeral for Moses. Only Elisha saw the translation of Elijah, and, in fact, no one saw the death and burial of Moses except God.

THE DOUBLE PORTION

"And it came to pass, when they were gone over, that Elijah said unto Elisha, Ask what I shall do for you, before I be taken away from you. And Elisha said, I pray you, let a double portion of your spirit be upon me. And he said, You have asked a hard thing: nevertheless, if you see me when I am taken from you, it shall be so unto you; but if not, it shall not be so" (II Ki. 2:9-10).

In essence, Elisha was asking for a double portion of the Spirit of God that was on Elijah.

The word *hard* in the Hebrew actually means, "You have made a great or hard claim." The bane of the modern church is that we make a much lesser claim or no claim at all. As believers, understanding that we are serving a great God, we should, as well, stake a great claim. As it regards the last phrase of Verse 10, the great question should be, even to modern believers, "What do you see?" Do we see the miracle-working power of God, or do we see other things?

A GREAT CLAIM

Verse 9 proclaims Elijah requesting of Elisha, *"Ask what I shall do for you, before I be taken away from you."*

That's quite a request!

That request, in fact, is asked of the whole church. The answer in the last few years has been very revealing: Money, fame, prestige, influence, recognition, approval, dominion, and more. Precious few have answered as Elisha, *"Let a double portion of your spirit be upon me."* Actually, Elisha was asking for the portion of the firstborn. The request expresses the greatness of the appetite of the heart of Elisha for spiritual power. In other words, Elijah's response, *"a hard thing,"* was in actuality an approval of Elisha's request. Elisha would then continue in the spirit in which Elijah had been functioning from the very beginning—*"if you see me,"* speaking of his coming translation. Elisha's faith that had remained so very close thus far would have little difficulty in the remainder of the distance.

WHAT IS THE ANOINTING OF THE HOLY SPIRIT?

Jesus said:

The Spirit of the Lord is upon Me (we learn here of the absolute necessity of the person and work of the Holy Spirit within our lives), *because He has anointed Me* (Jesus is the ultimate Anointed One; consequently, the anointing of the Holy Spirit actually belongs to Christ, and the anointing we have actually comes by His authority [Jn. 16:14]) *to preach the gospel to the poor* (the poor in spirit); *He has sent Me to heal the broken hearted* (sin breaks the heart, or else, is responsible for it being broken; only Jesus can heal this malady), *to preach deliverance to the captives* (if it is to be noticed, He didn't say to 'deliver the captives,' but rather 'preach deliverance,' which refers to the Cross [Jn. 8:32]), *and recovering of sight to the blind* (the gospel opens the eyes of those who are spiritually blind), *to set at liberty them who are bruised* (the vicissitudes of life at times place a person in a mental or spiritual prison; the Lord alone, and through what He did at the Cross, can open this prison door),

THE YEAR OF JUBILEE

To preach the acceptable year of the Lord (it is believed that the day on which Jesus delivered this message was the first day of the Year of Jubilee) (Lk. 4:18-19) (The Expositor's Study Bible).

The word *anointed* in the Greek is *shrio* and means "to consecrate to an office or spiritual service."

When the Lord calls someone for a particular task, whatever it might be, at the same time, He will give an anointing to that person to carry out the task, which refers to the help of the Holy Spirit. That anointing, or help, will be predicated somewhat on one's consecration and dedication to the Lord, and above all, on one's faith being properly placed in Christ and what He did for us on the Cross. The anointing and work of the Holy Spirit upon a person is, pure and simple, the prerogative of the Spirit and not man.

THE HOLY SPIRIT

The Scripture says: *"But all these* (gifts of the Spirit) *work that one and the selfsame Spirit* (refers to the fact that all of the abilities and powers of the gifts are produced and operated by the energy of the Spirit), *dividing to every man severally as He* (the Holy Spirit) *will.* (All the distribution is within the discretion of the Holy Spirit, which means that men or women cannot impart spiritual gifts to other individuals. That is the domain of the Spirit alone!)" (I Cor. 12:11).

So, the idea that a preacher can lay hands on somebody else and impart to that person his anointing is ridiculous to say the least. It cannot be done.

And yet, it is perfectly proper for younger preachers, or any preacher for that matter, to ask the Lord to give them the anointing that is obvious upon someone else that is such a blessing to the body of Christ. Whether the Lord will answer such a petition or not is strictly His domain; yet, it is perfectly proper to ask.

Jesus said, *"If you then, being evil, know how to give good gifts unto your children: how much more shall your heavenly Father give the Holy Spirit to them who ask Him?"* (Lk. 11:13).

We have far too many preachers in the modern church who make our Lord be much too humanized and man much too deified. While our Lord is both God and man, still, we as human beings are man and will never be otherwise. In other words, there is no such thing as human beings becoming gods, despite what the Mormons say.

THE LITTLE GOD SYNDROME

There has been an error perpetrated in the last few years as it regards the place and position of believers. Some preachers have even taught that believers are deity, and some have, as well, taken the words of Christ and claimed them for believers. I am speaking of when the high priest asked Jesus the question, *"Are you the Christ, the Son of the Blessed?"* Jesus then answered, *"I am."* These preachers are claiming that we as believers can say the same thing. Such borders on blasphemy!

Jesus' answer constituted a bold declaration of who He was. The pronoun *I* was used for emphasis. It was saying, "As for Myself in contradistinction to all others," meaning that He alone could say "I am," and no one else can (Mk. 14:61-62).

As well, some have attempted to use the answer given by Christ when He quoted the law to the Pharisees, by saying, *"Is it not written in your law* (presents the Lord taking up one illustration from among many in the Scriptures that the union between man and God lay at the heart of their law; by Jesus using the word *your,* He was not implying that the law was not His; actually, there is not a shadow of disrespect cast on the law by the pronoun, but it is used in such a sense that His hearers may identify with it), *I said, you are gods?* (This is taken from Psalm 82:6; the word *gods* is used here in the sense of magistrates and prophets appointed and energized by the Word of God. In this case, it did not refer to deity)" (Jn. 10:34).

THE WORD OF FAITH DOCTRINE

Jesus used the Greek word *theos,* which can mean either "the Supreme Divinity" or "a magistrate." He was using it here as a magistrate.

The foolishness of believers declaring themselves to be little gods stems from the confession teaching. This teaching comes from the Word of Faith doctrine, which, in reality, is no faith at all, at least that God will recognize. The teachers of this doctrine claim that once a person comes to Christ, he then has a franchise on doing whatever he desires or being whatever he desires. It all hinges on his faith and his confession. Instead of avidly seeking the will of God about matters and, thereby, the leading of the Holy Spirit, they teach that whatever it is they desire, whatever it is they want, or whatever direction they take, it automatically becomes the will of God.

A PERSONAL EXPERIENCE

Years ago, I had the occasion to come to know a young preacher who was very readily immersed in the Word of Faith doctrine. He resigned his church and in speaking with him one day, I asked him where he was going to build a church, as he had indicated this was what he had set out to do.

He named a particular place.

I then asked him, "Are you sure you have the mind of the Lord on this matter?"

I knew a little bit about the situation, at least when he named the city and the reason he was going there.

He looked at me in a peculiar way and said, "What do you mean 'seek the Lord'? Whatever it is I decide to do, that is the will of God."

If I remember correctly, I told him that he had better have the mind of God before he made such a move, or it could be catastrophic. He really did not answer me, but by his demeanor and spirit, I knew that he was of the frame of mind that, in essence, he was a little god.

He went to the city in question, got into one more royal mess so to speak, and ultimately wound up in prison.

What did he learn from all of this?

I do not know, for I did not speak with him about the situation thereafter.

However, the illustration I've just given characterizes far too many in today's religious climate. I use the word *religious* simply because what is being done is not of God.

THE APOSTLE PAUL

On Paul's second missionary journey, we find Paul and Silas going in a certain direction; however, at a point in time, the Holy Spirit stopped them.

The Scripture says: *"Now when they had gone throughout Phrygia and the region of Galatia, and were forbidden of the Holy Spirit to preach the Word in Asia, after they were come to Mysia, they assayed to go into Bithynia: but the Spirit suffered them not"* (Acts 16:6-7).

We find here the Holy Spirit charting the course and not Paul. To be sure, if the Holy Spirit doesn't chart the course, then nothing is going to be done for the Lord.

The modern Word of Faith doctrine places the Holy Spirit in a subservient role, actually making Him the servant of the individual. In other words, whatever it is I want to do, the Holy Spirit will then help me to do such. Let me say it again: if it were not for a downright ignorance of such direction, it would be blasphemy!

Incidentally, ultimately, the Lord gave Paul a vision of where he was to go. It would be a place called Macedonia, which was in Greece, actually, the first occasion of the gospel being preached on European soil (Acts 16:9-10).

SANCTIONED BY THE LORD

Getting back to our original subject, Elisha asked Elijah that for which the great prophet could not give, but yet, which was sanctioned by the Lord. The Lord, through Elijah, would grant the request, but with one stipulation: *"If you see me when I am taken from you, it shall be so unto you; but if not, it shall not be so."*

Whatever it was that the Lord put in Elisha's heart, it pertained to him seeing Elijah, and more particularly, when the great prophet would be translated. In fact, the Lord had impressed upon Elisha some days earlier that he must not leave the side of Elijah. More than likely, he did not know the reason, but he did know what the Lord had spoken to his heart, which the Lord undoubtedly did. Now he knew why!

THE TRANSLATION OF ELIJAH

"And it came to pass, as they still went on, and talked, that, behold, there appeared a chariot of fire, and horses of fire, and parted them both asunder; and Elijah went up by a whirlwind into heaven. And Elisha saw it, and he cried, My father, my father, the chariot of Israel, and the horsemen thereof. And he saw him no more: and he took hold of his own clothes, and rent them in two pieces" (II Ki. 2:11-12).

In the original Hebrew, it says, *"And Elijah went up in a storm into the heavens."* There is no mention of a whirlwind, for only two of the seed of Adam—Enoch and Elijah—have passed from earth without dying. Elijah had been the strength of Israel—not its army, not its king, etc. Likewise, the strength of any nation belongs to those who are truly born again and Spirit-filled.

Elisha tearing the clothes portrays the fact that he was no longer a learner but was now the prophet.

SPIRIT HORSES

Elijah and Elisha were on the eastern side of the Jordan River, with that body of water having just opened miraculously at the behest of the great prophet. Elijah and Elisha were conversing at this time, about what, we aren't told.

All of a sudden, it happened.

The Scripture says, *"Behold, there appeared a chariot of fire, and horses of fire, and parted them both asunder; and Elijah went up by a whirlwind* (storm) *into heaven."*

That which was invisible to the naked eye became visible to Elisha. He literally saw a chariot of fire, and horses of fire. In fact, this progression *"parted them both asunder."*

The word *fire* in the Hebrew as here used is *esh* and means "that which is literal or figurative." In this instance, it is used in the figurative sense. In other words, the chariot and the horses looked like fire. As should be understood, these were spirit horses, which were actually pulling a chariot.

Some claim that Elijah really did not go up into heaven in the chariot, but rather followed; however, the implication is the opposite. The Lord took the great prophet home to glory in a chariot of fire.

HEAVEN

Before the Cross, which paid the terrible sin debt that man owed but could not pay, when believers died, they were not taken to heaven, but rather down into paradise, which was next door to hell so to speak. Jesus said that there was a great gulf that separated paradise (Abraham's bosom) from hell itself (Lk. 16:26).

So, where did Elijah go? Did he go up into heaven as it regards the abode of God, or down into paradise?

Every evidence is that he was taken directly to heaven without going to paradise.

Approximately 900 years later, both Moses and Elijah appeared on the Mount of Transfiguration and conversed with our Lord.

In fact, they were seen by Peter, James, and John, who had accompanied the Lord to the top of the mountain. Jesus was there, transfigured before them, which means that a light, actually a living light so to speak, literally emanated from His person. It was not on Him, but rather from Him. This portrayed who and what He actually was, which was and is deity, despite His human frame, i.e., the incarnation, God becoming man (Lk. 9:28-31). Actually, our Lord, Moses, and Elijah *"spoke of His decease which He should accomplish at Jerusalem"* (Lk. 9:31).

THE CROSS

In essence, the Cross was the topic of their conversation on the Mount of Transfiguration, which means that this was the topic of conversation in heaven as well!

If it was the topic of conversation then, before the fact, how much should it be the topic of conversation now, considering it is after the fact? I think the answer is obvious!

Moses was a type of the law, thereby, when he died, he went to paradise, which was in the heart of the earth (Lk. 16:19-31).

Elijah was a type of the new covenant under Christ and, thereby, a type of the rapture. When he was translated, he was taken to heaven, the abode of God, and not paradise in the heart of the earth.

Incidentally, Elijah, along with Enoch, will yet come back to this earth, and they will preach the gospel and will do so as the prophets they were and are.

This will take place at about the midpoint of the great tribulation (Mat. 24:21). They will minister for approximately three and a half years and will be a sore thorn in the side of the Antichrist, but their ministry will, no doubt, turn many in Israel to Christ. While the Antichrist will repeatedly try to kill them during that three and a half years, he will not be successful until the very end of that period when the Lord will allow the great prophets to then be killed (Rev., Chpt. 11).

ENOCH AND ELIJAH

Malachi, the last great prophet before Christ prophesied, stating, *"Behold, I will send you Elijah the prophet before the coming of the great and dreadful day of the LORD"* (Mal. 4:5).

Following are the notes from The Expositor's Study Bible regarding this passage:

> The phrase, 'Behold, I will send you Elijah the prophet,' does not refer to the coming of John the Baptist, who only came in the spirit of Elijah. It actually refers to 'Elijah the prophet,' who was translated about 500 years before the time of Malachi, and who will be sent back to the earth by the Lord in the midst of the coming great tribulation.

> At that time, he and Enoch of Revelation 11:3 will be used of God mightily as they prophesy in Jerusalem. Their ministry will last for the entirety of the last three and a half years of the great tribulation. Both will be killed by the Antichrist at the end of that period, 'when they shall have finished their testimony.' However, after three and a half days, Enoch and Elijah will be resurrected and raptured (Rev. 11:11-12).

> As John the Baptist prepared the way for the first advent of Christ, these two, Elijah and Enoch, will prepare the way for the second coming of Christ.

THE SECOND COMING

> The phrase, 'Before the coming of the great and dreadful day of the Lord,' addresses the coming great tribulation, and more specifically, the second coming. It will be a 'great day' for God's people and a 'dreadful day' for His enemies!"

Malachi went on to say, "And he shall turn the heart of the fathers to the children, and the heart of the children to their fathers, lest I come and smite the earth with a curse" (Mal. 4:5-6).

Also from the notes of The Expositor's Study Bible:

> The first phrase proclaims 'Elijah' and 'Enoch' beginning the process, in the latter half of the great tribulation, of 'turning the hearts of the fathers to the children, and the hearts of the children to their fathers.'

The 'fathers' speak of the patriarchs and prophets of old.

AMEN

The phrase, "*Lest I come and smite the earth with a curse,*" proclaims the obvious fact that there is no word following curse in the last verse of the old covenant, meaning there is more to follow. Thank God! In contrast, the word *amen* follows the last words of the book of Revelation, closing out the canon of Scripture, because after grace, which is the theme of the ministry of Christ, there is nothing left to be said but Amen. Thank

God. The world was not left with the curse, but Jesus Christ came and *"redeemed us from the curse of the law, being made a curse for us"* (Gal. 3:13) (Mal. 4:6).

Some claim that Enoch will not be the second witness of Revelation, Chapter 11. They claim the second witness will be Moses because he appeared with Elijah on the Mount of Trans-figuration. While that is possible, we must allow the Scripture to be the final word. The Scripture says, *"And as it is appointed unto men once to die* (due to the fall, all men are under the sentence of death, and, in fact, all have died spiritually, which means to be separated from God), *but after this the judgment* (the answer to the spiritual death of man is Christ and what He did at the Cross; if Christ the Saviour is rejected, all will face Christ the judge; for as death is inevitable, the judgment is inevitable as well)" (Heb. 9:27). This pertains to all of human-ity with the exception of those who will go in the rapture (I Thess. 4:13-18).

The only two men on earth who have never died are Enoch and Elijah because they were translated. However, to fulfill this passage, both will come back and minister in Jerusalem, as stated, in the latter half of the great tribulation. At the con-clusion of that time frame, they will be killed. This will satisfy the Scriptures.

THE CHARIOT OF ISRAEL, AND
THE HORSEMEN THEREOF

The first words of Elisha after the translation of Elijah

were, *"My father, my father, the chariot of Israel, and the horsemen thereof."*

In effect, he was stating that the strength of the nation was not its army, not its king, not its wise men, and not its gold or silver. Its strength was this prophet. It is the same presently as it regards nations, wherever they might be. According to the number of true believers in a respective country, accordingly will be its strength and power. Of course, as a whole, nations never admit this and would consider it to be humorous if they heard this statement made; nevertheless, it is true!

Sadly, it is my personal thought that the church is weaker now than it has been at any time since the Reformation. Fewer people are being saved, fewer believers are being baptized with the Holy Spirit, fewer are being truly healed by the power of God, and fewer are living a victorious life than ever before. Why?

The modern church has left the Holy Spirit because it has left the Cross. In fact, the two, the Cross and the Holy Spirit, go hand in hand.

THE HOLY SPIRIT AND THE CROSS

Listen to Paul: *"For the law of the Spirit of life in Christ Jesus has made me free from the law of sin and death"* (Rom. 8:2).

The following is the way this Scripture was actually written by Paul.

He said, *"For the law of the Spirit of the life in Christ*

Jesus has set me free from the law of the sin and of the death."

The Holy Spirit works exclusively within the framework of the Cross of Christ, which gives Him the legal right to do all that He does, typified by the phrase, *"in Christ Jesus."* Anytime that Paul uses the term *in Christ Jesus,* or one of its several derivatives, such as "in Christ," etc., without exception, he is speaking of what Christ did at the Cross.

Regrettably and sadly, the Cross has been abandoned and, likewise, the Holy Spirit. This means that the modern church is powerless and, thereby, with no fruit.

Holy Spirit-filled believers are the strength of this nation or any nation. Regrettably, the church has precious few of that type anymore.

THE RIPPING OF THE CLOTHES

What statement was Elisha making when he took his own mantle and tore it in two pieces?

Inasmuch as he had seen Elijah depart this mortal coil, he knew that his request was granted, and, thereby, he was no longer the learner but now the prophet. He would now take up the mantle of Elijah.

THE MANTLE OF ELIJAH

He took up also the mantle of Elijah that fell from him, and went back, and stood by the bank of Jordan; And he took the mantle of Elijah that fell from him, and smote the waters, and said, Where is the LORD God of Elijah? and when he also had smitten the waters, they parted hither and thither: and Elisha went over. And when the sons of the prophets which were to view at Jericho saw him, they said, The spirit of Elijah does rest on Elisha. And they came to meet him, and bowed themselves to the ground before him. And they said unto him, Behold now, there be with your servants fifty strong men; let them go, we pray you, and seek your master: lest peradventure the Spirit of the LORD has taken him up, and cast him upon some mountain, or into some valley. And he said, You shall not send. And when they urged him till he was ashamed, he said, Send. They sent therefore fifty men; and they sought three days, but found him not. And when they came again to him, (for he tarried at Jericho,) he said unto them, Did I not say unto you, Go not? (II Ki. 2:13-18).

The mantle was the outer garment worn by the individual and was similar to a robe.

The Lord proclaimed to Elisha that He was with him by enabling him to repeat Elijah's last miracle, and thus gave him an assurance that He would be with him henceforth in his prophetic ministry.

Evidently, these sons of the prophets didn't understand what they saw regarding Elijah, that is, if they had seen anything at all, so they ventured the opinion that the body of Elijah would be found nearby.

Elisha waited at Jericho until the 50 men returned from their vain search and then reminded them of his advice to them, which had been to not start on this useless errand.

THE DOUBLE PORTION

Evidently, the outer garment of Elijah had been left behind when he was translated into heaven.

By Elisha seeing this, he apparently felt that this act was carried out by the Lord and that he should take the mantle, which was, no doubt, correct.

This act performed by the Lord was, in essence, saying that now the request of Elisha had been granted. He had a double portion of the spirit of Elijah.

The question should be asked regarding the modern ministry: How many mantles, which are truly of God, are being left behind for younger preachers to take up?

Not many, I'm afraid!

While the anointing cannot be passed to another, unless the Lord does such (which He most definitely sometimes does), still, older ministers, full of the Holy Spirit, definitely chart a course that is meant to be followed.

A PERSONAL EXPERIENCE

The Lord was gracious and kind enough to me to have me cross the path of a tremendous man of God, who left a marked influence on my life and ministry—an influence for the good.

I saw the Holy Spirit in his life as I had never seen it in anyone else's. I saw and sensed the anointing of the Spirit upon his ministry as I had not witnessed previously.

While I had the privilege of preaching several campmeetings with him, by and large, I was not around him a great deal, and what I did learn, I learned mostly through his tapes. His name was A. N. Trotter. I saw in his life that which I wanted. I saw in his ministry that which I strongly desired. He charted the course, and I did my best to try to follow.

If the Lord tarries and ultimately takes me home to glory, likewise, I want to leave a mantle of power and the anointing of the Spirit that can be taken up by my son, my grandson, and as many as possible of the other preachers of the gospel over whom I might have even a modicum of influence.

WHERE IS THE LORD GOD OF ELIJAH?

This, the Jordan River, was the first test of faith. As stated, the mantle of Elijah being left said to Elisha that his petition had been answered, and answered in full.

Now, he tested the waters.

He came to the Jordan River, took the mantle that fell from the shoulders of Elijah, and smote the waters. He then shouted, *"Where is the Lord God of Elijah?"*

He was to find that the Lord would be the same to him as He had been to the great prophet because then, *"the waters, they parted hither and thither: and Elisha went over."*

EASTER CAMPMEETING

In our Easter Campmeeting of 2007, a message in tongues and interpretation went forth in the morning service. Dave Smith, who has been on the staff here for many years, gave the interpretation.

Part of the interpretation said, "The world is asking, 'Where is the Lord God of Elijah?'"

The message continued, "The church is asking, 'Where is the Lord God of Elijah?'"

When those words went forth, the congregation, along with this evangelist, literally shook and trembled.

About a week later, I was in my car, and Donnie and Frances were on the air over SonLife Radio recounting the happenings of the campmeeting.

Donnie related the situation that I've just mentioned, and once again, the presence of God filled the car.

HE IS STILL A MIRACLE-WORKING GOD

I believe the Lord was saying to us that He is the same today as He was during the time of Elijah and Elisha. He is still a miracle-working God. He is still able to open the Jordan River and, in fact, anything that needs to be done.

This means that the church should believe God for miracles, should believe God for many, many souls to be saved, should believe God for many believers to be baptized with the Holy Spirit, should believe God for His Word to go out over the entirety of the world, and should believe God for this Message of the Cross to be delivered to the church, which will always effect deliverance. He is telling us that the Jordan will open, the fire will fall from heaven, and victories of unprecedented proportions will be won. He is looking for men and women of faith, but faith in Christ and what Christ has done for us at the Cross.

THE SONS OF THE PROPHETS

Whether the sons of the prophets saw the opening of the Jordan when Elisha struck it with the mantle, we aren't told in Scripture; however, they knew enough to bow themselves to the ground before him, which means that they realized that Elisha now was the one on whom the anointing had fallen. They knew this much.

And yet, despite his telling them that they were wasting their time looking for Elijah, they proceeded anyway.

Unbelief is the greatest problem that plagues the church. Unbelief is the greatest problem that plagues preachers. It is unbelief that keeps most from accepting the Message of the Cross. They simply do not believe that what Jesus did at Calvary answers every question, solves every problem, and meets every need. They would rather trust in the world. The Holy Spirit through the great prophet Jeremiah said, *"For My people have committed two evils; they have forsaken Me, the fountain of living waters, and hewed them out cisterns, broken cisterns, that can hold no water"* (Jer. 2:13).

POISONED WATER

"And the men of the city said unto Elisha, Behold, I pray you, the situation of this city is pleasant, as my lord sees: but the water is naught, and the ground barren" (II Ki. 2:19).

The ground was barren because of the poisoned water. Jericho was the city of the curse (and by God at that) simply because of its heathen worship in the days of Joshua. As well, the world is cursed because of sin. It could be as Jericho, a pleasant place, but instead, the water is poisoned and the ground barren, spiritually speaking.

The second great miracle of Elisha's ministry was about to unfold. He went into the city of Jericho and was met by its elders, who somehow now knew that he had taken the place of the great prophet Elijah. At any rate, they related to him the problem that plagued the city. The ground was barren, and it seems that it was barren because the water, which evidently came from an underground river, was poisoned. That affected the land, which made it difficult, if not impossible, for agriculture. As they related the problem to him, no doubt, the Lord told him what to do, even though the Scripture doesn't explicitly say.

THE NEW CRUSE

"And he said, Bring me a new cruse, and put salt therein. And they brought it to him" (II Ki. 2:20).

Vessels of this nature then were made of clay, with this particular vessel serving as a type of the One who would later come, namely the Lord Jesus Christ. It pictured the incarnation, God becoming flesh.

John the Beloved wrote:

In the beginning (does not infer that Christ as God had a beginning because as God, He had no beginning, but rather refers to the time of creation [Gen. 1:1]) *was the Word* (the Holy Spirit through John describes Jesus as 'the eternal logos'), *and the Word was with God* ('was in relationship with God,' and expresses the idea of the Trinity), *and the Word was God* (meaning that He did not cease to be God during the incarnation; He 'was' and 'is' God from eternity past to eternity future).

The same was in the beginning with God (this very person was in eternity with God; there is only one God, but manifested in three persons—God the Father, God the Son, God the Holy Spirit).

All things were made by Him (all things came into being through Him; it refers to every item of creation one by one, rather than all things regarded in totality); *and without Him was not anything made that was made* (nothing, not even one single thing, was made independently of His cooperation and volition).

And the Word was made flesh (refers to the incarnation, 'God becoming man'), *and dwelt among us* (refers to

Jesus, although perfect, not holding Himself aloft from all others, but rather lived as all men, even a peasant), *(and we beheld His glory, the glory as of the only begotten of the Father,)* (speaks of His deity, although hidden from the eyes of the merely curious; while Christ laid aside the expression of His deity, He never lost the possession of His deity) *full of grace and truth* (as 'flesh' proclaimed His humanity, 'grace and truth' His deity) (Jn. 1:1-3, 14) (The Expositor's Study Bible).

NEW

Besides that, this cruse was new, symbolizing the fact that even though Jesus Christ came to this world as a man, still, He was a man as there had never been such a man. After witnessing Jesus calm the angry storm of Galilee, the disciples asked the question, *"What manner of man is this, that even the wind and the sea obey Him?* (The disciples were right! The wind and sea did obey Him, and so does everything else. So why should we fear?)" (Mk. 4:35-41).

THE SALT

"And he went forth unto the spring of the waters, and cast the salt in there, and said, Thus says the LORD, I have healed these waters; there shall not be from thence any more death or barren land" (II Ki. 2:21).

The Holy Spirit evidently told Elisha to put salt into this new cruse. Salt is a type of the incorruptible Word of God.

In fact, Jesus was and is the living Word. As well, as a man, He learned the Word, practiced the Word, and, in fact, everything He did was by the Word as no other human being who has ever lived.

He said Himself, *"Man shall not live by bread alone, but by every Word that proceeds out of the mouth of God* (Jesus was quoting Deuteronomy 8:3; man is a spiritual being as well as a physical being, therefore, dependent on God)*"* (Mat. 4:4).

David said, *"For You have magnified Your Word above all Your name"* (Ps. 138:2).

His name means His reputation and character for faithfulness and goodness. His Word is His promise. In that future day, His performance will exceed His promise, thereby, magnifying His Word above all His name.

THE BIBLE

"And he went forth unto the spring of the waters, and cast the salt in there, and said, Thus says the LORD, I have healed these waters; there shall not be from thence any more death or barren land. So the waters were healed unto this day, according to the saying of Elisha which he spoke" (II Ki. 2:21-22).

The Bible is the only revealed truth in the world today and, in fact, ever has been. It is the single most important thing on the face of the earth. A proper understanding of its tenets of faith is the single most important thing for the believer.

That's the reason we urge every believer to get a copy of The Expositor's Study Bible. There is no study Bible in the world, we believe, that will open up the Scripture as this Bible will.

This was a simple thing done by Elisha in taking the cruse with salt in it and pouring it into the spring of the waters.

Please understand the following: The source of the water of this world, so to speak, is poisoned. One can plant flowers around the well, can make a golden pump, and can have parades and do all types of things, but, still, the water will not change simply because for it to be changed, it must be changed at the source. That's the reason that all of man's efforts fall short. It is the Word of the Lord alone that is believed and acted upon that will solve the problem of broken humanity.

Jericho was cursed, hence, the poisoned water, but the Word of God was able to lift the curse, as the Word of God alone is able to lift the curse.

THUS SAYS THE LORD, I HAVE HEALED THESE WATERS

The Word of the Lord was enough. The waters were healed and remain healed unto this day.

Sometime ago, Frances and I were in the city of Jericho. As we were leaving from the ruins of the old city where Joshua marched, the guide pointed toward a well nearby and said, "This is where Elisha healed the waters so long, long ago."

More than likely, this was the same place, even though, of course, the well was different. Wells very seldom ever change locations due to the underground current that feeds the current. He went on to say, "The water is still clean, fresh, and pure."

When people go to the Lord, and that's what the elders of the city of Jericho did when they went to Elisha, good things happen. When we try to address things outside of the Lord and His name, there are no good things that will take place.

The healing of these waters is very special to me in a spiritual sense. Concerning this experience that took place in the city of Jericho, the Lord moved greatly upon my heart, which, in effect, was a revelation.

A PERSONAL EXPERIENCE

It was a Friday night in November 1991. I had begun two prayer meetings a day (morning and evening) a few days before, and a few of us had gathered that evening for the nightly prayer meeting.

Just before we went to prayer, I read the account from the Word of God of the great miracle that transpired at Jericho, telling how the Lord through Elisha healed the waters. I commented on it for a few moments, and then we went to prayer.

Almost immediately, the presence of God filled my heart. It was as if the Holy Spirit portrayed to me that happening that took place in Jericho so long, long ago. It was as though I was there listening to Elisha and seeing what he did as it regarded the new cruse and the salt.

Then the Lord began to speak to my heart. I knew it was the Lord, and of that, I have no doubt.

I WILL HEAL YOU, AND I WILL
HEAL THIS MINISTRY

He said to me, "As I healed the poisoned waters of Jericho, I will heal you, and I will heal this ministry." He even delineated the various departments of the ministry—the church, the television ministry, the missions ministry, etc. For a period of time, possibly 30 minutes or more, as the Spirit of God swept through my soul, it was as though my very insides would erupt as I sobbed, experiencing the presence of God. When the Lord moves upon an individual, and it is no doubt that it is the Lord, it is a powerful thing. There is no way that words can describe it. To those of you who have experienced that of which I speak, you know what I'm talking about; otherwise, you don't.

Beautifully and strangely enough, the presence of the Lord didn't lift when we finished the prayer meeting. It lingered on me for the entirety of the evening. Actually, I awakened about midnight. I remember that simply because I looked at my watch. The presence of God was still on me. Truthfully, I went to sleep with it still lingering on my heart. The next morning when I awakened and arose, the presence of the Lord was still there. It remained until almost noon the next day.

I've never had such to happen before or since.

THE PROMISE

The Lord had given me a promise. He said that He would heal me and that He would heal this ministry.

As I dictate these notes, quite a number of years have passed. To be sure, He has done with me exactly as He said that He would. The healing concerning myself and concerning this ministry began with the revelation of the Cross in 1997, a revelation, incidentally, that continues to expand even unto this present hour, and I think it will never stop.

Then in 2005, the Lord told me to develop The Expositor's Study Bible. To this hour, it has sold over 2 million copies. It is, I believe, one of the most helpful study Bibles in the world today.

And then in 2010, the Lord instructed me to begin the Sonlife Broadcasting Network. We now go into 280 million homes by cable and by satellite. Then, counting the Internet, it reaches another billion homes, that is, if they so desire to receive the programming.

I might quickly add that the network is growing almost daily. I think this network is the fastest growing network in the world and, in fact, ever has been. It is that way because the Lord is in it, and all of this is just a preparation time for what is about to happen.

I believe that we are going to see the greatest moving of the Holy Spirit, concluding with hundreds of thousands, if not millions, of people brought into the kingdom of God. I believe the Lord has told me this is going to happen.

We are now in the beginning stages, but we are very close to the Holy Spirit working as never before.

The Scripture then says, *"So the waters were healed unto this day, according to the saying of Elisha which he spoke."*

THE JUDGMENT OF GOD

The close of II Kings, Chapter 2 portrays the judgment of God falling on some 42 young men, with them being killed by two she bears.

The translation here is unfortunate. The Hebrew word translated "little children" probably would have been better translated "young men."

As is obvious, we are given very little information concerning this incident. The Scripture merely says, *"There came forth little children out of the city* (Beth-el), *and mocked him, and said unto him, Go up, you bald head; go up, you bald head."*

Elisha then placed a curse upon them in the name of the Lord. We know the Lord was in sympathy with what was done simply because almost immediately *"there came forth two she bears out of the wood, and tore forty and two children of them."*

Some would claim that these were extreme measures and not indicative at all as it regards a God of love; however, as stated, we are only given scant information here. More than likely, much more was said and done by these young men in their wickedness than is given to us in the sacred text.

One thing is certain: The Lord would never have done such if the occasion had not warranted the act.

I can see far down the mountain,
Where I have wandered many years,
Often hindered on my journey,
By the ghosts of doubts and fears,

Broken vows and disappointments,
Thickly strewn along the way,
But the Spirit has led unerring,
To the land I hold today.

ELISHA

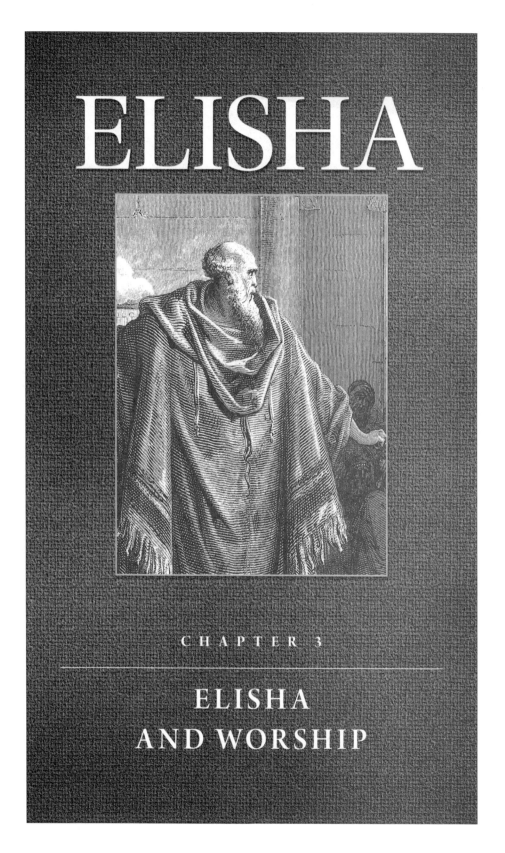

CHAPTER 3

ELISHA
AND WORSHIP

ELISHA AND WORSHIP

"NOW JEHORAM THE SON of Ahab began to reign over Israel in Samaria the eighteenth year of Jehoshaphat king of Judah, and reigned twelve years. And he wrought evil in the sight of the LORD; but not like his father, and like his mother: for he put away the image of Baal that his father had made. Nevertheless he cleaved unto the sins of Jeroboam the son of Nebat, which made Israel to sin; he departed not therefrom" (II Ki. 3:1-3).

SIN

The next few pages give us an idea of the spiritual condition of the northern confederation of Israel where Elisha had been called as a prophet.

Jehoram, the new king of Israel, removed the obscene idol erected by his father but resolutely held onto the great sin of Jeroboam, that is, the golden calf.

Sin principally means the substitution of a god other than

the Lord Jesus Christ. In one way or another, that's what it amounts to.

Any sin that a person may commit, be it a sin of passion or a sin of pride, is the substitution of another god in the place of our Lord. As Christians, we oftentimes fail to equate our sin with the idol worship of Israel, such as Baal or Chemosh. We picture in our minds Israel of old kneeling down to these heathenistic idols, and we congratulate ourselves on our great consecration in that we are far more spiritually enlightened. However, any sin, be it pride, lust, jealousy, or lying, is the substitution of another god in the place of the Lord. Our sin is just as hideous in the eyes of God as the sins of Israel of old, and more so. John said, *"Little children, keep yourselves from idols"* (I Jn. 5:21).

ANOTHER JESUS

The Holy Spirit through the apostle Paul said:

But I fear, lest by any means, as the serpent beguiled Eve through his subtilty (the strategy of Satan), *so your minds should be corrupted from the simplicity that is in Christ.* (The gospel of Christ is simple, but men complicate it by adding to the message.) *For if he who comes preaching another Jesus* (a Jesus who is not of the Cross), *whom we have not preached* (Paul's message was 'Jesus Christ and Him crucified'; anything else is 'another Jesus'), *or if you receive another spirit* (which is produced by preaching another Jesus), *which you have not received* (that's not what you received when we preached the true gospel to you), *or another gospel, which you have not accepted* (anything other than 'Jesus Christ and Him crucified' is 'another gospel'), *you might well bear with him.* (The apostle is telling the Corinthians they have, in fact, sinned because they tolerated these false apostles who had come in, bringing 'another gospel' that was something other than Christ and the Cross) (II Cor. 11:3-4) (The Expositor's Study Bible).

THE CROSS OF CHRIST

Millions presently claim fidelity to the Lord Jesus Christ but ignore the Cross or even repudiate the Cross. Paul referred to this as another Jesus.

This tells us the following: If the Cross is ignored or repudiated, then whatever Jesus is being promoted is not the Jesus of the Bible but a Jesus of one's own fabrication.

Let's say it another way: One cannot divorce Jesus from the Cross, and we are speaking of what He there did. That's the reason Paul said, *"We preach Christ crucified"* (I Cor. 1:23). Most of the modern church has done exactly that— they have divorced Jesus from the Cross. While they mention the Cross as it regards salvation, it is only in a sentimental way, which means they really do not understand the Cross at all as it regards our sanctification—our daily life and living.

Now, please understand that when we talk about the Cross, we aren't talking about the wooden beam on which

Jesus died. We are speaking of the benefits of the Cross, which are multitudinous. In other words, we are speaking of that which Jesus there did, the price He paid, and the victory that He there won. Incidentally, it was a victory that was total. These are benefits that will accrue to the believer forever and forever. That's the reason that Paul referred to it as the *"everlasting covenant"* (Heb. 13:20).

THE BELIEVER AND THE CROSS

The believer must understand that for every single thing we receive from the Lord, irrespective of what it is, the Cross is the means by which this is given to us. Our Lord Jesus Christ is the source of all these things, and the Cross of Christ is the means.

The Scripture says this of Christ:

> *In the last day, that great day of the feast* (spoke of the eighth day of the Feast of Tabernacles), *Jesus stood and cried, saying, If any man thirst, let him come unto Me, and drink* (presents the greatest invitation ever given to mortal man). *He who believes on Me* (it is 'not doing,' but rather 'believing'), *as the Scripture has said* (refers to the Word of God being the story of Christ and Him crucified; all the sacrifices pointed to Christ and what He would do at the Cross, as well as the entirety of the tabernacle and temple and all their appointments), *out of his belly* (innermost being) *shall flow rivers of living water*

(speaks of Christ directly and believers indirectly).

THE HOLY SPIRIT

(But this spoke He of the Spirit (Holy Spirit), *which they who believe on Him should receive* (it would begin on the day of Pentecost): *for the Holy Spirit was not yet given* (He has now been given); *because that Jesus was not yet glorified)* (Jn. 7:37-39).

The time of which John wrote was shortly before the crucifixion. When Jesus died on the Cross and was resurrected three days later, He was raised with a glorified body, which was one of the signs that all sin had been atoned. This now made it possible for the Holy Spirit to come in a new dimension.

In a sense, when our Lord said, *"Out of his belly* (innermost being) *shall flow rivers of living water,"* He was referring back to the smitten rock.

The Scripture says concerning that time:

And the LORD said unto Moses, Go on before the people, and take with you of the elders of Israel; and your rod, wherewith you smote the river, take in your hand, and go. Behold, I will stand before you there upon the rock in Horeb; and you shall smite the rock, and there shall come water out of it, that the people may drink. And Moses did so in the sight of the elders of Israel (Ex. 17:5-6).

THE ROCK

The rock was a type of Christ (I Cor. 10:1-4). The rock being smitten typified the Cross (Isa 53:4). The water coming out of the rock was a type of the Holy Spirit (Jn. 7:37-39); however, the water, i.e., the Holy Spirit, was not available until the rock (Christ) was smitten (crucified – Jn. 14:16-20). In fact, Christ, the Cross, our faith, and the Holy Spirit constitute the basis of Christianity (Gal., Chpt. 5).

The Holy Spirit, as I think these passages amply portray, works entirely within the framework of the Cross of Christ. In other words, He will not work outside of those parameters. It is the Cross that has given Him the latitude and liberty to work within our lives, in fact, to do all the things that He does (Rom. 8:2).

The Holy Spirit and the Cross of Christ are so inseparable that it's impossible to rightly understand one without rightly understanding the other.

At the turn of the 20th century, the Holy Spirit began to fall upon men and women all over this planet, fulfilling the great prophecy of Joel as it regarded the latter rain (Joel 2:23, 28).

IF THE HOLY SPIRIT IS REJECTED, BY AND LARGE, THE CROSS IS ALSO REJECTED

Even though multiple thousands of Baptists, Methodists, etc., were baptized with the Holy Spirit with the evidence of speaking with other tongues as the Spirit of God gave the utterance (Acts 2:4), still, those particular denominations as a whole rejected the outpouring of the Holy Spirit.

In those days, some of these denominations preached the Cross, at least the part they knew, and did so rather strongly; however, presently, with an exception here and there, they preach much of nothing. The point is that if you reject the Holy Spirit, by and large, you have, as well, rejected the Cross. Those who accepted the outpouring of the Holy Spirit came to be referred to as Pentecostals, and by the power of the Holy Spirit, they touched the world for Christ. Sadly, little by little, the Pentecostal world has also rejected the Cross, and as a result, they are rejecting the Holy Spirit as well.

In fact, when they began to embrace humanistic psychology, which began in the 1960s, that's when they began to abandon the Cross. Now, sadly and regrettably, for the most part, they preach much of nothing.

Once again, the point is that if you reject the Holy Spirit, there is no way that you can at the same time have the Cross and all of its benefits. Likewise, if you reject the Cross, you have at the same time rejected the Holy Spirit.

SPIRITUAL ADULTERY

Regrettably, most modern Christians have never even heard the term "spiritual adultery." Consequently, they have no idea what it means.

Paul explained this in the first four verses of Chapter 7 of

Romans. Please allow me to quote it from The Expositor's Study Bible:

> *Know you not, brethren* (Paul is speaking to believers), *(for I speak to them who know the law,)* (he is speaking of the law of Moses, but it could refer to any type of religious law), *how that the law has dominion over a man as long as he lives?* (The law has dominion as long as he tries to live by law. Regrettably, not understanding the Cross regarding sanctification, virtually the entirety of the modern church is presently trying to live for God by means of law. Let the believer understand that there are only two places he can be, grace or law. If he doesn't understand the Cross as it refers to sanctification, which is the only means of victory, he will automatically be under law, which guarantees failure.) *For the woman which has an husband is bound by the law to her husband so long as he lives* (presents Paul using the analogy of the marriage bond); *but if the husband be dead, she is loosed from the law of her husband* (meaning that she is free to marry again if she so desires).

TWO HUSBANDS

> *So then if, while her husband lives, she be married to another man, she shall be called an adulteress* (in effect, the woman now has two husbands, at least in the eyes of God; following this analogy, the Holy Spirit through Paul

will give us a great truth; many Christians are living a life of spiritual adultery; they are married to Christ, but they are, in effect, serving another husband, 'the law'; it is quite an analogy!): *but if her husband be dead* (the binding force of the law is dead by virtue of Christ having fulfilled the law in every respect), *she is free from that law* (if the husband dies, the woman is free to marry and serve another; the law of Moses, being satisfied in Christ, is now dead to the believer, and the believer is free to serve Christ without the law having any part or parcel in his life or living); *so that she is no adulteress, though she be married to another man* (presents the believer as now married to Christ and no longer under obligation to the law).

DEAD TO THE LAW

Wherefore, my brethren, you also are become dead to the law (the law is not dead per se, but we are dead to the law because we are dead to its effects; this means that we are not to try to live for God by means of 'law,' whether the law of Moses or laws made up by other men or of ourselves; we are to be dead to all law) *by the body of Christ* (this refers to the crucifixion of Christ, which satisfied the demands of the broken law we could not satisfy; but Christ did it for us; having fulfilled the law in every respect, the Christian is not obligated to law in any fashion, only to Christ and what He did at the Cross); *that you should be married to another* (speaking of Christ), *even to Him who is raised from the dead* (we are raised with Him in newness of life, and we should ever understand that Christ has met, does meet, and shall meet our every need; we look to Him exclusively, referring to what He did for us at the Cross), *that we should bring forth fruit unto God* (proper fruit can only be brought forth by the believer constantly looking to the Cross; in fact, Christ must never be separated from the work of the Cross; to do so is to produce 'another Jesus' [II Cor. 11:4]) (Rom. 7:1-4).

THE STATE OF SPIRITUAL ADULTERY

The idea of this analogy given by the Holy Spirit through Paul is that if the believer places his faith in anything except Christ and the Cross, and that exclusively, such a believer is living in a state of spiritual adultery, which causes all types of problems, as should be obvious.

To be sure, the Holy Spirit will not function in that type of situation, as again should be obvious. While He doesn't leave the believer and continues to do all He can to help such a believer, still, He is greatly limited as to what He can do. Such a believer will find *"works of the flesh"* becoming predominant within his life, which causes all kinds of problems and could even cause the individual to ultimately lose his way (Gal. 5:19-21).

To more properly understand the statement of Paul the

apostle as it regards spiritual adultery, I would strongly rec-
ommend that you obtain for yourself The Expositor's Study
Bible and our study guide from the Cross of Christ series
titled, *"Spiritual Adultery."*

WHETHER YOU BE IN THE FAITH

Let's now go back to the activity of Jehoram, the king
of Israel. While he did put away the image of Baal out of
Israel, which, within itself, admittedly was a notable achieve-
ment, still, the Scripture says, *"He cleaved unto the sins of*
Jeroboam the son of Nebat, which made Israel to sin; he
departed not therefrom."

Regrettably, the sin of the modern church is that it has not
departed from law, and to be sure, such definitely is a sin.

Paul said: *"Examine yourselves, whether you be in the*
faith (the words, 'the faith,' refer to 'Christ and Him crucified,' with the Cross ever being the object of our faith); *prove*
your own selves. (Make certain your faith is actually in the
Cross and not other things.) *Know you not your own selves,*
how that Jesus Christ is in you (which He can only be by our
faith expressed in His sacrifice), *except you be reprobates?*
(Rejected)" (II Cor. 13:5) (The Expositor's Study Bible).

AN UNHOLY ALLIANCE

And Mesha king of Moab was a sheepmaster, and ren-
dered unto the king of Israel an hundred thousand

> *lambs, and an hundred thousand rams, with the wool. But it came to pass, when Ahab was dead, that the king of Moab rebelled against the king of Israel. And King Jehoram went out of Samaria the same time, and numbered all Israel. And he went and sent to Jehoshaphat the king of Judah, saying, The king of Moab has rebelled against me: will you go with me against Moab to battle? And he said, I will go up: I am as you are, my people as your people, and my horses as your horses. And he said, Which way shall we go up? And he answered, The way through the wilderness of Edom* (II Ki. 3:4-8).

The lambs and the rams were tribute rendered by the king of Moab each year to the king of Israel.

The words uttered by Jehoshaphat in Verse 7 were probably a common formula, expressive of willingness to enter into the closest possible alliance.

The incurable insubjection of the natural will, even in a Christian, to the Word of the Lord is seen in Jehoshaphat. Despite two severe lessons from God, for the third time, he united with the religious world in a "laudable" enterprise. The results would be that he nearly lost his life.

AN OLD SIN IS AN EASY SIN

This seemed to be a weakness of Jehoshaphat—his joining alliance with the king of Israel—which was not the will of God.

Three times he did this:

1. He joined Ahab to recover Ramoth and nearly lost his life, and was sharply rebuked by the prophet Jehu.
2. He united with Ahab's son, Ahaziah, in shipbuilding, but his ships were broken.
3. Now he united with Jehoram, Ahaziah's brother, in making war upon their neighbors, with the result that he once again nearly lost his life.

So, Verse 7 says that Jehoram requested of Jehoshaphat his help against the king of Moab. Jehoshaphat agreed by saying, "*I am as you are, my people as your people.*" As stated, an old sin is an easy sin. As with every Christian, it is easy for Satan to maneuver us down a path well traveled.

The believer is *in* the world, but he is to never be *of* the world. We do not march to its drumbeat; we do not function according to its precepts; its ways are not our ways; and its methods are not our methods. That, among many other reasons, is why it is so wrong for the modern church to adopt the marketing ways of the world in order to build the church. While we may succeed in filling the pews with warm bodies, that is about all that we will do. There will be little or no spiritual growth. In fact, most of the people entering into modern churches presently are not even born again.

SIN

Sin is rarely mentioned anymore, and the Cross is anathema because to mention the Cross, as hireling preachers

68 | ELISHA JIMMY SWAGGART

say, might offend the unbelievers. So, the gospel, if one would refer to it as gospel, has been so watered down that it is mostly a motivational appeal at present. While in some cases it may be a morality appeal, it is a morality without Christ and what He did at the Cross. As such, there could never be any true morality because the power of what Jesus did at the Cross is denied.

Admittedly, the "morality message" and the "motivational message" are very appealing to the carnal ear. They sound good! They appeal to self, in effect, stating that whatever problems that self might have, they can be rectified by certain things being done. What are those things?

So-called modern Christians are told to change their habits. In other words, sin is reduced to merely a bad repetition. If someone has repeatedly done something wrong, he is told that if he will change that habit, whatever it might be, and start to do right, the problem will be solved.

THE PROBLEM IS SIN

Chapter 6 of Romans is where the Holy Spirit through Paul tells us how to live a victorious life. Unless we understand this chapter, unless its rudiments are in our hearts, and unless we abide by what it teaches us, we simply cannot be victorious in our life and living for the Lord.

Of course, this chapter functions on the premise that the individual is truly a believer, i.e., born again. All the teaching in the world is not going to do the unredeemed any good.

Let's say it again. The individual must be born again.

Jesus said: *"Verily, verily, I say unto you, Except a man be born again* (the term, 'born again,' means that man has already had a natural birth but now must have a spiritual birth, which comes by faith in Christ and what He has done for us at the Cross, and is available to all), *he cannot see the kingdom of God* (actually means that without the new birth, one cannot understand or comprehend the 'kingdom of God')" (Jn. 3:3) (The Expositor's Study Bible).

So, as it regards victorious living, trying to explain the great plan of God to the unbeliever is a waste of time.

ROMANS, CHAPTER 6

The Holy Spirit through Paul began Chapter 6 of Romans, the great chapter of victory over the world, the flesh, and the Devil, by telling us that sin is the problem.

He said: *"What shall we say then?* (This is meant to draw attention to Romans 5:20.) *Shall we continue in sin, that grace may abound?* (Just because grace is greater than sin doesn't mean that the believer has a license to sin.) *God forbid* (presents Paul's answer to the question, 'Away with the thought, let not such a thing occur'). *How shall we, who are dead to sin* (dead to the sin nature), *live any longer therein?* (This portrays what the believer is now in Christ)" (Rom. 6:1-2) (The Expositor's Study Bible).

Now, if the problem with the believer is sin, and it most definitely is, then the preacher must deal with it. If he doesn't because it's not a good marketing approach, meaning he has adopted the ways of the world, then whoever it is he attracts, he's not going to do them any good, as should be overly obvious. Regrettably, that's the story of most modern churches.

Paul tells us that sin is the problem, and then he tells us that the Cross of Christ is the answer to that problem.

THE CROSS OF CHRIST

Once again, listen to the great apostle:

Know you not, that so many of us as were baptized into Jesus Christ (plainly says that this baptism is into Christ and not water [I Cor. 1:17; 12:13; Gal. 3:27; Eph. 4:5; Col. 2:11-13]) *were baptized into His death?* (When Christ died on the Cross, in the mind of God, we died with Him; in other words, He became our substitute, and our identification with Him in His death, which is done by faith, gives us all the benefits for which He died; the idea is that He did it all for us!) *"Therefore we are buried with Him by baptism into death* (not only did we die with Him, but we were buried with Him, as well, which means that all the sin and transgression of the past were buried; when they put Him in the tomb, they put all of our sins into that tomb as well): *that like as Christ was raised up from the dead by the glory of the Father, even so we also should walk in newness of life* (we died with Him, we were buried with Him, and His resurrection was our resurrection to a 'newness of life').

RESURRECTION LIFE

> *For if we have been planted together* (with Christ) *in the likeness of His death* (Paul proclaims the Cross as the instrument through which all blessings come; consequently, the Cross must ever be the object of our faith, which gives the Holy Spirit latitude to work within our lives), *we shall be also in the likeness of His resurrection* (we can have the 'likeness of His resurrection' i.e., 'live this resurrection life,' only as long as we understand the 'likeness of His death,' which refers to the Cross as the means by which all of this is done) (Rom. 6:3-5) (The Expositor's Study Bible).

So, once again, if the preacher doesn't mention the Cross because it may offend people, then he has forfeited the entirety of the gospel. Let us say it again: Sin is the problem, and the Cross is the solution, in fact, the only solution.

So, if we ignore these two fundamentals of the faith, we have ignored the gospel, and whatever it is we are giving to the people is something that we've made up out of our own minds or borrowed from the minds of others.

This will set no one free, deliver no one, and save no one, meaning that such a message is less than useless, but regrettably, the prattle of man is basically what the modern church is giving to the people.

As Jehoshaphat made an alliance with Jehoram, which

again would cause him to almost lose his life, likewise, the modern church has and is making alliances with the world. The results now will be no different than the results then.

IS THERE NOT HERE A PROPHET OF THE LORD?

"So the king of Israel went, and the king of Judah, and the king of Edom: and they fetched a compass of seven days' journey: and there was no water for the host, and for the cattle that followed them" (II Ki. 3:9).

"The cattle that followed them," actually constituted the baggage animals, i.e., the horses that carried the necessities of the soldiers.

Verse 9 proclaims the difficulties of their seven days' journey, for the Scripture says there was no water for the host.

We have here a dichotomy as it regards Jehoram, the king of the northern confederation of Israel, and Jehoshaphat, the king of the southern confederation of Judah and Benjamin.

HERE IS ELISHA

And the king of Israel said, Alas! that the LORD has called these three kings together, to deliver them into the hand of Moab! But Jehoshaphat said, Is there not here a prophet of the LORD, that we may inquire of the LORD by him? And one of the king of Israel's servants answered and said, Here is Elisha the son of Shaphat, which poured water on the hands of Elijah. And Jehoshaphat said, The

> *Word of the* LORD *is with him. So the king of Israel and*
> *Jehoshaphat and the king of Edom went down to him*
> (II Ki. 3:10-12).

As stated, Verse 10 proclaims Jehoram, although an idol worshipper, blaming the Lord for their predicament.

Verse 11 proclaims Jehoshaphat doing the very opposite. He asked, *"Is there not here a prophet of the* LORD*?"* The answer was immediate: *"Here is Elisha the son of Shaphat."* Then a strange statement of identification was made about Elisha. It says, *"Which poured water on the hands of Elijah."*

To pour water on the hands of anyone is the action of a servant. Public and brilliant ministries must be preceded by humble and hidden ones. This is God's method of teaching disciples. He desires those whom He will use mightily in the future to pour water on the hands of those who are being mightily used at the present. If they cannot function in the realm of servant ministry, then they will not be fit for use at a later time.

SPIRITUAL LEADERSHIP BEFORE THE CROSS

Before the Cross, the Lord's method of dealing with people and leading them was somewhat different than compared to now.

What did the Cross have to do with all of this? Jesus went to the Cross and, thereby, atoned for all sin, and did so by the giving of Himself in sacrifice. Until then, the sin debt remained on all. Even though the sacrificial system was in place, having been instituted immediately after the fall (Gen., Chpt. 4), still, that only served as a stopgap measure.

Paul plainly told us, *"For it is not possible that the blood of bulls and of goats should take away sins"* (Heb. 10:4).

The word *impossible* is a strong one. It means that there is no way forward through the blood of animals. As well, it applies to all efforts other than the Cross that are made by man to address the problem of sin.

The sacrifice of clean animals such as lambs did give man a limited access to God, but only a limited access. Before the Cross, the Holy Spirit could not enter into the hearts and lives of believers to abide there permanently. He did come into the hearts and lives of some in order to help them fulfill a mission, but that was the limit.

THE LIMITED MANNER OF THE HOLY SPIRIT

Actually, when believers died before the Cross, they were not taken to heaven simply because the sin debt remained upon them inasmuch as animal blood was insufficient to remove it. Their souls and their spirits were instead taken to paradise, where they were there comforted (Lk. 16:19-31). Yet, at least in a sense, they remained captives of Satan.

Naturally, Satan was hoping that he would ultimately get them into the burning side of hell, but, of course, the Cross foiled his plans, with our Lord delivering all of these people out of paradise. Now, when believers die, they instantly go to heaven (Eph. 4:8-15). Due to the limited manner of the Holy Spirit before the Cross, the Lord by and large led His people by the means of the prophet. That's the reason that Jehoshaphat asked for the prophet. While the kings were titular leaders of the people, especially the southern confederation of Judah, still, it was mostly the prophet to whom the Lord spoke and whose words were to be followed, at least those who were truly prophets of God.

Regrettably, there were many false prophets then as there are many false prophets now.

LEADERSHIP SINCE THE CROSS

Speaking of the time frame after the Cross, there are still prophets, even until this present time. This means that, in a sense, the office is the same as it was before the Cross, with one exception: Now, it is the apostle who stands in the position of leadership as it regards the church. The office of the apostle did not exist before the Cross.

What are the earmarks of a true apostle?

Even though there are a number of earmarks, we find from our study of the book of Acts and the epistles that the greatest earmark of all is the message given by the apostle. While those who are not apostles may preach the same message—whatever it is that the Holy Spirit then wants and desires—still, it is the apostle who will be given the authority to proclaim a certain message. It will be to such an extent that it is undeniable, at least by honest, seeking hearts.

It should be understood that man cannot appoint apostles. This is a prerogative of the Holy Spirit alone. The Holy Spirit sees a certain lack in the church and gives the apostle the appropriate message to address that lack, whatever it might be. However, the greatest difference since the Cross than before the Cross is that now the Holy Spirit comes into the heart and life of each person at conversion to abide permanently (Jn. 14:16-17).

This means that the Holy Spirit is not limited to just a few individuals but is available to lead and guide every single believer, whomever that believer might be.

MADE POSSIBLE BY THE CROSS

Jesus said:

Howbeit when He, the Spirit of truth, is come (which He did on the day of Pentecost), *He will guide you into all truth* (if our faith is properly placed in Christ and the Cross, the Holy Spirit can then bring forth truth to us; He doesn't guide into some truth, but rather 'all truth'): *for He shall not speak of Himself* (tells us not only what He does but whom He represents); *but whatsoever He shall hear, that shall He speak* (doesn't refer to lack of knowledge, for the Holy Spirit is God, but rather He will proclaim the work of Christ only): *and He will show you things to come* (pertains to the new covenant, which would shortly be given).

He shall glorify Me (will portray Christ and what Christ did at the Cross for dying humanity): *for he shall receive of Mine* (the benefits of the Cross), *and shall show it unto you* (which He did when He gave these great truths to the apostle Paul [Rom., Chpts. 6-8, etc.]).

All things that the Father has are Mine (has always been the case; however, due to the Cross, all these things can now be given to the believer as well): *therefore said I, that He shall take of Mine, and shall show it unto you* (the foundation of all that the Holy Spirit reveals to the church is what Christ did at the Cross [Rom. 6:3-14; 8:1-11; I Cor. 1:17-18, 21, 23; 2:2; Gal., Chpt. 5; 6:14; Col. 2:10-15]) (Jn. 16:13-15) (The Expositor's Study Bible).

With the present work of the Holy Spirit—all made possible by the Cross and available to every believer—I think it is easily ascertained as to how much better it is now than then. Each believer has the prerogative of having the Holy Spirit lead and guide him 24 hours a day, seven days a week.

What a privilege! The sadness is that we take so little advantage of this.

THE BELIEVER, THE CROSS, AND THE HOLY SPIRIT

The greatest reason of all that most believers have such little help from the Holy Spirit, when, in reality, He desires to do much, much more, is simply because of a lack of understanding of the Cross of Christ. We must first of all understand that the Holy Spirit works exclusively within the framework of the finished work of Christ. In other words, it is what Jesus did at the Cross that gives the Holy Spirit the legal right to do all that He does. We must understand that, know that, and comprehend that (Rom. 8:2).

THE CROSS IS THE MEANS

Understanding that, we must without fail place our faith exclusively in Christ and the Cross, for this is demanded by the Holy Spirit. The entirety of Chapter 6 of Romans is given over to this very principle. We are told in that chapter, as previously stated some pages back, that sin is the problem, and the Cross of Christ is the answer to sin, in fact, the only answer.

If one properly understands the Word of God, one will properly see that the Cross of Christ is the foundation principle of the entirety of the Word, and we speak of Genesis 1:1 through Revelation 22:21. The story of the Bible is the story of Jesus Christ and Him crucified. One might say that the story of Jesus Christ and Him crucified is the story of the Bible.

Jesus Christ is the source of all things, while the Cross is the means by which these things are given unto us. Thus, our faith in that finished work then gives the Holy Spirit latitude to work within our hearts and lives and, thereby, to do things which He alone can do.

ELISHA THE PROPHET

"And Elisha said unto the king of Israel, What have I to do with you? get you to the prophets of your father, and to the prophets of your mother. And the king of Israel said unto him, No: for the LORD *has called these three kings together, to deliver them into the hand of Moab. And Elisha said, As the* LORD *of Hosts lives, before whom I stand, surely, were it not that I regard the presence of Jehoshaphat the king of Judah, I would not look toward you, nor see you"* (II Ki. 3:13-14).

Elisha regarded it as incumbent upon him to rebuke the monarch from Israel who, though he had *"put away the image of Baal that his father had made,"* still *"wrought evil in the sight of the* LORD*"* and *"cleaved unto the sins of Jeroboam the son of Nebat"* (II Ki. 3:2-3).

In effect, Verse 14 states that Jehoram and the king of Edom owed their lives to Jehoshaphat.

Without a doubt, Elisha was one of the greatest prophets who had ever lived. He had been trained, so to speak, by none other than Elijah. He had witnessed the greatest phenomenon in human history—the translation of a human being from earth to heaven, and that by a chariot of fire pulled by horses of fire. I think the phenomenon of such speaks for itself.

While he received the double portion of Elijah's spirit in Judah, his primary mission was to the northern kingdom of Israel.

Had it not been for the prophet Elisha, this situation concerning Jehoram and Jehoshaphat could have turned out badly.

In Verse 14, as stated, Elisha said, *"Were it not that I regard the presence of Jehoshaphat the king of Judah, I would not look toward you, nor see you."*

There is no way that a church, a religious denomination, a fellowship, a city, or a country can understand how blessed it is if God's anointed is in their midst. Only because of Jehoshaphat would God move. So, in effect, Jehoram and the king of Edom owed their lives to Jehoshaphat.

Denominations and fellowships owe their blessings to men of God who are among them, and not to a man-made hierarchy. Entire nations owe their blessings to men of God in their midst, of whom they have little or no knowledge. Even for 10 righteous men, God would have spared Sodom and Gomorrah. How much does he withhold judgment from people, cities, and even nations because of the children of God in their midst!

MUSIC AND SINGING, THE HIGHEST FORM OF PRAISE

"But now bring me a minstrel. And it came to pass, when the minstrel played, that the hand of the LORD came upon him" (II Ki. 3:15).

The Holy Spirit, no doubt, moved upon Elisha to request a minstrel. Most probably, these were musicians and singers who sang and played the songs. When this happened, the Scripture says, *"The hand of the* LORD *came upon him"*— meaning Elisha.

Likewise, when David played, the evil spirits that troubled Saul departed from him.

Why?

It was because of the anointing of the Holy Spirit on David and upon the musicians mentioned in this passage.

There are seven major religions in the world, of which Christianity is one (actually, Christianity is not really a religion but a relationship with a person, Christ Jesus). Of these seven major religions, there is only one that has a songbook, and that is Bible Christianity. In fact, the others have nothing to sing about.

THE LONGEST BOOK IN THE BIBLE

As we mentioned, music and singing, that is, if it's of the Lord, are the highest forms of praise and worship.

How do we know that?

The Lord devoted the longest book in the Bible to music and singing, and we speak of Psalms. These are 150 songs, which were all authored by the Holy Spirit and given to David and others.

Spirit anointed singing and music proclaim petition, prayer, praise, and prophecy, which makes this so very, very important. That's the reason that Satan has done everything within his power to subvert and to hinder music and singing in the modern church. He has, by and large, succeeded in doing so.

It must first of all be understood that Spirit directed singing and music are not for the unbeliever, but rather for the believer. The Spirit of the Lord most definitely may use music and singing, as He has many times, to touch the unredeemed and even to bring some to salvation. Still, music and singing anointed by the Holy Spirit are for the believer. If the words of the song are right, and the melody is correct, the Lord will use it and, in fact, has used such music and singing untold numbers of times. He does this to encourage, to lift up, to strengthen, and to show the way to untold numbers of believers.

A PERSONAL EXPERIENCE

When I was 8 years old, having been saved and baptized with the Holy Spirit only a short time, I asked the Lord to give me the talent to play the piano. I will never forget that night.

To make the story brief, the Lord not only gave me the talent but, as well, gave me an understanding of what music and singing should be like, in other words, that which is sanctioned by the Holy Spirit. Over 16 million of our albums and CDs have been sold all around the world.

The Lord, in fact, has used our music, and, as well, what presently comes from Family Worship Center, to bless untold thousands, even millions. We give Him all the praise and all the glory.

If music and singing do not glorify the Lord, then it's not sanctioned by the Holy Spirit. To be frank, music and singing that is inspired by the Holy Spirit will in some way elicit praise and worship in the heart of the listener, that is, if he knows the Lord. While that person may not become emotionally involved at the moment, he will most definitely feel it in his heart and in his spirit.

Unfortunately, modern church music has become a business instead of a form of worship. In other words, money is the object.

JESUS IS THE ONE

To give one example, of which we could give many, please allow me to relate the following: In the year 2000, the Lord instructed me to purchase radio stations all over the country, and He even told me what type of programming that I should use. Everything had to come from Family Worship Center. That meant that we would not sell time to preachers but would look to the audience to provide the means that was needed to operate the stations.

Now, please understand that when the Lord told me to secure the stations, we didn't have a dime of money, and I'm not exaggerating. We had nothing.

The ministry at that time owned two stations, the mother station in Baton Rouge, Louisiana, and a powerful AM station in Bowling Green, Ohio. Then we purchased another station in Atlanta, Texas, a 50,000-watt FM giant.

To our dismay, the station in Atlanta, Texas, kept going off the air. There was no engineer in that part of the world, and we had to send an engineer all the way from Baton Rouge, which was terribly expensive.

We found that the transmitter needed to be completely overhauled, for which we had no money to get it done.

We were on radio for an hour and a half every morning, Monday through Friday, teaching the Word of God. On the particular morning in question, when our program ended, David Whitelaw walked into the room and said, "Atlanta is off the air again."

THE MOVING OF THE HOLY SPIRIT

I got in the car, drove up to McDonald's to get something for breakfast, and to say the least, I was about as discouraged as a person could ever be. We were patching up the transmitter, trying to make it work, with no money to buy a new one and no money to actually get it properly repaired. I did not know what to do!

As I was pulling into the line to place my order at McDonald's, all of a sudden over our mother station here in Baton Rouge, the song came on the air, a song I had known basically all of my life:

> *Jesus is the one,*
> *Yes He's the only one,*
> *Let Him have His way,*

Until the day is done.
When He speaks you know,
The dark clouds will have to go.
Just because He loves you so.

All of a sudden, the Spirit of the Lord filled the car, and somehow I knew that the Lord was going to take care of the situation. To be sure, He did, as He always does.

Something of that nature has taken place many times in my life and ministry as the Lord used a song to minister to me and countless others. However, if some of the stuff that goes under the guise of Christian music had been coming over the air that day, there would have been no blessing of the Lord and no moving of the Holy Spirit on such.

I'll go back to that night that the Lord answered my prayer by giving me the talent to play the piano. He also gave me an understanding of music regarding what the Holy Spirit wants and desires. As a result, we have seen untold thousands, perhaps even millions, touched by the grace and glory of the Lord through our songs. Once again, we give the Lord all the glory.

THE MIRACLE

"And he said, Thus says the Lord, *Make this valley full of ditches"* (II Ki. 3:16).

In the dryness of that wilderness, the Lord said, *"Make this valley full of ditches."* Faith obeyed, even though this was the dry season when rain was highly unlikely; however, *"with God all things are possible"* (Mk. 10:27).

No matter how sinful or wicked the situation and no matter how dry the spiritual desert, faith, despite the scoffing, will make the valley full of ditches. They will preach the Word of God so to speak, and the Word will not return void. It will accomplish its intended purpose. Just because there is no water in the ditch, do not sell it short.

FILL WITH WATER

"For thus says the LORD, You shall not see wind, neither shall you see rain; yet that valley shall be filled with water, that you may drink, both you, and your cattle, and your beasts. And this is but a light thing in the sight of the LORD: He will deliver the Moabites also into your hand" (II Ki. 3:17-18).

Verse 17 says, *"Thus says the LORD."* The prophet then proclaimed, *"You shall not see wind, neither shall you see rain,"* but then the pronouncement was made, *"yet that valley shall be filled with water, that you may drink."* Most of the time, the church cannot believe what it cannot see. The writer of Hebrews said that faith is the *"evidence of things not seen"* (Heb. 11:1).

A LIGHT THING

From the statement made in Verse 18, *"And this is but*

a light thing in the sight of the Lord," the announcement must have had a startling effect. Unbelief always looks at the circumstances, while faith looks to God. Not only would there be plenty of water, but *"He will deliver the Moabites also into your hand."*

FILL WITH WATER

"And you shall smite every fenced city, and every choice city, and shall fell every good tree, and stop all wells of water, and mar every good piece of land with stones. And it came to pass in the morning, when the meat offering was offered, that, behold, there came water by the way of Edom, and the country was filled with water" (II Ki. 3:19-20).

Verse 20 says, *"Behold, there came water by the way of Edom."*

Josephus said, "That the storm burst at a distance of three days journey from the Israelite camp, however, this at best can only be conjectured. Irrespective, ever how far it was from the Israelites, they could not see the rain, neither was there any wind, but the water still came."

When one reads the Bible, one sees immediately that God is a God of miracles. With that being the case, and it most definitely is, we should believe Him presently for great and mighty things.

In one of our campmeetings, there was a message in tongues and interpretation that was given. The interpretation basically stated as the Lord spoke, *"Do not ask Me only for little things or small things. Ask Me for the impossible—for that which is far beyond your thinking."*

As that word was given, the Spirit of God wafted over the great congregation.

As believers, we ask too little, and we oftentimes ask too late. My grandmother taught me from the time I was a child, "Jimmy, God is a big God, so ask big."

I've never forgotten that. It has helped me to touch this world for Christ.

VICTORY

"And when all the Moabites heard that the kings were come up to fight against them, they gathered all who were able to put on armor, and upward, and stood in the border. And they rose up early in the morning, and the sun shone upon the water, and the Moabites saw the water on the other side as red as blood: And they said, This is blood: the kings are surely killed, and they have smitten one another: now therefore, Moab, to the spoil" (II Ki. 3:21-23).

The Moabites thought that Judah, Israel, and Edom had turned on each other because there had been bad blood in the past between these countries.

The smiting of the enemy can only be carried out by the believer as faith is evidenced in Christ and the Cross. The Holy Spirit, who alone can help, works entirely within the framework of the finished work of Christ.

The water was not from the general direction of the

Moabites because Verse 22 says, *"And the sun shone upon the water."* With the sun shining upon the water, the Moabites would see the water as red as blood.

Consequently, they thought that Israel was smitten and cried, *"To the spoil."* Likewise, when Satan saw the ground at the foot of Calvary red with blood, and the blood of Christ at that, he thought surely that heaven was totally defeated. Instead, it was his defeat.

THE CROSS ALONE IS THE ANSWER

"And when they came to the camp of Israel, the Israelites rose up and smote the Moabites, so that they fled before them: but they went forward smiting the Moabites, even in their country" (II Ki. 3:24).

Likewise, as Verse 24 says, *"The Israelites rose up and smote the Moabites."* Every victory is won by and through the blood of our Lord Jesus Christ, which was shed at Calvary. The Cross is the answer to man's ills, and the only answer to man's ills. There is no other! Sadly, the modern church little believes anymore in the effectiveness of the blood of Jesus Christ.

RELIGION

And they beat down the cities, and on every good piece of land cast every man his stone, and filled it; and they stopped all the wells of water, and felled all the good

> *trees: only in Kir-haraseth left they the stones thereof;*
> *howbeit the slingers went about it, and smote it. And*
> *when the king of Moab saw that the battle was too sore*
> *for him, he took with him seven hundred men who drew*
> *swords, to break through even unto the king of Edom:*
> *but they could not. Then he took his oldest son who*
> *should have reigned in his stead, and offered him for a*
> *burnt offering upon the wall. And there was great indig-*
> *nation against Israel: and they departed from him, and*
> *returned to their own land* (II Ki. 3:25-27).

In desperation, the king of Moab took his eldest son to offer him for a burnt offering upon the wall. Religion is a horrid business. It demands the physical and spiritual death of its victims, while Christianity demands death to the carnal man that the spiritual man may reign. Upon the offering up of the eldest son of the king of Moab to the fire god, terror struck the superstitious Israelites, and they hastened back to their own land.

This chapter is somewhat strange, and the reason is because God had no part in idolatrous Israel. He only came to their rescue because of Jehoshaphat, even though Jehoshaphat was out of the will of God at the time.

In this, we see the greatness of God's mercy and compassion, even when we're out of His will and wrongly directed.

Exalt the Lord, His praise proclaim;
All ye His servants, praise His name,
Who in the Lord's house ever stand
And humbly serve at His command.

The Lord is good, His praise proclaim;
Since it is pleasant, praise His name;
His people for His own He takes
And His peculiar treasure makes.

I know the Lord is high in state,
Above all gods our Lord is great;
The Lord performs what He decrees,
In heaven and earth, in depths and seas.

He makes the vapors to ascend
In clouds from earth's remotest end;
The lightnings flash at His command,
He holds the tempest in His hand.

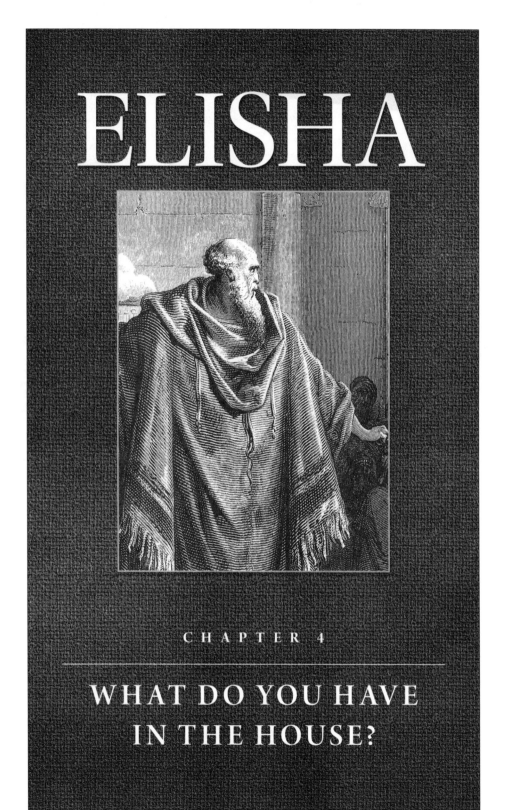

ELISHA

CHAPTER 4

WHAT DO YOU HAVE
IN THE HOUSE?

WHAT DO YOU HAVE IN THE HOUSE?

"NOW THERE CRIED A certain woman of the wives of the sons of the prophets unto Elisha, saying, Your servant my husband is dead; and you know that your servant did fear the LORD: *and the creditor is come to take unto him my two sons to be bondmen. And Elisha said unto her, What shall I do for you? tell me, what have you in the house? And she said, Your handmaid has not anything in the house, save a pot of oil"* (II Ki. 4:1-2).

WHAT DO YOU HAVE IN THE HOUSE?

There is some intimation that this woman's husband, one of the sons of the prophets, was known to Elisha. Many a Christian is like this widow. There is depression, poverty, and bondage in their lives instead of joy, wealth, and liberty. The truth is that the plight of this home was not God's will. It is God's will that we be in health and prosper, even as our souls do prosper (III Jn., Vs. 2). Satan never ceases in his efforts to deprive the child of God of his rightful inheritance in Christ Jesus.

For the Christian, the house is the physical body (I Cor. 3:16). The Holy Spirit, represented by the pot of oil, is supposed to fill the house. This woman had a small pot of oil but nothing else.

The Word of God is full of pictures, types, allegories, and symbols of God's great plan and design for the human race. With God being omniscient (all-knowing) and omnipotent (all-powerful), He is able to weave His plan into circumstances, happenings, prophets, people, and nations; consequently, Moses' ministry was a type of the law. Joshua's ministry was a type of grace. As well, Elijah's ministry was a type of the law, with Elisha's ministry being a type of grace. The sufficiency of grace in relation to man's folly and need appears in the miracles of Elisha. He is a savior to Israel and a healer to the Gentiles.

GRACE

In the previous chapter, living water, so to speak, is abundantly given to the three kings who are about to perish. This same grace now grants an overflowing provision of wealth to the impoverished widow. The succeeding miracles strikingly prove that "grace upon grace" is the measure that hastens to the help of needy and sinful men. These miracles characterize Elisha's ministry. The thirsty are refreshed, the poor and needy provided for, the childless made the joyful mother of children, the dead raised to life, the brokenhearted bound up, the hungry healed and fed, the leprous cleansed, and victory given over all the power of the enemy. Such is Christ to broken, sinful, and diseased humanity.

Verse 1 says, *"Your servant my husband is dead."*

As stated, there is some intimation that this woman's husband (one of the sons of the prophets) was known to Elisha. In these passages we see a striking miracle that is brought about. However, the question must be asked, if God would do such a thing as multiply the oil, why did not He heal this woman's husband?

THE GREAT QUESTIONS OF LIFE

Christians have pondered these questions from the very beginning. The answers are probably as varied as the people involved. God performs miracles in response to faith, need, and His will. Faith will never override the will of God. Was it the will of God for this man to die at this time?

We have to conclude that it was. And yet, the will of God is never arbitrary. It is much of the time based on variables, in other words, the faith, consecration, and purpose of the individual involved. Sometimes it is obvious, and sometimes, as in Job's case, it is not obvious.

It is quite possible for Christians, and we speak of true believers, to shorten their lives, and to do so by faith improperly placed, which refers to making the wrong thing the object of one's faith.

What do we mean by that?

The Holy Spirit explained this through the apostle Paul as it regarded the taking of that which we refer to as the Lord's Supper.

He said, *"Wherefore whosoever shall eat this bread, and drink this cup of the Lord, unworthily* (tells us emphatically that this can be done, and is done constantly, I'm afraid), *shall be guilty of the body and blood of the Lord* (in danger of judgment, subject to judgment).

EXAMINE OURSELVES

Paul continued:

But let a man examine himself (examine his faith as to what is its real object), *and so let him eat of that bread, and drink of that cup* (after careful examination). *For he who eats and drinks unworthily, eats and drinks damnation to himself* (does not necessarily mean the loss of one's soul, but rather temporal penalties, which can become much more serious), *not discerning the Lord's body.* (Not properly discerning the Cross refers to a lack of understanding regarding the Cross. All of this tells us that every single thing we have from the Lord comes to us exclusively by means of the Cross of Christ. If we do not understand that , we are not properly 'discerning the Lord's body.') *For this cause* (not properly discerning the Lord's body) *many* (a considerable number) *are weak and sickly among you* (the cause of much sickness among Christians), *and many sleep.* (This means that many Christians die prematurely. They don't lose their souls, but they do cut their lives short. This shows us, I seriously think, how important properly understanding the Cross actually is.) *For if we would judge ourselves* (we should examine ourselves constantly as to whether our faith is properly placed in the Cross of Christ), *we should not be judged* (with sickness and even premature death). *But when we are judged* (by the Lord because we refuse to judge ourselves), *we are chastened of the Lord* (divine discipline), *that we should not be condemned with the world* (lose our souls) (I Cor. 11:27-32).

I think the notes we have quoted from The Expositor's Study Bible amply explain what we addressed, but due to its vast significance, let us briefly say it again.

THE GREATEST PROBLEM
FOR THE CHILD OF GOD

The greatest problem is the believer not properly understanding the Cross of Christ, which is what all of this is all about as Paul gave it to us.

The believer must understand the following:

- We must understand that Jesus Christ is the source of everything that we receive from God (Jn. 14:6).

- The Cross of Christ is the means by which these things are given unto us (Rom. 6:1-14; I Cor. 1:17-18, 23; 2:2; Col. 2:10-15).
- We must without fail ever make the Cross of Christ the object of our faith. This is very, very important (Gal. 6:14; I Cor. 2:2; Col. 2:14-15).
- With Christ as our source and the Cross as our means, and Jesus Christ and Him crucified ever the object of our faith, the Holy Spirit, who works exclusively within the framework of the finished work of Christ, will then greatly help us (Rom. 8:1-11; Eph. 2:13-18; Acts 1:8).

THE CROSS OF CHRIST
AND THE MODERN CHURCH

The Cross of Christ, in essence, is the new covenant. There has been such a paucity of teaching and preaching in the last several decades as it regards the Cross of Christ that it falls out to believers not really understanding what Jesus did there for them. Most believers have at least a rudimentary knowledge of the Cross as it regards salvation. In fact, it could probably be said that the sentimental phrase, "Jesus died for me," pretty well explains their knowledge. Don't misunderstand; there is nothing greater in the world than the phrase we've just given.

However, when it comes to sanctification as it regards our life and living, most Christians don't have the foggiest idea of the part that the Cross plays in this. Consequently, the object of their faith runs the gamut from A to Z. It is mostly anchored up in themselves. In other words, the object of their faith is self even though they do not really understand such. In fact, I think it can be said that the only place that faith can be if it's not in the Cross of Christ is self. With that being the case, which constitutes the flesh, Paul boldly stated, *"So then they that are in the flesh cannot please God"* (Rom. 8:8).

This refers to the believer attempting to live his Christian life by means other than faith in Christ and the Cross.

FAITH COMES BY HEARING

The teaching we are giving in this volume as it regards the Cross of Christ has never been heard or read by most believers. And yet, this is the staple of the Word of God, which is the foundation of the faith. It's not something new because the entirety of the Bible is given over to Jesus Christ and Him crucified. However, as stated (and we make the case again), the modern church knows next to nothing about the Cross of Christ simply because it is no longer preached and taught.

The Scripture plainly says, *"So then faith comes by hearing* (it is the publication of the gospel which produces faith in it), *and hearing by the Word of God* (faith does not come simply by hearing just anything, but rather by hearing God's Word, and that Word taught correctly, and then believing that Word)" (Rom. 10:17) (The Expositor's Study Bible).

FALSE DOCTRINE

A short time ago over his television program, one very popular preacher was addressing those with addictions. He said, "It's all in your mind." He then went on to postulate that if they would just start thinking differently, then these addictions could be easily overcome, whether it be nicotine, gambling, alcoholism, etc.

Sadly and regrettably, that is the so-called gospel that is being preached in most churches presently. Such a direction completely ignores what the Bible tells us about what the problem is, which is sin, and the solution to that problem, which is the Cross of Christ.

What does the Bible say as it regards this mind over matter bit, this "think and grow rich" philosophy, and this "mentally developing" your character?

The Holy Spirit through Paul said:

For I delight in the law of God (refers to the moral law of God ensconced in the Ten Commandments) *after the inward man* (refers to the spirit and soul of man which has now been regenerated).

ANOTHER LAW

But I see another law in my members (the law of sin and death desiring to use my physical body and my mind as an instrument of unrighteousness), *warring against the law of my mind* (this is the law of desire and willpower), *and bringing me into captivity to the law of sin* (the law of sin and death) *which is in my members* (this means that it will function through my members and make me a slave to the law of sin and death; this will happen to the most consecrated Christian if that Christian doesn't constantly exercise faith in Christ and the Cross, understanding that it is through the Cross that all powers of darkness were defeated [Col. 2:14-15]) (Rom. 7:22-23) (The Expositor's Study Bible).

Now, Paul here plainly tells us that the law of my mind is woefully insufficient as it regards overcoming sin. As a child of God, it is my will and desire, i.e., my mind, that I overcome sin; however, that desire is not strong enough to overcome sin within itself.

This means that no matter how much I may try to change my thinking, it's not going to overcome sin.

TWO MORE LAWS

The great apostle now gives us two more laws. He said:

There is therefore now no condemnation (guilt) *to them which are in Christ Jesus* (refers back to Romans 6:3-5 and our being baptized into His death, which speaks of the crucifixion), *who walk not after the flesh* (depending on one's personal strength and ability or great religious efforts in order to overcome sin) *but after the Spirit* (the

Holy Spirit works exclusively within the legal confines of the finished work of Christ; our faith in that finished work, i.e., 'the Cross,' guarantees the help of the Holy Spirit, which guarantees victory). *For the law* (that which we are about to give is a law of God devised by the Godhead in eternity past [I Pet. 1:18-20]; this law, in fact, is 'God's prescribed order of victory') *of the Spirit* (Holy Spirit, i.e., 'the way the Spirit works') *of life* (all life comes from Christ, but through the Holy Spirit [Jn. 16:13-14]) *in Christ Jesus* (any time Paul uses this term or one of its derivatives, he is, without fail, referring to what Christ did at the Cross, which makes this 'life' possible) *has made me free* (given me total victory) *from the law of sin and death* (these are the two most powerful laws in the universe; the 'law of the Spirit of life in Christ Jesus' alone is stronger than the 'law of sin and death'; this means that if the believer attempts to live for God by any manner other than faith in Christ and the Cross, he is doomed to failure) (Rom. 8:1-2) (The Expositor's Study Bible).

In these passages, the great apostle tells us how to overcome sin, which is the only way that we can overcome sin. It is by and through the law of the Spirit of life in Christ Jesus.

As we've already stated, that law is the only law in the universe that is stronger than the law of sin and death.

This means that all the mental gymnastics in the world is not going to change anything.

VARIOUS LAWS

In Chapter 7 of Romans, we find several laws listed, which are very, very important. Now please understand that these are laws that were devised by the Godhead, meaning that they will function exactly as they were devised. The four laws are:

1. The law of Moses. The heartbeat of this law is the Ten Commandments (Ex. 20:1-17; Rom. 7:12). This is the moral law of God and is incumbent upon every human being. While Jesus fulfilled the law in every respect in His life and living and, as well, addressed the broken law by giving Himself in sacrifice on the Cross of Calvary (Col. 2:14-15), still, the moral code of God is incumbent upon all believers. And yet, we keep that moral code not by addressing it as law, but by placing our faith exclusively in Christ and the Cross. This then gives the Holy Spirit latitude to work within our lives, which automatically keeps the law. As a child of God, we aren't to think about law, even the moral law, in any capacity. Let me state it again: The moral law has already been kept in Christ. Our faith in Him and what He did for us at the Cross guarantees us the keeping of this moral code, and the doing of such without even giving it a thought. Concerning this, Paul also said:

I am crucified with Christ (as the foundation of all victory; Paul here takes us back to Romans 6:3-5): *nevertheless I live* (have new life); *yet not I* (not by my own strength and ability), *but Christ lives in me* (by virtue of me dying with Him on the Cross and being raised with Him in newness of life): *and the life which I now live in the flesh* (my daily walk before God) *I live by the faith of the Son of God* (the Cross is ever the object of my faith), *who loved me, and gave Himself for me* (which is the only way that I could be saved) (Gal. 2:20) (The Expositor's Study Bible).

2. The law of sin and death. This is the second most powerful law in the universe and came about as a result of the fall (Rom. 7:21; Gen., Chpt. 3). There is only one way that one can overcome the law of sin and death, and that is by and through the law of the Spirit of life in Christ Jesus.

3. The law of the mind. This is the law of desire and willpower (Rom. 7:23). While it is most definitely greatly enhanced once the person is born again, still, it is not strong enough within itself to bring about victory that one desires and, in fact, must have. It wants and desires that which God wants and desires, and we continue to speak of the born-again individual, but within itself doesn't have the power to bring it about.

4. The law of the Spirit of life in Christ Jesus. This is the strongest law in the universe (Rom. 8:2). It alone can get one victory over the law of sin and death. Regrettably, believers seem to have a difficult time understanding this.

So, what is this law of the Spirit of life in Christ Jesus?

The key is found in the phrase "in Christ Jesus." Anytime Paul uses that term or one of its derivatives, such as "in Christ," "in the Lord," etc., he is speaking, and without exception, of what Christ did on the Cross.

This means that the Holy Spirit works exclusively within the framework, i.e., the parameters, of the finished work of Christ, i.e., the Cross. Please understand that the Scripture tells us that this is a law, meaning that it will function according to the way it has been devised.

The problem is that the modern church is trying to overcome the law of sin and death by the law of the mind, which cannot be done. While the law of the mind (our will) is most definitely important, still, within itself, it is insufficient. To be sure, there must be a willing mind and a willing heart, and we speak of believers trying to overcome sin; however, that within itself is insufficient. Our faith—and it is all by faith— must always be placed without exception in the Cross of Christ. In the Cross alone is the victory (Heb. 8:6; 9:14, 28).

WHOSOEVER WILL!

Many Christians confuse the *"whosoever will"* of Revelation 22:17 with the *"law of the mind"* in Romans. They are two different things.

The *"whosoever will"* of Revelation 22:17 pertains to the invitation given to the unredeemed to come to Christ. People who aren't saved know nothing about the Lord. They don't know anything about a law of the mind, or anything else that is spiritual for that matter. So, the Holy Spirit is saying that any person who is unsaved, any person who is without God, or any person who is lost can come to Christ and be saved if they "will."

Paul said, *"For whosoever* (anyone, anywhere) *shall call upon the name of the Lord shall be saved"* (Rom. 10:13).

So, while the will and a little faith, which is supplied by the Holy Spirit, are all that is necessary as it regards the sinner coming to Christ, that is not referring to the believer.

As we have stated, while the will, or the mind, of the believer is most definitely important, as ought to be obvious, still, that alone (which I believe we have sufficiently explained) is not sufficient within itself. While our will most definitely must be engaged in the proper way, still, it is our faith in Christ and the Cross that gives us the victory, and that alone.

THE CREDITOR IS COME

Far too many Christians are subject to the "creditor." There is depression, poverty, and bondage in the life instead of joy, wealth, and liberty. Even though the death of this man may or may not have been the will of God, still, the plight of this home was definitely not God's will. It is God's will that we be in health and prosper even as our souls do prosper (III Jn., Vs. 2).

Satan never ceases in his efforts to deprive the child of

God of his rightful inheritance in Christ Jesus.

THE WILL OF GOD

It is the will of God for every believer to *"grow in grace and the knowledge of the Lord."* We can do that only in one way, and that is by placing our faith exclusively in Christ and the Cross. Our spiritual growth is the single most important thing in our life and living. This we must understand.

IS IT ALWAYS THE WILL OF GOD TO HEAL THE SICK?

I believe the Lord will give us physical strength, in other words, bless us physically, if we will but trust Him. However, at the same time, divine healing is always predicated on the wisdom of God. While it is always the will of God, I believe, for the Lord to heal the sick, at times, it may not be His wisdom. At any rate, anytime the sickness comes near our door, we should ask the Lord, in fact, avidly seek Him, for divine healing. We should also understand that there is no such thing as divine healers, which means that men cannot heal anyone, but there most definitely is such a thing as divine healing, which, of course, comes from the Lord. A long time ago the Lord said, *"For I am the LORD who heals you"* (Ex. 15:26). That promise was real then, and that promise is real today. The Bible says, *"Jesus Christ the same yesterday, and today, and forever"* (Heb. 13:8).

FINANCIAL PROSPERITY

I believe it is the will of God for every believer to prosper financially. The truth in many cases is that we have not because we ask not. Then all too often, *"You* (we) *ask, and receive not, because you* (we) *ask amiss, that you* (we) *may consume it upon your* (our) *lusts"* (James 4:3).

The idea is that we do not at times properly ask, and then at other times, our motives aren't right.

The believer must settle it in his mind once and for all that the Lord wants to bless us financially. He desires to do that. If we understand that and believe that, most of the battle has already been won.

Now it's up to us to commit our ways to the Lord, avidly seek His face, believe Him to bless us in whatever endeavor we may be engaged, and to be sure, He most definitely will do such (Mk. 11:24; Jn. 14:14; 15:7).

It is not the will of God for creditors to be knocking at the door of the child of God. It is the will of God, as stated, *"that you may prosper and be in health, even as your soul prospers"* (III Jn., Vs. 2).

WHAT DO YOU HAVE IN THE HOUSE?

Even though Elisha was speaking of the woman's domicile, as is obvious, still, believers now constitute the "house" of the Holy Spirit.

Paul said, *"Know you not that you are the temple of God*

(house—where the Holy Spirit abides), *and that the Spirit of God dwells in you?* (That makes the born-again believer His permanent home)" (I Cor. 3:16). The question broadened can apply to us as well. It is as follows:

- What we have in the house, which is the temple of the Holy Spirit, may be detrimental to our walk with God and, thereby, hinder that which we can receive from God. Jesus would cleanse the temple. Perhaps our temples need cleansing as well.
- And yet, what we have in the house as a child of God is the Holy Spirit. It is represented by the pot of oil. Sadly, most Christians are using everything except the Holy Spirit—the pot of oil. Yet, the pot of oil, which is so lightly regarded by human wisdom or overlooked totally as the rock in the case of Israel (Num. 20:8), responds at once when appealed to, and the house is filled with *"life more abundant."*

THE HOLY SPIRIT IS GOD

Please understand that due to the fact that the Holy Spirit is God, the believer has nothing more important than the privilege of His help.

Concerning this, Jesus said, *"And I will pray the Father, and He shall give you another Comforter* ('parakletos,' which means 'one called to the side of another to help'), *that He may abide with you forever* (before the Cross, the Holy

Spirit could only help a few individuals, and then only for a period of time; since the Cross, He lives in the hearts and lives of all believers, and does so forever)" (Jn. 14:16).

As stated, the Holy Spirit is given to us for many and varied reasons, but He is to help us in all things. The way to have that help on a constant basis is for the believer to place his faith exclusively in Christ and the Cross and understand that this is the way the Spirit works (Rom. 8:2).

What a privilege to serve as the house of the Lord! What a privilege to have His help on a constant, never-ending basis.

EMPTY VESSELS, BORROW NOT A FEW

"Then he said, Go, borrow you vessels abroad of all your neighbors, even empty vessels; borrow not a few" (II Ki. 4:3).

If there is a problem among believers, it is that we borrow too few vessels, so to speak.

The Christian life should be and, in fact, can be one of expectancy. The believer should expect the Lord to do great and mighty things each and every day. We should get up each morning with a spirit and an attitude of anticipation. The question should ever be, "What is the Lord going to do today?"

We should expect great things, good things, and bountiful things because that's what is promised in His Word.

In order to receive, our vessels must be empty, and I speak of being empty of doubt, unbelief, jealousy, envy, malice, or sin of any sort. Only then can the Lord fill these vessels.

EMPTY VESSELS AND THE CROSS

The only way that the believer can be emptied of the works of the flesh is by our faith being placed exclusively in Christ and the Cross, which then gives the Holy Spirit liberty to work within our lives. What needs to be done, we do not have the capacity within ourselves to get done. Now, that's hard for believers to understand and to accept; but it happens to be true!

It is the Holy Spirit alone who can make of our lives what our lives ought to be. What can we do in order to give Him the liberty and latitude that He must have?

As we have stated over and over again, but simply because it seems to be difficult to accept, the believer must place his faith exclusively in Christ and the Cross.

That's why Paul said, *"But God forbid that I should glory* (boast), *save in the Cross of our Lord Jesus Christ* (what the opponents of Paul sought to escape at the price of insincerity is the apostle's only basis of exultation), *by whom the world is crucified unto me, and I unto the world.* (The only way we can overcome the world, and I mean the only way, is by placing our faith exclusively in the Cross of Christ, and keeping it there.)"

THE CROSS OF CHRIST

The apostle then went on to say:

For in Christ Jesus neither circumcision availeth any-thing, nor uncircumcision (blows all of man's religious ceremonies to pieces), *but a new creature* (new in every respect, which can only be brought about by trusting Christ and what He did for us at the Cross). *And as many as walk* (to direct one's life, to order one's conduct) *according to this rule* (the principle of the Cross), *peace be on them, and mercy* (which comes only by means of the Cross), *and upon the Israel of God.* (This refers to all who look to the Cross for their redemption. They alone are the true Israel.) *From henceforth let no man trouble me* (don't listen to these false teachers): *for I bear in my body the marks of the Lord Jesus.* (This concerns the persecution he suffered because of the 'offence of the Cross' [Gal. 5:11].) *Brethren, the grace of our Lord Jesus Christ* (which comes by our faith in the Cross) *be with your spirit.* (We worship the Lord in Spirit and in truth, and the Cross is that truth.) *Amen* (empty of works of the flesh, the Holy Spirit will then fill the empty vessels) (Gal. 6:14-18) (The Expositor's Study Bible).

THE OUTPOURED SPIRIT

"And when you are come in, you shall shut the door upon you and upon your sons, and shall pour out into all those vessels, and you shall set aside that which is full" (II Ki. 4:4).

The great miracle here performed by the Lord through the

prophet Elisha was a portrayal, so to speak, of the outpouring of the Holy Spirit, which would come about 900 years later.

As long as there were empty vessels, the miracle oil poured from the vessel, and continued to pour. As should be understood, and without a doubt, this was a miracle!

If it is to be noticed, the Lord told Elisha to tell this widow woman that when all the empty vessels were gathered, she should, *"shut the door upon you and upon your sons, and shall pour out into all those vessels, and you shall set aside that which is full."*

The baptism with the Holy Spirit is not for the world. It is only for those who are redeemed, who know the Lord; thereby, there is a select few with a shut door, so to speak, between this group and the world. Unless one has been born again and made the Lord Jesus Christ the Saviour of one's soul, one cannot be baptized with the Holy Spirit (Jn. 14:17).

This oil was not to be poured out beneath the inquisitive gaze of the unredeemed of that time, hence, the command that the door was to be shut. As well, it should be understood that the world, and even most of the modern church, does not understand at all the baptism with the Holy Spirit.

THE BAPTISM WITH THE HOLY SPIRIT

It is understandable that the world does not comprehend this tremendous gift, which was made possible by what Jesus did at the Cross, but it is a sad shame when most of the church doesn't understand it either. In fact, most of the church has rejected that which, in a sense, is the sustainer of life.

Jesus said:

In the last day, that great day of the feast (spoke of the eighth day of the Feast of Tabernacles), *Jesus stood and cried, saying, If any man thirst, let him come unto Me, and drink* (presents the greatest invitation ever given to mortal man). *He who believes on Me* (it is not 'doing,' but rather, 'believing'), *as the Scripture has said* (refers to the Word of God being the story of Christ and Him crucified; all the sacrifices pointed to Christ and what He would do at the Cross, as well as the entirety of the tabernacle and temple and all their appointments), *out of his belly* (innermost being) *shall flow rivers of living water* (speaks of Christ directly and believers indirectly).

THE INDWELLING OF THE SPIRIT

(But this spoke He of the Spirit (Holy Spirit), *which they who believe on Him should receive* (it would begin on the day of Pentecost): *for the Holy Spirit was not yet given* (He has now been given); *because that Jesus was not yet glorified.)* (The time of which John wrote was shortly before the crucifixion. When Jesus died on the Cross and was resurrected three days later, He was raised with a glorified body, which was one of the signs that all sin had been atoned, now making it possible for

the Holy Spirit to come in a new dimension) (Jn. 7:37-39) (The Expositor's Study Bible).

There are many great things that one could say when speaking of the Cross as it involves the believer. However, the greatest of all, I think, other than all sin being atoned, is that the Cross made it possible for the Holy Spirit to come and dwell in the hearts and lives of all believers, thereby, giving us His eternal help. Without that help, we could not be what we ought to be, but thank God, we do have His help.

GO, SELL THE OIL, PAY THE DEBT, AND LIVE

"So she went from him, and shut the door upon her, and upon her sons, who brought the vessels to her; and she poured out. And it came to pass, when the vessels were full, that she said unto her son, Bring me yet a vessel. And he said unto her, There is not a vessel more. And the oil stayed. Then she came and told the man of God. And he said, Go, sell the oil, and pay your debt, and you and your children live of the rest" (II Ki. 4:5-7).

The following constitutes, at least in part, that which the Holy Spirit is here telling us.

GO

Unfortunately, most believers are attempting to "go" without the Holy Spirit. Such constitutes a waste of time.

From my many, many years of studying the Word of God, as well as these many years of experience, it is my personal belief that unless one is baptized with the Holy Spirit with the evidence of speaking with other tongues, that one is not going to do much of anything for the Lord.

If it is to be noticed, Jesus did not suggest to His followers that they be baptized with the Holy Spirit; it was rather a command.

The Scripture says:

And, being assembled together with them (speaks of the time He ascended back to the Father; this was probably the time of the 'above five hundred' [I Cor. 15:6]), *commanded them* (not a suggestion) *that they should not depart from Jerusalem* (the site of the temple where the Holy Spirit would descend), *but wait for the promise of the Father* (spoke of the Holy Spirit which had been promised by the Father [Lk. 24:49; Joel, Chpt. 2]), *which, said He, you have heard of Me* (you have also heard Me say these things [Jn. 7:37-39; 14:12-17, 26; 15:26; 16:7-15). *For John truly baptized with water* (merely symbolized the very best baptism believers could receive before the day of Pentecost); *but you shall be baptized with the Holy Spirit not many days hence* (spoke of the coming day of Pentecost, although Jesus did not use that term at that time) (Acts 1:4-5) (The Expositor's Study Bible).

SELL THE OIL

Of course, this was literal oil of which Elisha spoke and, thereby, could be sold. As it regards the type that this represents, it tells us that the Holy Spirit is the only currency, so to speak, that will spend in the bank of heaven. We must ever consider that the Holy Spirit works entirely within the framework of the Cross of Christ; therefore, our faith must ever be placed in Christ and what He has done for us at the Cross. With that being done, the Holy Spirit will work mightily on our behalf. Please remember that the Holy Spirit never glorifies Himself, and neither are we to glorify Him, but rather, He glorifies Christ. This refers not only to the person of Christ but, as well, to what Christ has done, meaning the Cross (Jn. 16:13-15).

PAY THE DEBT

This refers to the fact that every believer owes a debt to every person who does not know Christ. In fact, Jesus paid the debt at Calvary's Cross that we owed to God, a debt so monstrous that it was impossible for us to pay. He paid it, and paid it in totality. Yet, we do owe a debt as believers to all of humanity.

Listen to what Paul said:

> *I am debtor* (true of every believer) *both to the Greeks* (Gentiles) *and to the barbarians; both to the wise, and*

to the unwise (to all people, whomever they might be and wherever they might be). *So, as much as in me is, I am ready to preach the gospel to you who are at Rome also. For I am not ashamed of the gospel of Christ* (is said in reference to the Cross): *for it is the power of God unto salvation to every one who believes; to the Jew first, and also to the Greek* (through the Cross, and the Cross alone, man is reconciled unto God) (Rom. 1:14-16) (The Expositor's Study Bible).

That debt can be paid to lost humanity by the believers allowing the Holy Spirit to flow through them uninterrupted, that it may fill their vessels, even as our vessels have been filled.

AND LIVE

The believer is to be baptized with the Holy Spirit and have his faith exclusively in Christ and the Cross. This gives the Holy Spirit liberty to work within his life, and, thereby, he is poured out to a dying world.

Such will provide life to the giver and to the one to whom the gift is given. Unfortunately, the modern church seems to be looking in every direction instead of that of the Holy Spirit.

As a result, there is no life in such a direction. Life is found only in obedience to the Word (Mat. 4:4).

A MAN OF GOD

> *And it fell on a day, that Elisha passed to Shunem,*
> *where was a great woman; and she constrained him to*
> *eat bread. And so it was, that as oft as he passed by,*
> *he turned in thither to eat bread. And she said unto*
> *her husband, Behold now, I perceive that this is an holy*
> *man of God, which passes by us continually. Let us*
> *make a little chamber, I pray you, on the wall; and let*
> *us set for him there a bed, and a table, and a stool, and*
> *a candlestick: and it shall be, when he comes to us, that*
> *he shall turn in thither. And it fell on a day, that he*
> *came thither, and he turned into the chamber, and lay*
> *there* (II Ki. 4:8-11).

This woman was wealthy, yet she did not allow her riches to lift her up in pride, as often happens to so many. Rather, she allowed it to draw her closer to God. She was wise to bless the man of God, and she, in effect, would greatly bless herself.

From the four verses just given, we learn some tremendous truths.

We learn that it is a man of God who is to be supported, and not rather organizations, etc. There is nothing wrong with organizations, providing there are men and women of God in those organizations; however, all too often, that isn't the case. It is probably correct that there are any number of religious denominations in this nation and around the world in which there is not one single man or woman of God.

Consequently, such should not be supported.

Please understand that a person is not a man or a woman of God simply because he has been elected to an office in a denomination.

While there are some few who most definitely may fit the criteria, it is not necessarily so because they have been elected to such and such an office. We must remember that. God does not work in denominations or organizations, but rather individual people. We need to understand that.

THE KEY TO ALL BLESSINGS

The key to all blessings from the Lord is for us to support His work, which we can only do by supporting men and women of God; however, we must make doubly certain that those we are supporting are truly men and women of God. There are untold numbers who claim to be but really aren't. Jesus said you'll know them, whether they be false or true, by their fruit.

He said:

> *Beware of false prophets, which come to you in sheep's clothing, but inwardly they are ravening wolves* ('beware of false prophets' is said in the sternest of measures! there will be and are false prophets and are some of Satan's greatest weapons). *You shall know them by their fruits* (this is the test as given by Christ as it regards identifica-

tion of false prophets and false apostles). *Do men gather grapes of thorns, or figs of thistles?* (It is impossible for false doctrine, generated by false prophets, to bring forth good fruit.) *Even so every good tree brings forth good fruit; but a corrupt tree brings forth evil fruit* (the good fruit is Christlikeness, while the evil fruit is self-likeness).

THE GOOD TREE

A good tree cannot bring forth evil fruit, neither can a corrupt tree bring forth good fruit (the 'good tree' is the Cross, while the 'corrupt tree' pertains to all of that which is other than the Cross). *Every tree that brings not forth good fruit is hewn down, and cast into the fire* (judgment will ultimately come on all so-called gospel other than the Cross [Rom. 1:18]). *Wherefore by their fruits you shall know them* (the acid test). *Not every one who says unto me, Lord, Lord, shall enter into the kingdom of heaven* (the repetition of the word 'Lord' expresses astonishment, as if to say: 'Are we to be disowned?'); *but he who does the will of My Father which is in heaven* (what is the will of the Father? Verse 24 tells us).

WHAT IS THE WILL OF THE FATHER?

Many will say to Me in that day, Lord, Lord, have we not prophesied in Your name? and in Your name have cast out devils (demons)? *and in Your name done many wonderful works?* (These things are not the criteria, but rather faith in Christ and what Christ has done for us at the Cross [Eph. 2:8-9, 13-18]. The Word of God alone is to be the judge of doctrine) And then will I profess unto them, I never knew you (again we say, the criteria alone is Christ and Him crucified [I Cor. 1:23]): *depart from Me, you who work iniquity* (we have access to God only through Christ, and access to Christ only through the Cross, and access to the Cross only through a denial of self [Lk. 9:23]; any other message is judged by God as 'iniquity' and cannot be a part of Christ [I Cor. 1:17]). *Therefore whosoever hears these sayings of Mine, and does them, I will liken him unto a wise man, which built his house upon a rock* (the 'rock' is Christ Jesus, and the foundation is the Cross [Gal. 1:8-9]) (Mat. 7:15-24) (The Expositor's Study Bible).

Every believer should support the work of God, but for those whom God has especially blessed in a financial sense, their obligation is even greater. To be sure, the Lord blesses for purpose and reason. Unfortunately, many believers can give to the Lord what they should give when it is of small denomination. However, when it is large, many back away, thinking it's too much to give.

This woman who helped Elisha was termed by the Holy Spirit as "great," meaning that she was wealthy. Thank God that she allowed the Lord to use her; consequently, the account of her experience is given to us in the Word of God.

BLESSING

As would be obvious, this woman was blessed immeasurably by what she did for the Lord. Our giving should bear the following in mind:

Paul said, *"I speak not by commandment* (the grace of 'giving' cannot be by 'commandment,' or it is no longer giving), *but by occasion of the forwardness of others* (proclaims grandly that giving inspires giving), *and to prove the sincerity of your love.* (If we truly love God, we will give liberally to His work)" (II Cor. 8:8) (The Expositor's Study Bible).

We are encouraged to expect God to bless our giving.

Paul also said: *"But this I say, He which sows sparingly shall reap also sparingly* (if we give little to the Lord, He will bless little); *and he which sows bountifully shall reap also bountifully.* (If we give bountifully, He will bless bountifully. This is a promise of the Lord)" (II Cor. 9:6) (The Expositor's Study Bible).

We must also understand that it is God who judges what is bountiful and what is sparing. In other words, the little woman who gave two mites gave bountifully because that was all she had. If the Lord gives us a promise, and He most definitely did here, then we are to expect that promise to be fulfilled. The Lord desires that we have such expectation.

While we definitely do not give from a motivation of getting, still, we are to most definitely expect His blessings. In fact, we are encouraged to do so (Mat. 21:21-22; Mk. 11:24; Jn. 14:14; 15:7).

This great woman of Shunem ascertained that Elisha was a holy man of God, and she determined to be a blessing to him.

She did so by actually adding a room to her house and furnishing it in order that he might have a place to stay when he came that way. Such did not go, as stated, unrecognized by the Lord.

Once like a slave in prison I dwelt,
No freedom from my sorrow I felt,
But Jesus came and listened to me,
And glory to God, He set me free.

ELISHA

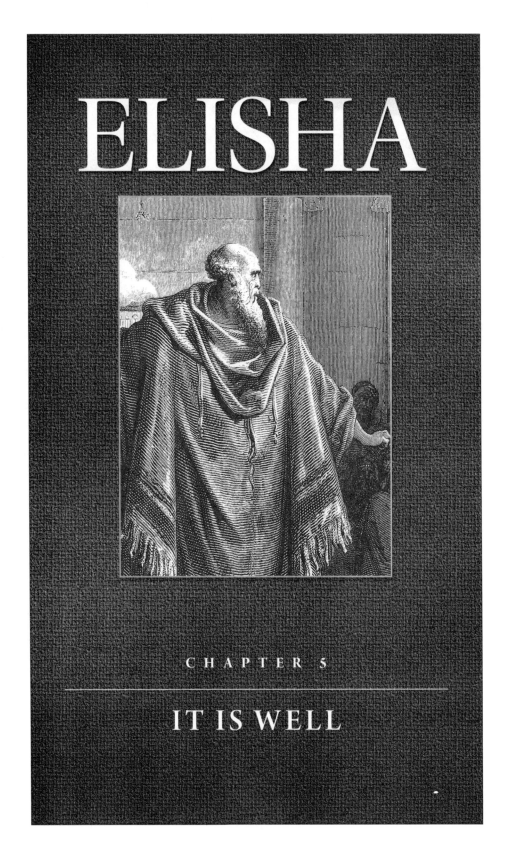

CHAPTER 5

IT IS WELL

IT IS WELL

"AND HE SAID TO Gehazi his servant, Call this Shunam-
mite. And when he had called her, she stood before him.
And he said unto him, Say now unto her, Behold, you have
been careful for us with all this care; what is to be done for
you? would you be spoken for to the king, or to the captain
of the host? And she answered, I dwell among my own peo-
ple. And he said, What then is to be done for her? And
Gehazi answered, Verily she has no child, and her husband
is old. And he said, Call her. And when he had called
her, she stood in the door. And he said, About this season,
according to the time of life, you shall embrace a son. And
she said, No, my lord, you man of God, do not lie unto your
handmaid. And the woman conceived, and bore a son at
that season that Elisha had said unto her, according to the
time of life" (II Ki. 4:12-17).

WHAT IS TO BE DONE FOR YOU?

The kindness this woman showed to Elisha and his servant

Gehazi had no ulterior motive behind the act. Actually, even though she was asked what she might desire, she, in effect, answered "nothing." Her motives were pure. All too often, giving is done from a basis of greed. In other words, "What will I get in return?"

Like Sarah of old, the woman was incredulous. When told that she would have a child, she could not believe the good tidings and thought the prophet was only raising hopes to disappoint them; however, she would find out that the Lord never deceives anyone.

For her kindness shown to the prophet, the Lord would reward her graciously and despite the age of her husband, He would miraculously give her a son. This, no doubt, was the greatest thing that could have ever happened to them.

THE LORD WILL NEVER OWE ANYONE ANYTHING

It can be said from the experience of this Shunammite woman, and countless others in the Word of God, that the Lord never allows good things done for Him to go unrewarded. As well, that which He gives in turn is always far greater than what we have done for Him. Listen to the words of Christ:

He who receives a prophet in the name of a prophet (because he is a true prophet) *shall receive a prophet's reward; and he who receives a righteous man in the name of a righteous man* (because he is a righteous man) *shall receive a righteous man's reward* (one on a righteous mission). *And whosoever shall give to drink unto one of these little ones* (newest believer) *a cup of cold water only in the name of a disciple* (because he is a follower of Christ), *verily I say unto you, he shall in no wise lose his reward* (a reward is guaranteed!) (Mat. 10:41-42) (The Expositor's Study Bible).

While there definitely was an expense for this woman and her husband to build a room onto their house and to furnish it so that Elisha and Gehazi would have a place to stay when they came in that direction, it would prove to be the greatest investment they ever made. That's exactly the way it is as it regards the work of God.

Anything and everything that we give to the work of the Lord is an investment that will bring forth eternal dividends, not only in this life but in the one to come. In other words, there is a double-barreled return, so to speak.

THE LESSON WE SHOULD LEARN

That's the reason that Paul said, *"And to remember the words of the Lord Jesus, how He said, It is more blessed to give than to receive"* (Acts 20:35).

These words are not recorded in the Gospels; however, we know that only a tiny part of what Jesus said and did is recorded. Peter or one of the other apostles who were with Jesus evidently related this to Paul.

The old adage is true: You cannot outgive God!

This woman was told that despite the age of her husband, *"About this season, according to the time of life, you shall embrace a son."*

To be frank, the word was so fantastic, so incredulous, and, in fact, so unbelievable that she could not bring herself to accept what was being said. She was to find very shortly that the promise was no joke.

It doesn't matter who we are, what our circumstances might be, or what difficulties may seem to lie in the path. The truth is this: We serve a miracle-working God. This means that He can do anything. When we entered into His economy, we entered into a miracle economy that is not subject to the variances of the ways of this world. God can create something out of nothing. As we have previously stated, as believers, we should live in a state of believing, i.e., a state of expectation and a state of anticipation, wondering what great and glorious thing that God is going to do next. Those who give to His work and those who support His work can expect His greatest and His best, in other words, His miraculous.

SATAN WILL ATTEMPT TO TAKE AWAY THAT WHICH THE LORD HAS GIVEN

"And when the child was grown, it fell on a day, that he went out to his father to the reapers. And he said unto his father, My head, my head. And he said to a lad, Carry him to his mother. And when he had taken him, and brought

*him to his mother, he sat on her knees till noon, and then
died. And she went up, and laid him on the bed of the
man of God, and shut the door upon him, and went out"*
(II Ki. 4:18-21).

The child evidently died of sunstroke.

Her laying the dead child on the bed of the man of God
evidently meant that she reasoned that if the Lord through
Elisha could give her the child, then the child could be raised
from the dead through Elisha.

It is evident from this that this woman was a person of
great faith.

Receiving from the Lord is one thing but keeping what
we have received is another thing. To begin with, Satan will
do everything within his power to keep us from receiving
anything. Not being successful at that, he will do everything
within his power to take what we have received. He is just
as zealous in the latter as he is in the former. If he is able to
take what we have received, it's not at all easy or simple to
get it back. One need only look at the scenario before us of
this little boy having died, which would necessitate his being
raised from the dead. While that most definitely happened,
one would have to readily admit that such is not a common
occurrence. So, we must guard diligently that which the Lord
has given us.

Paul said this: *"Wherefore take unto you the whole
armor of God* (because of what we face), *that you may be
able to withstand in the evil day* (refers to resisting and
opposing the powers of darkness), *and having done all, to*

stand. (This refers to the believer not giving ground to Satan, not a single inch.)" (Eph. 6:13) (The Expositor's Study Bible).

Most read this passage given by Paul in a wrong light. Most take it to mean that the believer is backed against the wall, so to speak, and that there he must make a stand, somewhat with a fortress mentality.

It doesn't mean that at all! It means that Satan is not to gain one single inch against us and is not to take anything from us that is ours. In other words, and as stated, the believer is not to give ground, not a single inch.

VICTORY AND THE CROSS

For the type of victory of which I speak—and to be frank, there is no other kind—the believer must understand that Jesus Christ is the source of all things that are given to us, and the Cross is the means by which these things are given. In that capacity, the Holy Spirit superintends it all.

Victory is found in the Cross, and only in the Cross. I am adamant regarding this subject because that's what the Lord told me when the revelation of the Cross was given to me. I have found out from the Word of God and from experience that this is most definitely the case.

The Lord spoke to me that morning hour in 1997 and said, "The answer for which you seek is found in the Cross."

He then said a second time, with a slight variation, "The *solution* for which you seek is found in the Cross."

And then, a third time, He said the following, "The answer

for which you seek is found *only* in the Cross."

To be frank, Satan respects nothing but the Cross of Christ because it was there where he was totally and completely defeated (Col. 2:10-15).

I'm going to show you something from the Word of God that most believers do not know. To be sure, this is something very, very important!

SATAN CAN OVERRIDE THE WILL OF A BELIEVER AND FORCE HIM TO DO SOMETHING HE DOESN'T WANT TO DO IF HIS FAITH IS IMPROPERLY PLACED!

Read the heading again. Most believers have never seen such a statement, and most would not believe what is stated. I'll prove it to you from the Word of God. If the believer's faith is placed in anything except the Cross of Christ, then Satan will be able to push that believer into doing something he is trying not to do. This is true despite the fact that he is trying with all of his might, power, and strength not to fail.

Most would read that and think that if that is the case, then the believer is not responsible.

Oh yes he is!

He is responsible because He is not subscribing to God's prescribed order of victory, but rather to something else entirely. In other words, the believer is responsible for taking the wrong direction, which is unscriptural and ties the hands of the Holy Spirit.

PROVIDING THE BELIEVER IS
FOLLOWING THE WORD OF GOD ...

Most believers erroneously believe that while Satan could force the issue before they were saved, thereby, forcing them to do something they didn't want to do, now that they're saved, he can no longer do such.

That is definitely correct, providing the believer is following the Word of God.

Please understand that God has a prescribed order, and that order is found in Romans, Chapter 6. If we follow that order, we can expect victory; otherwise, it will be defeat. Most believers have the erroneous idea that before they were saved, Satan could, in fact, override their will and force them into doing things that they did not want to do. However, now that they are saved, they think that Satan cannot do such.

It is true that he cannot, providing, as stated, that we are functioning after the Word of God. However, if we aren't functioning after the Word of God, meaning that we are functioning after the flesh, no matter how hard we try otherwise, Satan most definitely will override our will and force us to do things we don't want to do.

Most believers, and especially preachers, are loath to admit that, but it happens to be true.

IS SIN A MATTER OF CHOICE?

Yes it is, but only in a particular manner.

For many, many years, while in a particular religious denomination, when someone did something wrong, I would hear preachers say, "They wanted to do that."

They intimated that all the person had to do was just simply say no, walk away, and the deed would not be done.

Is that correct?

No it isn't!

The choice that the believer has is whether he accepts God's way or accepts another way. That is the choice. If we make the wrong choice, thereby deciding for some way other than that which is scriptural, the choice is no longer ours. In other words, Satan will force us into a position that we are trying to avoid.

Please allow me to state once again that this doesn't mean that the believer is not responsible. Every believer is responsible for his or her sin. It is our responsibility to know what the Word of God says about the matter and then obey what it does say.

THE SEVENTH CHAPTER OF ROMANS

This chapter, Chapter 7 of Romans, proves 100 percent what I say. It is the experience of the apostle Paul after he was saved, baptized with the Holy Spirit, and called to be an apostle. Not understanding the Message of the Cross at that time, which no one else did either because this revelation had not yet been given, Paul attempted to live for God by means of the flesh. In other words, he looked at the Ten Commandments and then set about to try to keep them, thinking that he surely could do such since he was born again; however, he was to find to his dismay that he couldn't. He said:

> *For that which I do* (the failure) *I allow not* (should have been translated, 'I understand not'; these are not the words of an unsaved man as some claim, but rather a believer who is trying and failing): *for what I would, that do I not* (refers to the obedience he wants to render to Christ, but rather fails; why? as Paul explained, the believer is married to Christ but is being unfaithful to Christ by spiritually cohabiting with the law, which frustrates the grace of God; that means the Holy Spirit will not help such a person, which guarantees failure [Gal. 2:21]); *but what I hate, that do I* (this refers to sin in his life which he doesn't want to do and, in fact, hates, but finds himself unable to stop; unfortunately, due to the fact of not understanding the Cross as it refers to sanctification, this is the plight of most modern Christians) (Rom. 7:15).

WILLPOWER

The great apostle then dealt with willpower. He said:

> *For I know that in me, (that is, in my flesh,) dwells no good thing* (speaks of man's own ability, or rather the lack thereof in comparison to the Holy Spirit, at least when it comes to spiritual things): *for to will is present with me*

(Paul is speaking here of his willpower; regrettably, most modern Christians are trying to live for God by means of willpower, thinking falsely that since they have come to Christ, they are now free to say no to sin; that is the wrong way to look at the situation; the believer cannot live for God by the strength of willpower; while the will is definitely important, it alone is not enough; the believer must exercise faith in Christ and the Cross, and do so constantly; then he will have the ability and the strength to say yes to Christ, which automatically says no to the things of the world); *but how to perform that which is good I find not* (outside of the Cross, it is impossible to find a way to do good) (Rom. 7:18) (The Expositor's Study Bible).

GOD'S PRESCRIBED ORDER OF VICTORY

The following has been given elsewhere in this volume, but due to the great significance of what is said here, permit us to use it again in this extremely abbreviated form. It will set the tone for what we are saying:

- Focus: the Lord Jesus Christ (Jn. 14:6).
- Object of faith: the Cross of Christ (Rom. 6:3-5; I Cor. 1:17-18, 23; 2:2; Gal. 6:14).
- Power source: the Holy Spirit (Rom. 8:1-11).
- Results: victory (Rom. 6:14).

Now, let's use the same formula but in the way that it's attempted by most modern Christians:

- Focus: works (Rom. 4:4).
- Object of faith: performance (Rom. 8:8).
- Power source: self (Lk. 9:23).
- Results: defeat (Rom. 7:15).

In short, God's prescribed order of victory is the Cross of Christ. The believer is to place his faith exclusively in Christ and what He did at the Cross and not allow it to be moved to something else.

With this being done and maintained, the Holy Spirit will then grandly help us to do that which needs to be done, without whom it cannot be done.

GOD'S PRESCRIBED ORDER

Subscribing and adhering to God's prescribed order guarantees that Satan cannot override your will and force you to do something you don't want to do. The Holy Spirit will guarantee that this will not happen, but otherwise, it will!

The Shunammite woman took the dead body of her son and laid his body on the bed of the man of God. The son was probably 4 or 5 years old and had died of sunstroke. The Scripture says that she then *"shut the door upon him, and went out."*

Why did she do this?

She correctly reasoned in her mind that God, through Elisha, had performed a miracle in giving her this son, especially considering that her husband was long since past the age of being able to father a child. With that being the case, she, no doubt, believed that God, through Elisha, could raise the child from the dead.

IT IS WELL!

> *And she called unto her husband, and said, Send me, I pray you, one of the young men, and one of the asses, that I may run to the man of God, and come again. And he said, Wherefore will you go to him today? it is neither new moon, nor Sabbath. And she said, It shall be well. Then she saddled an ass, and said to her servant, Drive, and go forward; slack not your riding for me, except I bid you. So she went and came unto the man of God to Mount Carmel. And it came to pass, when the man of God saw her afar off, that he said to Gehazi his servant, Behold, yonder is that Shunammite: Run now, I pray you, to meet her, and say unto her, Is it well with you? is it well with your husband? is it well with the child? And she answered, It is well* (II Ki. 4:22-26).

Evidently the father didn't know the child had died, and his wife not telling him shows that she believed the child would be raised from the dead.

Elisha suspected that something was wrong because only faith could answer, *"It is well!"*

Why did this dear lady answer in this manner, *"It is well,"* when her child was dead? Should we, as well, call those things that be not as though they are?

Can we change things that we do not desire by confessing the opposite of what actually is?

Was the woman telling the truth when she said in answer to the question concerning her child, *"It is well"*?

Let's look at these questions one by one.

WHY DID THIS WOMAN ANSWER, "IT IS WELL"?

She knew, as stated, that the Lord, through Elisha, had given her this child. She knew it took a miracle for his conception to be brought about. So she reasoned in her mind, and rightly so, that if the Lord had done this thing, and He most definitely had, then somehow, some way, it would turn out all right, despite the fact that the child had died.

She definitely was not functioning from the position of presumption. She had reason to believe as she did and, therefore, to answer as she did.

SHOULD WE CALL THOSE THINGS THAT BE NOT AS THOUGH THEY WERE?

The apostle Paul said:

(As it is written, I have made you a father of many nations [Gen. 12:1-3; 17:4-5],) *before Him whom he believed, even God* (refers to Abraham believing God), *who quickens the dead* (makes spiritually alive those who are spiritually dead), *and calls those things which be not*

as though they were (if God has said it to us personally, we can call it; otherwise, it is presumption). *Who against hope believed in hope* (a description of Abraham's faith as it regarded the birth of Isaac), *that he might become the father of many nations; according to that which was spoken* (the promise of God), *So shall your seed be* (Gen. 15:5). *And being not weak in faith* (strong faith), *he considered not his own body now dead, when he was about an hundred years old* (no longer able to father children), *neither yet the deadness of Sarah's womb* (placed her in the same situation as her husband): *He staggered not at the promise of God through unbelief* (he did not allow difficulties to deter him from the intended conclusion); *but was strong in faith, giving glory to God* (his faith came from the Word of God); *And being fully persuaded* (no turning back) *that, what He* (God) *had promised, He was able also to perform* (whatever it was, God could do it) (Rom. 4:17-21) (The Expositor's Study Bible).

Once again, we come back to the will of God. Abraham knew that God had promised him and Sarah a son. So, on that premise, and that premise alone, he could *"call those things which be not as though they were."*

If we as believers think that we can confess things into existence that the Lord has not promised, then we are sadly mistaken. The Lord will not allow His Word to be used against Himself.

Let's look at that under the next heading.

CAN WE AS BELIEVERS BRING THINGS INTO EXISTENCE BY A PROPER CONFESSION?

Once again, we go back to the will of God. If the Lord has promised us something, then it's perfectly proper for us to begin confessing that thing, at least within reason. However, the mistaken idea that is presented presently by many is that we as believers can confess into existence that which we want or desire. This is not upheld by Scripture. As stated, the Lord will not allow His Word to be used against Him, which means to be used against His will.

What do we mean by that statement?

For instance, Jesus said: *"Therefore I say unto you, What things soever you desire, when you pray, believe that you receive them, and you shall have them"* (Mk. 11:24).

What did Jesus mean by that statement?

The idea is that one seeking to do the will of God will want only what God desires. For the most part, ascertaining the will of God in that is not difficult. The believer can definitely have that which he so desires, but only on the premise of it being the will of God.

Even as it regards the will of God, there are times that certain things may be His will but not His wisdom. In other words, the Lord may want to do something for us, but because of certain situations, He knows that it would be best for that thing not be carried out presently, whatever it might be. Any believer in his right mind wants only the perfect will of God.

A PERSONAL EXPERIENCE

Sometime back, I was asking the Lord about a certain thing. I made mention to Him what I wanted, but then quickly stated that only He knew all the ins and outs of the situation, and if what I wanted was not His will, then by all means, His will had to be paramount.

Things can look so good on the surface and seem to be the right thing to do, but if it's not the will of God, it's not going to turn out that way. We must be mature enough in the Lord that we seek only the will of God, desire only the will of God, and settle for nothing less than the will of God. Concerning this, Paul said:

> *I beseech you therefore, brethren* (I beg of you please), *by the mercies of God* (all is given to the believer, not because of merit on the believer's part, but strictly because of the 'mercy of God'), *that you present your bodies a living sacrifice* (the word 'sacrifice' speaks of the sacrifice of Christ and means that we cannot do this which the Holy Spirit demands unless our faith is placed strictly in Christ and the Cross, which then gives the Holy Spirit latitude to carry out this great work within our lives), *holy* (that which the Holy Spirit alone can do), *acceptable unto God* (actually means that a holy physical body, i.e., 'temple,' is all that He will accept), *which is your reasonable service.* (Reasonable if we look to Christ and the Cross, otherwise, impossible!)

TRANSFORMED

And be not conformed to this world (the ways of the world): *but be you transformed by the renewing of your mind* (we must start thinking spiritually, which refers to the fact that everything is furnished to us through the Cross and is obtained by faith and not works), *that you may prove what is that good* (is put to the test and finds that the thing tested meets the specifications laid down), *and acceptable, and perfect, will of God* (this presents that which the Holy Spirit is attempting to bring about within our lives and can only be obtained by ever making the Cross the object of our faith) (Rom. 12:1-2) (The Expositor's Study Bible).

WE MUST TURN FROM GEHAZI TO ELISHA

And when she came to the man of God to the hill, she caught him by the feet: but Gehazi came near to thrust her away. And the man of God said, Let her alone; for her soul is vexed within her: and the LORD has hid it from me, and has not told me. Then she said, Did I desire a son of my lord? did I not say, Do not deceive me? Then he said to Gehazi, Gird up your loins, and take my staff in your hand, and go your way: if you meet any man, salute him not; and if any salute you, answer him not again: and lay my staff upon the face of the child. And the mother of the child said, As the LORD lives, and as your soul lives, I will not leave you. And he arose, and followed her. And Gehazi passed on before them, and laid the staff upon the face of the child; but there was neither voice, nor hearing. Wherefore he went again to meet him, and told him, saying, The child is not awaked (II Ki. 4:27-31).

Elisha knew something was wrong with the woman, but he didn't know exactly what. Gehazi, who represented religion, *"thrust her away,"* as religion must! But Elisha, who represented grace, said, *"Let her alone."* Oh, that somehow we would turn from Gehazi to Elisha! Her son was given to her by the Lord, and she did not expect the Lord to take him away.

The Shunammite would not be satisfied with whatever the servant was to do. She wanted Elisha to go where her child was, and so he did!

What purpose Elisha had in mind regarding the staff upon the child, we aren't told. Perhaps we could say that it represented ceremony, which means that a dead staff laid upon a dead face cannot give life. Religious ceremonies, however scriptural, are paralyzed in the presence of death. Religion has never set anyone free. Ceremonies have never set anyone free. It is only the power of Jesus Christ, made available to us through the Cross and given by the Holy Spirit, that can bring life (Jn. 7:37-39). Perhaps Elisha conducting himself as he did toward the dead child was meant to symbolize the fact that Jesus could not save mankind by passing a decree. He saved man by becoming one with man (Isa. 7:14).

TAKE UP YOUR SON

This, without a doubt, is one of the greatest miracles recorded in the Word of God.

This woman, as it regarded her need, went to the man of God, i.e., Elisha. Men and women of God, and we speak of those who are truly of God, are the strength of the church and the strength of a nation.

In fact, there is no way that the worth of such could even remotely be estimated, but somehow, we get our eyes off of that which is given by God onto that which is devised by men. I speak of denominations, organizations, etc.

There's really nothing wrong with these particular things, not normally, as it regards their existence. They can be helpful to the work of God, but we must never forget that religious denominations and organizations are not sacrosanct. There is nothing holy about them. They are merely tools that can be used to hinder or help the work of God, according to how they are used.

DENOMINATIONS AND DENOMINATIONALISM

As we've already stated, there is nothing wrong with believers forming a denomination or belonging to a denomination, providing the doctrine is scriptural; however, as it regards denominationalism, this is wrong, very wrong!

What is denominationalism?

Denominationalism is very much akin to racism. Racism

projects the idea that if anyone is not of the color desired, that person is then looked at as inferior as far as intellectualism, intelligence, etc. is concerned.

Denominationalism is very similar. It projects the idea that association with the denomination in question gives one a spiritual edge. In other words, one is spiritually elite if one belongs to that particular denomination. Then such becomes sin. That is denominationalism.

Unfortunately, most denominations, even those which are begun correctly, soon drift into denominationalism.

I was a part of a particular denomination for many, many years. There are still many godly people and preachers in that particular group. However, little by little, they have drifted toward denominationalism.

INFERIOR?

The last few years I was associated with that group, I started hearing statements such as, "While others may be believers, if they are where they ought to be, they will be with us."

Of course, that implied that if one was not a member of that particular denomination, then they were inferior. Again we state, that is denominationalism.

Then I heard statements such as, "Any move that God brings about will begin with this denomination. If it doesn't begin with this denomination, then we have to look at it as not being of God."

Once again, those who believe such have placed themselves in a superior position, which is extremely displeasing to the Lord.

It is not denominations or organizations that accomplish the work of God, but rather men and women of God. We must never forget that!

THE MIRACLE

There are eight recorded incidents in the Bible of individuals being raised from the dead. They are:

1. The son of the widow of Zarephath was raised from the dead by Elijah (I Ki. 17:17-24).
2. The son of the Shunammite raised from the dead by Elisha (II Ki. 4:18-37).
3. The man raised from the dead when his corpse touched the bones of Elisha (II Ki. 13:20-21).
4. Jesus raised the man from the dead from the city of Nain (Lk. 7:11-16).
5. Jesus raised the daughter of Jairus from the dead (Lk. 8:40-56).
6. Jesus raised Lazarus from the dead (Jn. 11:33-45).
7. Peter raised Tabitha from the dead in the city of Joppa (Acts 9:36-43).
8. Paul raised the young man from the dead at Troas (Acts 20:7-12).

Augustine said that Jesus raised others from the dead who were not recorded, which may very well have been the case.

As John the Beloved closed out his great gospel, he said, *"And there are also many other things which Jesus did* (speaks, no doubt, of the many miracles He performed, some which are not recorded in any of the four gospels), *the which, if they should be written every one* (lends credence to the idea that there were far more miracles performed by Jesus and not recorded than those which were recorded), *I suppose that even the world itself could not contain the books that should be written. Amen"* (Jn. 21:25) (The Expositor's Study Bible).

Christ is infinite, the earth finite; hence, the supposition of the verse is most reasonable.

THE NUMBER EIGHT

As stated, there are eight recorded incidences in the Bible of people being raised from the dead. Eight is also the number of resurrection.

There is yet to come the greatest resurrection of the dead the world has ever known, and by far. I speak of the rapture of the church when all the dead in Christ who have ever lived will be raised in a moment, in the twinkling of an eye. Paul said:

> *For the Lord Himself shall descend from heaven with a shout* (refers to 'the same Jesus' which the angels proclaimed in Acts 1:11), *with the voice of the archangel* (refers to Michael, the only one referred to as such [Jude, Vs. 9]), *and with the trump of God* (doesn't exactly say

God will personally blow this trumpet, but that it definitely does belong to Him, whoever does signal the blast): *and the dead in Christ shall rise first* (the criterion for being ready for the rapture is to be "in Christ," which means that all who are truly born again will definitely go in the rapture) (I Thess. 4:16) (The Expositor's Study Bible).

THE RESURRECTION

As is obvious, the accounts we have given of individuals being raised from the dead do not include Christ, inasmuch as He is in a class all to Himself. Also, there may very well have been other people raised from the dead during the church age, but the Bible accounts are those in which we are the most interested.

Why?

The main purpose and reason is the fact that inasmuch as the power of God was able to raise the dead during Bible times, this shows us that the Lord will be able, as well, to raise the sainted dead at the time of the resurrection.

The miracle of the little boy being raised from the dead by Elisha was indisputable. As well, the little boy had been dead for at least one or two days.

One can well imagine the joy that filled the heart of the mother when Elisha said to her, *"Take up your son."*

The Scripture then says, *"Then she went in, and fell at his feet, and bowed herself to the ground, and took up her son, and went out"* (II Ki. 4:35-37).

THE FAMINE IN THE LAND

And Elisha came again to Gilgal: and there was a dearth in the land; and the sons of the prophets were sitting before him: and he said unto his servant, Set on the great pot, and seethe pottage for the sons of the prophets. And one went into the field to gather herbs, and found a wild vine, and gathered thereof wild gourds his lap full, and came and shred them into the pot of pottage: for they knew them not. So they poured out for the men to eat. And it came to pass, as they were eating of the pottage, that they cried out, and said, O you man of God, there is death in the pot. And they could not eat thereof (II Ki. 4:38-40).

Elisha offered God's provision, for surely the gospel occupies a great container. One man was not satisfied with that which the Lord had provided, so he went out into the field to gather herbs, and the herbs were from a wild vine.

These herbs of the wild vine represent all false doctrine. Men are ever trying to add to the Word of God, but it only brings death.

The herbs were poison—all false doctrine brings death in one way or the other. Sadly, much, if not most, doctrine in the church presently is unscriptural.

In fact, if every doctrine is not built exclusively upon the Cross of Christ, then in some way, it is spurious (I Pet. 1:18-20).

THE MEAL

"But he said, Then bring meal. And he cast it into the pot; and he said, Pour out for the people, that they may eat. And there was no harm in the pot" (II Ki. 4:41).

The meal is a type of the Word of God, which was and is the only answer for the *"death in the pot."* When will we quit trying to take away or add to the Word of God? Every time it brings death.

As it regarded Judah and Israel of those days, anything, such as a drought or a famine, signified terrible spiritual declension. In other words, God at times would bring such upon the land because of Judah and Israel forsaking Him and His way. The occasion of this incident was no exception.

Presently, if the facts be known, how many storms and catastrophes brought on by the elements could be attributed to the spiritual declension of the nation? Possibly, not all would fall into that category, but most definitely, some would.

THE ONLY PLACE FOR SIN IS
AT THE FOOT OF THE CROSS

The Scripture plainly says, *"The wages of sin is death"* (Rom. 6:23). Of course, it is speaking here of spiritual death, which means separation from God, but at the same time, the word can be broadened to mean other things also.

God created this world and, thereby, owns it and all that is therein. As well, He has total control over everything. He has plainly told us and, in fact, the entirety of mankind, at least if men will only read the Word, that sin will bring on terrible catastrophes. Mankind ignores that and reaps the terrible results. He sows to the wind and reaps the whirlwind (Hos. 8:7).

As it applies to nations, it also applies to individuals. The only place for sin is at the foot of the Cross. Otherwise, we reap what we sow (Gal. 6:7).

SONS OF THE PROPHETS

Evidently, this was some type of school as it regarded prophets. And yet, we hear next to nothing from these individuals, except as they were related to Elisha.

While the Lord may have most definitely used some of these young men, and, no doubt, did, of that the Scripture is silent. Those who were truly used of God are those who are truly called of God. There were not many God-called prophets then, and there aren't many God-called prophets now. There are many who go under the heading, but it is an office to which they have appointed themselves instead of being appointed by the Lord.

The prophet is basically a preacher of righteousness, who is generally used by God to call the nation, the church, and the people to repentance. Sometimes the Lord uses prophets to foretell events, such as He did with Isaiah, Jeremiah, Ezekiel, etc. Of course, He has also done such to foretell future events through many, many others, as well, but, as stated, the greater thrust of the true prophet is to be a preacher of righteousness.

THE MESSAGE OF THE PROPHET

Most of the time, the message of the prophet is negative; consequently, true prophets are not too very much appreciated. People do not enjoy being told that they are wrong, that they are heading in the wrong direction, and that what they're doing is going to destroy them.

Not only do they reject the message, but most of the time, they reject the messenger as well. Therefore, most false prophets have a message that appeals to people. In other words, the people are being told what they want to hear instead of what they need to hear. To be sure, the people in an apostate church always reward handsomely the false prophet.

Paul said:

For the time will come when they will not endure sound doctrine ('sound doctrine' pertains to overriding principles: the salvation of the sinner and the sanctification of the saint; the Cross is the answer for both, and is the only answer for both); *but after their own lusts shall they heap to themselves teachers, having itching ears* (refers to the people who have ears that 'itch' for the smooth and comfortable word, and are willing to reward handsomely the man who is sufficiently compromising to speak it;

hearers of this type have rejected the truth and prefer to hear the lie);

THE TRUTH

And they shall turn away their ears from the truth (those who follow false teachers not only turn away their ears from the truth, but see to it that their ears are always in a position such that they will never come in contact with the truth), *and shall be turned unto fables.* (If it's not the 'Message of the Cross,' then it is 'fables' [I Cor. 1:18].)

But watch thou in all things (carries the idea of watching one's own life, ministry, and the doctrine which we are proclaiming), *endure afflictions* (carries the idea of not allowing hardships, difficulties, or troubles to hinder one's carrying forth of one's ministry; it is a sharp command given with military snap and curtness; Wuest says, 'How we in the ministry of the Word need that injunction today. What a "softy" we sometimes are, afraid to come out clearly in our proclamation of the truth and our stand as to false doctrine, fearing the ostracism of our fellows, the ecclesiastical displeasure of religious leaders so-called, or even the cutting off of our immediate financial income.' ['I would rather walk a lonely road with Jesus than be in a crowd, without His fellowship']), *do the work of an evangelist* (keep trying to get people saved), *make full proof of your ministry* (does it match up with the Word of God?) (II Tim. 4:3-5) (The Expositor's Study Bible).

WATCHMEN?

Concerning false prophets, the great prophet Isaiah said:

His watchmen are blind: they are all ignorant, they are all dumb dogs, they cannot bark; sleeping, lying down, loving to slumber. (The idea, as presented by the Holy Spirit, is that Israel lost her way because of these 'blind watchmen,' i.e., false prophets! Israel forfeited all the great promises because of these 'dumb dogs' that 'cannot bark,' which means they do not preach the truth or warn of false doctrine.) *Yes, they are greedy dogs which can never have enough, and they are shepherds who cannot understand: they all look to their own way, every one for his gain, from his quarter.* (In Jesus' day, these 'watchmen' were called 'blind guides' of the gospel [Mat. 15:14; Lk. 6:39]. They did not have the spiritual discernment which would enable them to lead people aright. Instead of acting as faithful watchdogs who give warning of the approach of danger by their barking, they remain apathetic and utter no warning at all. It is as if they pass their lives in sleep. Not only do they fail in the way of neglect of duty, but they are actively culpable. Being worldly and not spiritually minded, they are 'greedy' after gain, i.e., 'greedy dogs.') *Come you, say they, I will fetch wine, and we will fill ourselves with strong drink; and tomorrow shall be as this day, and much more abundant.* (The prophets of Isaiah's time, as well as the time of Christ, were not only negligent of their duty, and covetous, but they were given to excess regarding entertainment. Such crucified their Saviour when He came, and such today reject their Saviour who has come!) (Isa. 56:10-12) (The Expositor's Study Bible).

THE SUPPLY

And there came a man from Baal-shalisha, and brought the man of God bread of the firstfruits, twenty loaves of barley, and full ears of corn in the husk thereof. And he said, Give unto the people, that they may eat. And his servitor said, What, should I set this before an hundred men? He said again, Give the people, that they may eat: for thus says the Lord, *They shall eat, and shall leave thereof. So he set it before them, and they did eat, and left thereof, according to the Word of the* Lord (II Ki. 4:42-44).

A man brought some food, and Elisha told those in charge, *"Give unto the people, that they may eat."* The man that was doing the serving looked at the small amount of food and the 100 men who were to take of the food and complained that it was not nearly enough. Elisha said again, *"Give the people, that they may eat: for thus says the* Lord, *They shall eat, and shall leave thereof."*

The Lord evidently multiplied the food. It must be remembered that the same power that multiplied this food multiplied the loaves and fish regarding Christ. Men judge our Lord the same as the prophet's servant judged the barley cakes. They do not believe that He can satisfy the hunger of their hearts. However, all that the world offers can never satisfy man's hunger. Jesus alone can satisfy and give even more. So, there was plenty, and there was even some left, exactly as the Lord through the prophet said it would be.

GIVE UNTO THE PEOPLE THAT THEY MAY EAT

Who this man was who brought this food, *"twenty loaves of barley,"* we aren't told. However, there was no doubt that it was the Lord who instructed him to do this.

Whenever the Lord supplies something, actually anything, the miracle—and it is a miracle—does not stop with the supply. The Lord is able to multiply what is given, and to do so abundantly, to meet the need, whatever the need might be.

Consequently, as believers, we must never complain about the supply. Rather, we must understand that it is a miracle to supply and, as such, it will meet the need, irrespective as to what the need might be.

We serve a miracle-working God, who is able to take from or add to. It remains only that we believe Him.

As believers, we must understand that this great and glorious gospel, which looks so insufficient to the world, is, in fact, a miracle supply and can meet the need of anyone, whomever it might be.

The command is that we *"give unto the people, that they may eat."*

Do you believe that what Jesus did at the Cross meets every need, answers every question, solves every problem, breaks every bondage of darkness, and cleanses from all sin?

DO YOU BELIEVE ...?

Well, if you believe it, hold up the Cross of Christ as the answer and the solution for the ills, the needs, and the perversions of mankind. Give it with assurance that whatever the need is, that need will most definitely be met.

We must understand that there was not a question that was not answered at Calvary. There was not a problem that wasn't solved at Cavalry. There wasn't a sickness that wasn't healed at Calvary. There wasn't a sin that wasn't washed clean at Calvary. There wasn't a bondage that wasn't broken at Calvary. There wasn't a life that could not be changed because of Calvary.

No, the gospel is most definitely not insufficient. It is the problem of unbelief on the part of the ministry. Too many preachers simply do not believe that what Jesus did at the Cross solves every problem, cleanses from all sin, breaks every bondage, and answers all questions. By not believing it, they set something else before the people instead of the gospel of Jesus Christ and what He did at Calvary.

Irrespective, the Word still goes out, *"Give unto the people, that they may eat."*

IT WILL BE ENOUGH AND MORE!

"And his servitor said, What, should I set this before an hundred men? He said again, Give the people, that they may eat: for thus says the LORD, *They shall eat, and shall leave thereof. So he set it before them, and they did eat, and left thereof, according to the word of the* LORD*"* (II Ki. 4:43-44).

The Lord multiplied the food until it was sufficient for all 100 men, with food left over. That is the same way with the gospel.

What Jesus did at the Cross is sufficient to meet every need, to quench every thirst, and to satisfy every hunger. After every bondage of darkness has been broken, there will still be a sufficient measure of the power of God remaining, for it cannot be exhausted, no matter the need.

Throw out the lifeline across the dark wave,
There is a brother whom someone can save;
Somebody's brother! Oh, who then will dare,
To throw out the lifeline, his peril to share?

Throw out the lifeline, with hand quick and strong,
Why do you tarry, why linger so long?
See! He is sinking, Oh hasten today,
And out with the lifeboat, away then away!

Throw out the lifeline to danger fraught men,
Sinking in anguish where you've never been:
Winds of temptation and billows of woe,
Will soon hurl them out where the dark waters flow.

Soon will the season of rescue be o'er,
Soon will they drift to eternity's shore,
Have then my brethren no time for delay,
But throw out the lifeline and save them today.

ELISHA

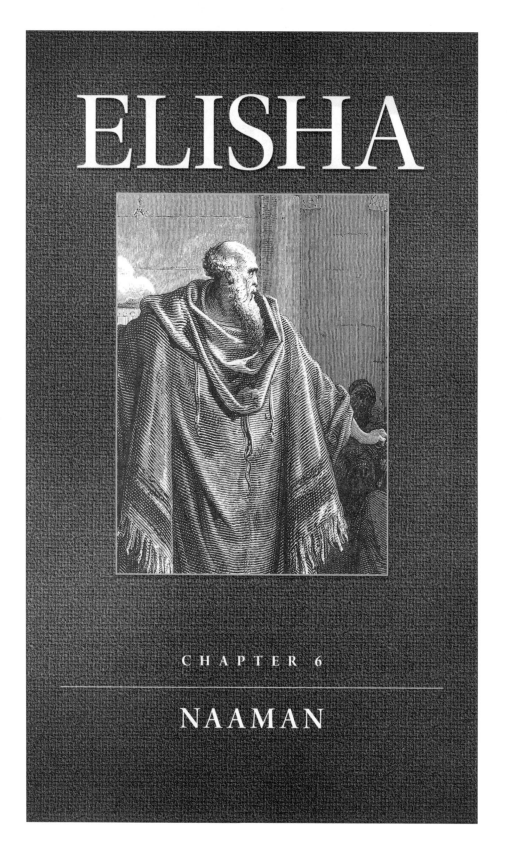

CHAPTER 6

NAAMAN

NAAMAN

"NOW NAAMAN, CAPTAIN OF the host of the king of Syria, was a great man with his master, and honorable, because by him the LORD had given deliverance unto Syria: he was also a mighty man in valor, but he was a leper" (II Ki. 5:1).

At this time, Naaman was one of the most powerful army commanders in the world. He was *"captain of the host of the king of Syria."* The Scripture also says that he was *"a great man with his master, and honorable"* and *"also a mighty man in valor."*

Even though Naaman was a worshipper of idol gods, still, the Lord used him to bring deliverance unto Syria, although Naaman would not have been aware of such. Despite all of that, he was a leper.

Leprosy in the Old Testament was a type of the spiritual condition of unregenerate man. There was no earthly cure for leprosy, just as there is no earthly cure for sin.

All of these great things said about Naaman did not save or heal him.

He was still a leper, and so are the untold millions in the world who think their state, status, and position mean something with God. They don't!

It is believed that Shalmaneser II, who headed up the great Assyrian Empire, had attacked Syria, threatening its independence, but was rebuffed by Naaman. Even though Naaman at this time would have had no knowledge of Jehovah, the God of Israel, still, the Lord would help him against the Assyrians in his defense of his native country of Syria. Then the Holy Spirit said several things about this man. He proclaimed that he was a great man, honorable, and a mighty man of valor. However, the Holy Spirit also said he was a leper.

LEPROSY

Leprosy in the Old Testament was a type of the spiritual condition of unregenerate man. Now, that doesn't mean that all who had leprosy were lost. It was just that what they had was a type of the sinful nature of man. Leprosy would gradually eat away the vitals, ultimately resulting in death, and there was no cure. Likewise, sin will eat away the vitals, resulting in spiritual death. As well, there is no earthly cure for sin.

Most of the world would think of Naaman's greatness—his honor and his valor—and would surmise that this would bring salvation. It did not then, and it does not now. The Holy Spirit is telling us here that irrespective of man's achievements, wealth, power, and position, still, he is an unregenerate, loathsome sinner on his way to eternal darkness, and none of these great things will save him, for he is a leper. This was Naaman's condition; it is, likewise, the condition of the world today.

Grace, of which Elisha was the instrument, having visited Israel, now reached out to the Gentile. We will find that the Lord would perform a notable miracle for Naaman. In fact, the entire story of Naaman is a picture of this present dispensation, even as the Lord Jesus Christ predicted in the synagogue at Nazareth.

THE WORD OF THE LORD

In His message, our Lord said:

But I tell you of a truth (will proclaim in no uncertain terms Israel's problem of self-righteousness resulting from pride), *many widows were in Israel in the days of Elijah, when the heaven was shut up three years and six months, when great famine was throughout all the land* (proclaims the time of Ahab and the great wickedness concerning the northern kingdom of Israel); *But unto none of them was Elijah sent, save unto Sarepta, a city of Sidon, unto a woman who was a widow* (she was a Gentile as well). *And many lepers were in Israel in the time of Elisha the prophet; and none of them was cleansed, saving Naaman the Syrian* (another Gentile).

And all they in the synagogue, when they heard these words, were filled with wrath (incensed that Jesus would hold up two Gentiles as examples of receiving from the Lord, while the Jews were shut out; He, in effect, was telling them that this is what would happen to Israel; the Gentiles would receive Him, but Israel would refuse Him; 'wrath' is generally the response of unbelief) (Lk. 4:25-28) (The Expositor's Study Bible).

THE GOSPEL

This great miracle that the Lord performed for Naaman is an illustration of the gospel. It tells us:

- The hopeless state of Naaman. He was a leper!
- The simplicity of the remedy given by the Lord.
- The worthlessness of the provisions suggested by Naaman.
- His anger when his plan of cure was rejected.
- His ultimate cleansing!

The first 19 verses of this chapter sing of mercy; the last eight, of judgment. The Psalmist desired to sing of both. Many preachers today desire to sing only of the first. A true preacher sings of both.

The use of the great covenant title, "Jehovah," in Verse 1, makes it clear that Naaman, even though a great chieftain, and even though a worshipper of idol gods, still was subject to Jehovah, as are all in this world and ever have been.

A LITTLE MAID

"And the Syrians had gone out by companies, and had brought away captive out of the land of Israel a little maid; and she waited on Naaman's wife. And she said unto her mistress, Would God my lord were with the prophet who is in Samaria! for he would recover him of his leprosy. And one went in, and told his lord, saying, Thus and thus said the maid that is of the land of Israel" (II Ki. 5:2-4).

This little maid would figure prominently in history. The Holy Spirit does not even give her name; however, her testimony would affect nations.

It would have been very easy for her to be bitter, morose, and angry toward God for His allowing her to be taken captive away from her land and family and made a slave in Syria, but she exhibited none of these evil traits. She retained her testimony. The things she did not understand, she left in the hands of God. What an example! When this little maid spoke unto her mistress regarding the great prophet Elisha in Samaria, in effect, she was saying, "I know somebody, who knows somebody, who knows what to do for you!"

Through her experience, this nameless girl (who was used by God so greatly) presents tremendous lessons for us to learn.

THINGS WE SHOULD LEARN

What we attempt to bring out should give encouragement to every single child of God. Satan is very adept at telling individuals that their lives are of no consequence regarding the work of God. However, this girl, even though a slave, would affect millions in a positive way by her testimony. Her tremendous accomplishment was that she was simply faithful. Let's look at her experience:

- From what little information we have regarding this young lady, we must conclude that she was close to the Lord. In other words, she was faithful, she was consecrated, she loved the Lord, and she was endeavoring with all of her strength to live for Him to the best of her ability.

- Yet, the Lord allowed the Syrians, who were idol worshippers, to take her captive and to make her a slave. We must not forget that it was the Lord who allowed this.

- It is certain that she did not enjoy at all being taken captive and made a slave and having to leave her family and the land that she knew. This should be overly obvious. However, instead of complaining, fretting, and blaming God, she put everything in His hands. She didn't question Him.

- It would have been very easy for her to become bitter and morose. After all, she had tried to live a consecrated life, so why did the Lord allow this thing to happen to her? There is no hint, however, that she questioned the Lord at all. Sometimes, bad things happen to good people, and the Lord allows them to happen.

- We must never forget that every single thing that

happens to a child of God is either caused by the Lord or allowed by the Lord. We belong to Him and are bought with a price, with that price being the shed blood of Jesus Christ at Calvary's Cross.

- There are things we do not understand that come to all of us in time, even the most consecrated of us. At these times, we are to place them in the hands of the Lord and seek to learn whatever lesson it is that is being taught. Above all, we must not become bitter or even complain.

- When the opportunity presented itself, this little maid was a faithful witness for the Lord, which fell out to a miracle being performed for Naaman. This, no doubt, brought peace between Syria and Israel, at least for a period of time. This young lady was the key in all of this.

THE TESTIMONY

As stated, Naaman was one of the most powerful men in the world at that particular time. By the providence of the Lord, this little maid had been placed in his home and was made to serve in whatever capacity that was deemed necessary.

In all of this, there is no evidence that the Lord explained to her why He allowed her to be taken captive and made a slave. Neither does He explain to us everything that He does. He expected her to trust Him, and He expects us to trust Him as well. We must understand that He is guiding us, even every footstep and every direction. Admittedly, at times we go wrong, but that's not God's fault, but rather ours. Even then, if we will recognize our wrong direction and repent of such, the Lord will bring us back to the right path.

When the news reached her ears that Naaman had contracted the dread disease of leprosy, the hour presented itself when she was with Naaman's wife. She said to her, *"Would God my lord were with the prophet who is in Samaria! for He would recover him of his leprosy."*

Of course, she was speaking of Elisha.

Now, think about what she has just said!

She knew Elisha, and she knew the power that he had with God. She believed in a God of miracles. So, why did the Lord allow her to be taken as a slave?

FORGIVE GOD?

As we have stated, there is no evidence that she ever asked the question of why she was allowed to be taken as a slave, and neither did she question God to any degree. Presently, there are millions of Christians who blame God for their circumstances.

Why didn't He deliver them? Considering some good things they have done for Him, or things which they thought were good, why didn't He bless them, even as He has blessed others, instead of allowing them to be in their present negative position?

The world of humanistic psychology, which, regrettably, has invaded the church, claims that in such circumstances, individuals should *forgive* God!

BLASPHEMY

Such thinking is not very much short of blasphemy. The idea a man should forgive God, insinuating that He has done something wrong to him, does not help the person, but rather drives him deeper into anger and bitterness. Basing one's efforts on a lie never helps.

To be sure, the Lord has never done anything wrong, bad, or hurtful to any of His children. He does allow things to happen, but it is for our good, even as with this little maid taken captive by the Syrians. Everything He does is always for a purpose and will always turn out to great blessing, that is, if we will trust Him, believe Him, and look exclusively to Him. If we complain, find fault, blame God, or question our circumstances, then we place ourselves in a position where we cannot be used by God. There are, as stated, millions of Christians right now who the Lord desires to use in a very important position, but they cannot be used, and it's for all the obvious reasons. They are bitter, morose, complaining, fault finding, and above all, deep down inside, they are angry at God.

In essence, as stated, this young lady told her mistress, "I know somebody, who knows somebody, who knows what to do for you."

Her witness would turn out to effect one of the greatest miracles recorded in the Word of God. In fact, it was so great and carried such implications that Jesus Himself mentioned it, to which we have already alluded (Lk. 4:27).

MONEY

> *And the king of Syria said, Go to, go, and I will send a*
> *letter unto the king of Israel. And he departed, and took*
> *with him ten talents of silver, and six thousand pieces*
> *of gold, and ten changes of raiment. And he brought*
> *the letter to the king of Israel, saying, Now when this*
> *letter is come unto you, behold, I have therewith sent*
> *Naaman my servant to you, that you may recover him of*
> *his leprosy. And it came to pass, when the king of Israel*
> *had read the letter, that he rent his clothes, and said,*
> *Am I God, to kill and to make alive, that this man does*
> *send unto me to recover a man of his leprosy? wherefore*
> *consider, I pray you, and see how he seeks a quarrel*
> *against me. And it was so, when Elisha the man of God*
> *had heard that the king of Israel had rent his clothes,*
> *that he sent to the king, saying, Wherefore have you rent*
> *your clothes? let him come now to me, and he shall know*
> *that there is a prophet in Israel* (II Ki. 5:5-8).

The amount of money taken by Naaman for his healing
would have been nearly $5 million in today's currency.
Man has ever tried to purchase something from God when,
in reality, the Lord has nothing for sale; it is all a free gift
(Jn. 3:16). If it was for sale, to be sure, we could not afford it.

As is obvious from Verse 7, unfortunately, that much of the
modern church is trying to evangelize the world by political
means, which are worse than useless. They are attempting

to establish some type of pseudo-Christian kingdom age philosophy. There is nothing in the Word of God that even remotely hints at such. Evangelism is carried on by the preaching of the gospel and by no other means (Mk. 16:15; I Cor. 1:17-18, 23; 2:2).

Evidently, it became obvious that the king of Israel was upset at such a request, so the news came to Elisha, and the prophet said, in effect, "Send him to me!"

KINGDOM AGE PHILOSOPHY

The king of Syria, who was totally unfamiliar with the ways of the Lord, sent Naaman to the king of Israel, saying to him, *"Behold, I have therewith sent Naaman my servant to you, that you may recover him of his leprosy."*

As should be obvious, the king of Israel, although occupying this high and lofty political office, could not recover anyone of anything. The modern church should read these passages very carefully because the modern church is attempting to establish the kingdom of God on earth by political means. It is referred to as "the new age philosophy," "kingdom age," "manifest sons of God," etc.

To be brief, the idea is that Christianity will come to terms with the other religions of the world and, thereby, establish a utopian paradise, and the church then will signal the Lord that He can now come back. What crass stupidity!

How could they hold such an opinion of themselves, thinking they can tell the Lord when He can come back!

POLITICAL MEANS

This is all to be done by political means, or at best, by using the ways of the world. Nothing can be further from the truth!

The truth is that instead of Christianity taking over the world, in most parts of the world, Christianity has already apostatized. This means that it is of precious little use anymore, at least as far as the power of God is concerned. True, there is a "true church" that has not apostatized. Its members are scattered all over the world, and they love the Lord supremely. However, as a whole, the church has apostatized, meaning that is of no further use to the kingdom of God. As believers, we have never been called upon to save society. Rather, we have been called upon to save men out of society. The truth is, society is doomed because of sin. It will only be saved at the second coming, which, of course, refers to the time that Jesus comes back. Then, the knowledge of the Lord shall cover the earth as the waters cover the sea (Isa. 11:9), but until then, the situation in this world is not going to get better, but rather worse.

THE LAST DAYS

Paul said:

This know also, that in the last days (the days in which we now live) *perilous times shall come.* (This speaks of difficult, dangerous times, which Christians living just before the rapture will encounter.) *For men* (those who call themselves Christians) *shall be lovers of their own selves, covetous, boasters, proud, blasphemers, disobedient to parents, unthankful, unholy, without natural affection, trucebreakers, false accusers, incontinent, fierce, despisers of those who are good, traitors, heady, highminded, lovers of pleasures more than lovers of God* (and remember, this is describing the end-time church, which has been totally corrupted [Mat. 13:33; Rev. 3:14-22]);

A FORM OF GODLINESS

Having a form of godliness (refers to all the trappings of Christianity, but without the power) *but denying the power thereof* (the modern church, for all practical purposes, has denied the Cross; in doing this, they have denied that through which the Holy Spirit works and in whom the power resides [Rom. 8:1-2, 11; I Cor. 1:18]): *from such turn away.* (No half measures are to be adopted here. The command is clear! It means to turn away from churches that deny or ignore the Cross) (II Tim. 3:1-5).

PAUL

Paul also said:

Now the Spirit (Holy Spirit) *speaks expressly* (pointedly), *that in the latter times* (the times in which we now live, the last of the last days, which began the fulfillment of end-time prophecies) *some shall depart from the faith* (anytime Paul uses the term 'the faith,' in short, he is referring to the Cross; so, we are told here that some will depart from the Cross as the means of salvation and victory), *giving heed to seducing spirits* (evil spirits, i.e., 'religious spirits,' making something seem like what it isn't), *and doctrines of devils* (should have been translated 'doctrines of demons'; the 'seducing spirits' entice believers away from the true faith, causing them to believe 'doctrines inspired by demon spirits') (I Tim. 4:1) (The Expositor's Study Bible).

THE TRUE MISSION OF THE CHURCH

The true church is to spend its time preaching the gospel to a hurting and dying world. Jesus said, *"Go ye into all the world* (the gospel of Christ is not merely a Western gospel, as some claim, but is for the entirety of the world), *and preach the gospel to every creature* ('preaching' is God's method, as is here plainly obvious; as well, it is imperative that every single person have the opportunity to hear; this is the responsibility of every believer)" (Mk. 16:15).

Jesus also said, *"All power is given unto Me in heaven and in earth* (this is not given to Him as Son of God; for, as God, nothing can be added to Him or taken from Him; it is rather a power, which He has merited by His incarnation and His death at Calvary on the Cross [Phil. 2:8-10]; this authority extends not only over men, so that He governs and protects the church, disposes human events, controls hearts and opinions; but the forces of heaven also are at His command; the Holy Spirit is bestowed by Him, and the angels are in His employ as ministering to the members of His body. When He said, 'all power,' He meant, 'all power!')

GO!

Go ye therefore (applies to any and all who follow Christ, and in all ages), *and teach all nations* (should have been translated, 'and preach to all nations,' for the word 'teach' here refers to a proclamation of truth), *baptizing them in the name of the Father, and of the Son, and of the Holy Spirit* (presents the only formula for water baptism given in the Word of God): *Teaching them* (means to give instruction) *to observe all things* (the whole gospel for the whole man) *whatsoever I have commanded you* (not a suggestion): *and, lo, I am with you always* (it is I, myself, God and man, who am—not 'will be'—hence, forever present among you, and with you as companion, friend, guide, Saviour, God), *even unto the end of the world* (should have been translated 'age'). *Amen* (it is the guarantee of My promise) (Mat. 28:19-20) (The Expositor's Study Bible).

Unfortunately, the modern church is presently being

filled with those who refer to themselves as "life coaches," or some other such stupidity. We aren't life coaches and never can be. The Holy Spirit alone is such. We are merely pipelines through which the Message of the Cross must be presented to a hurting and dying world. If we think of ourselves as more than that, then we think too much of ourselves.

WHAT KIND OF GOSPEL ARE WE TO PREACH?

We are to preach the Cross! Paul said, *"For Christ sent me not to baptize* (presents to us a cardinal truth), *but to preach the gospel* (the manner in which one may be saved from sin): *not with wisdom of words* (intellectualism is not the gospel), *lest the Cross of Christ should be made of none effect.* (This tells us in no uncertain terms that the Cross of Christ must always be the emphasis of the message)" (I Cor. 1:17) (The Expositor's Study Bible).

In fact, this one verse tells us that the Cross of Christ is the gospel. It does not merely contain the gospel or is not merely a part of the gospel but, in effect, is *the* gospel.

In Verse 17, we are clearly and plainly told what the gospel of Jesus Christ actually is. In brief, and as stated, it is the Cross of Christ, which refers to what He there did, with benefits that will never end. Hence, Paul also referred to it as *"the everlasting covenant"* (Heb. 13:20).

Let us say it again: "Jesus Christ is the source of all things we receive from God, and the Cross is the means by which these things are given to us, all superintended by the Holy Spirit."

PAUL

The great apostle also stated, *"For the preaching* (Word) *of the Cross is to them who perish foolishness* (spiritual things cannot be discerned by unredeemed people, but that does not matter; the Cross must be preached just the same, even as we shall see); *but unto us who are saved it is the power of God.* (The Cross is the power of God simply because it was there that the total sin debt was paid, giving the Holy Spirit, in whom the power resides, latitude to work mightily within our lives)" (I Cor. 1:18).

Paul continues, *"For after that in the wisdom of God the world by wisdom knew not God* (man's puny wisdom, even the best he has to offer, cannot come to know God in any manner), *it pleased God by the foolishness of preaching* (preaching the Cross) *to save them who believe.* (Paul is not dealing with the art of preaching here, but with what is preached.)

The apostle then said, *"But we preach Christ crucified* (this is the foundation of the Word of God and, thereby, of salvation), *unto the Jews a stumblingblock* (the Cross was the stumblingblock), *and unto the Greeks foolishness"* (I Cor. 1:21, 23) (The Expositor's Study Bible).

ONLY THE CROSS

To continue, the apostle then said:

And I, brethren, when I came to you, came not with excellency of speech or of wisdom (means that he depended not on oratorical abilities, nor did he delve into philosophy, which was all the rage of that particular day), *declaring unto you the testimony of God* (which is Christ and Him crucified). *For I determined not to know anything among you* (with purpose and design, Paul did not resort to the knowledge or philosophy of the world regarding the preaching of the gospel), *save Jesus Christ, and Him crucified* (that and that alone is the message, which will save the sinner, set the captive free, and give the believer perpetual victory) (I Cor. 2:1-2).

I think we have established that we as preachers of the gospel must preach the Cross. If we don't, we aren't really preaching the gospel.

THE CROSS OF CHRIST

If the mission of Christ had stopped at His virgin birth, although that was completely necessary, no one would have been saved. If the mission of Christ had been stopped at His perfect life, as necessary as that was, no one would have been saved. If the mission of Christ had stopped at His miracles and healings, as necessary as they were, no one would have been saved. The truth is, God became man and came to this world for one purpose and reason, and that was to go to the Cross. While everything He did was of extreme significance, as should be obvious, and played its part in the great redemption plan, still, it was the Cross where Satan was totally and completely defeated.

Sin gives Satan the legal right to hold man in bondage; however, when Jesus died on the Cross and gave Himself as a perfect sacrifice, which was required by God, He atoned for every sin—past, present, and future—at least for those who will believe. This took away Satan's legal right to hold anyone in bondage, but again, it applies only to those who place their faith and trust in Christ and what He did at the Cross.

THE VICTORY OF THE CROSS!

Paul also said:

Blotting out the handwriting of ordinances that was against us (pertains to the law of Moses, which was God's standard of righteousness that man could not reach), *which was contrary to us* (law is against us simply because we are unable to keep its precepts, no matter how hard we try), *and took it out of the way* (refers to the penalty of the law being removed), *nailing it to His Cross* (the law with its decrees was abolished in Christ's death, as if crucified with Him); *And having spoiled principalities and powers* (Satan and all of his henchmen were defeated at the Cross by Christ atoning for all sin, past, present, and future, at least for all who will believe; sin was the legal right Satan had to hold man in captivity; with all sin atoned, he has no more legal right to hold anyone in bondage), *He* (Christ) *made a show of them openly* (what Jesus did at the Cross was in the face of the whole universe), *triumphing over them in it.* (The triumph is complete, and it was all done for us, meaning we can walk in power and perpetual victory due to the Cross) (Col. 2:14-15) (The Expositor's Study Bible).

WHY A CROSS?

Could not God have redeemed humanity without becoming man and going to the Cross? Yes, He could have!

God is omniscient, meaning all-knowing; omnipotent, meaning all-powerful; and omnipresent, meaning that He is everywhere at the same time. Yes, He had and has the power to do whatever He desires to do. Yet, God will never do anything that is opposed to His nature, His character, or His being of pure holiness. Let me try to explain it in this manner: A nation can print money by the printing press, and it may seem to work, at least for awhile. However, very shortly, inflation will begin to cut through the fabric of such a nation, with the economy ultimately being destroyed.

No, if a nation is to conduct business as it should, it has to pay its way. If it spends more than it takes in, it has to somehow pay back that money. At the very least, it must continue to pay the interest on that which it borrows. In other words, there are no shortcuts. For sin to be properly addressed, God could not honestly remove it or its penalty by decree. Sin is an affront against God and all that is holy and righteous. Consequently, its penalty must be exacted.

THE PENALTY

Now, the problem with that is that man was totally unable to pay the penalty. So, if man was to be saved, God would have to perform the work correctly, and do so in totality. In other words, nothing must be left hanging.

The price that God demanded was far beyond silver and gold (I Pet. 1:18-20). It had to be the sacrifice of a perfect victim—one who was perfect in every respect—and that, man could not supply. Being born in sin, he was doomed even before he began. So, God would become man and do so for the purpose of going to the Cross. There the price would be paid, and only there would the price be paid.

SIN

The reason that it had to be a Cross, or even as the Scripture says, "a tree," is because of the following: Every type of sin, especially the worst types of sins, had to be addressed. Nothing could be left unattended. The price that would be paid had to cover every perversion, every evil, and every wickedness ever devised by the powers of darkness.

As it regarded certain types of crimes, the law of Moses, which, in reality, was the law of God, demanded that the individual be stoned to death and then his body placed on a tree, i.e., the Cross. And yet, his body could not remain on the tree after the sun had set but had to be taken down and buried.

For certain types of crimes, such an individual would be cursed by God, hence, the demands regarding his death, etc.

The Scripture says:

"And if a man have committed a sin worthy of death, and he be to be put to death, and you hang him on a tree: His body shall not remain all night upon the tree, but you shall in any wise bury him that day; (for he who is hanged is accursed of God;) that your land be not defiled, which the LORD your God gives you for an inheritance" (Deut. 21:22-23).

THE RELIGIOUS LEADERS OF ISRAEL

This is the reason that the religious leaders of Israel demanded that Jesus be put on the Cross (Mat. 27:23). They knew that one put on the tree was accursed of God, and so they reasoned that the people would then think, were He really the Messiah, God would never allow Him to be put on a Cross.

They did not realize that the Lord had foretold the event of the Cross some 1,500 years earlier as it concerned the brazen serpent on the pole (Num. 21:8-9).

It was necessary that Jesus go to the Cross in order that He might atone for all the sins of mankind, at least for all who will believe (Jn. 3:16). So, Jesus was made a curse on the Cross, not because of His sins, for He had none, but for the sin of the whole world, and for all time.

So, it had to be a Cross and for the reason of sin! (Jn. 1:29; Gal. 3:13).

THERE IS NO EARTHLY REMEDY FOR SIN

While there is a remedy, there is no earthly remedy. The remedy that is given to us is the Cross of Christ and was formulated by the Godhead from before the foundation of the world (I Pet. 1:18-20).

When the church leaves the Cross, it ceases to be of service to mankind. In fact, when the church leaves the Cross, it is worthless!

If that is correct, then that means that virtually the entirety of the church world is pretty much a waste of time. Unless the Cross of Christ is held up, there is no deliverance for mankind.

Let me give you a Bible example; I will quote from The Expositor's Study Bible (subheadings added):

> *And they journeyed from Mount Hor by the way of the Red Sea, to compass the land of Edom: and the soul of the people was much discouraged because of the way* (the 'way' is not always easy, but this difficult way was their own doing; if their fathers had believed the Lord, they would have been in the Promised Land approximately 38 years before).

THE ATTITUDE OF THE PEOPLE

And the people spoke against God, and against Moses, Wherefore have you brought us up out of Egypt to die in the wilderness? for there is no bread, neither is there any water; and our soul loathes this light bread (in other words, they hated the manna. They had the same heart of rebellion as their fathers. Wherever the believer finds himself, and no matter how difficult may seem the way at present, he must not complain. To do so presents a gross insult to the Lord, and for many and varied reasons. We should thank the Lord, and do so daily, irrespective of the circumstances. If the 'way' is hard, we should try to learn the lesson which the Lord is trying to teach us and ask Him to deliver us. He will!). *And the* LORD *sent fiery serpents among the people, and they bit the people; and much people of Israel died.* (It says that the 'LORD' sent these fiery serpents. Let all understand, everything which happens to a believer, be it negative or positive, is either 'caused' by the Lord or 'allowed' by the Lord. Believers belong to the Lord. As such, Satan can do nothing against us, unless the Lord allows it.)

THE FIERY SERPENT

Therefore the people came to Moses, and said, We have sinned, for we have spoken against the LORD, *and against you; pray unto the* LORD, *that He take away the serpents from us. And Moses prayed for the people.* (This is the first and only occasion on which the people directly asked for the intercession of Moses—Pulpit.) *And the LORD said unto Moses, Make thee a fiery serpent, and set it upon a pole* (the 'serpent,' i.e., 'sin and Satan,' was the reason for the Cross, and the pole was a type of the Cross): *and it shall come to pass, that every one who is bitten, when he looks upon it, shall live* (everyone who looks to Christ and the Cross has the sentence of death abated and, therefore, shall 'live'). *And Moses made a serpent of brass* (copper), *and put it upon a pole and it came to pass, that if a serpent had bitten any man, when he beheld the serpent of brass* (copper), *he lived* (approximately 400 years earlier, the Lord had shown Abraham the manner of salvation; it would be through the death of an innocent victim, namely the Son of God [Jn. 8:36]; it was to Moses, however, as recorded here, that the Lord proclaimed the way that the Son of God would die; it would be by the Cross, symbolized by the serpent on the pole) (Num. 21:4-9) (The Expositor's Study Bible).

WHY A SERPENT?

If it is to be noticed, the Lord told Moses to put a serpent on the pole—not a dove, not a lamb, etc., but a serpent.

Why a serpent?

It was for sin—our sin—that Jesus went to the Cross. His death was not an execution, but rather a sacrifice. The Cross was why He came, and why He went to the Cross was sin. It was not for His sin, for He had none, but it was for the sin of the entirety of the world, and for all time, at least for those who were then alive and all who had believed prior to the death of Christ.

Let us say it again: It was for sin—our sin—that Jesus went to the Cross. Satan is the author and the instigator of all sin. It would be at the Cross where Satan, plus all of his demon spirits and fallen angels, would be defeated, and defeated in totality (Col. 2:14-15). That's the reason there had to be a serpent on a pole.

As well, if it is to be noticed, the Lord told Moses to tell the people that anyone who had been bitten by a serpent must look on that pole. He didn't say anything about looking to the tabernacle, the gold or the silver that had been brought out of Egypt, or any other such thing. They had to look at the pole in order to be healed, delivered, and saved.

All of that was a type of the Cross of Christ. That's the reason that we unequivocally say that there is no answer but the Cross.

NO OTHER GOSPEL

That's the reason that Paul stated, and did so unequivocally:

"*But though we* (Paul and his associates), *or an angel from heaven, preach any other gospel unto you than that which we have preached unto you* (Jesus Christ and Him crucified), *let him be accursed* (eternally condemned;

the Holy Spirit speaks this through Paul, making this very serious)" (Gal. 1:8).

The apostle also said: *"Behold* ('mark my words!'), *I Paul say unto you* (presents the apostle's authority regarding the message he brings), *that if you be circumcised, Christ shall profit you nothing.* (This means if the believer goes back into law, and law of any kind, what Christ did at the Cross on our behalf will profit us nothing. One cannot have it two ways)" (Gal. 5:2) (The Expositor's Study Bible).

Sadly and regrettably, as it regards most of the modern church, it must be said, "Christ profits them nothing."

This solemnly means that if our faith is placed in anything except Christ and the Cross, our efforts are wasted. All that Jesus did at the Cross will avail us nothing! One cannot go in a wrong direction, and come out at the desired destination.

> *So Naaman came with his horses and with his chariot, and stood at the door of the house of Elisha. And Elisha sent a messenger unto him, saying, Go and wash in Jordan seven times, and your flesh shall come again to you, and you shall be clean. But Naaman was wroth, and went away, and said, Behold, I thought, He will surely come out to me, and stand, and call on the name of the LORD his God, and strike his hand over the place, and recover the leper. Are not Abana and Pharpar, rivers of Damascus, better than all the waters of Israel? may I not wash in them, and be clean? So he turned and went away in a rage. And his servants came near,*

*and spoke unto him, and said, My father, if the prophet
had bid you do some great thing, would you not have
done it? how much rather then, when he said to you,
Wash, and be clean? Then went he down, and dipped
himself seven times in Jordan, according to the saying of
the man of God: and his flesh came again like unto the
flesh of a little child, and he was clean* (II Ki. 5:9-14).

The intimation of Verse 9 is that there was quite an
entourage that came to the home of Elisha. Naaman expected
to be waited on, courted, and to receive every possible
attention, but Elisha didn't even come out himself and pray
for the commander. He just sent a messenger out to him and
told him what to do.

Naaman was a powerful man and thought he warranted
much more than this curt dismissal. Entire nations trembled
at his presence, after all, he was the mightiest military
chieftain on the face of the earth of that day.

All of this was pride, which is the crowning sin of the
human race. It is the reason that most never receive from
God. Every individual must come to the Lord the same
way—the great, the rich, the poor, the small. They are all the
same to the Lord—poor and wretched lepers.

Actually, the two rivers, Abana and Pharpar, were some of
the clearest streams in the world, so why this muddy Jordan?

This Jordan, at least at this time, was a type of Calvary.
Yes, it was muddy, and yes, there were other rivers much more
beautiful. However, there were no healing qualities in the

other rivers, as beautiful as they might have been, while there was a total healing and cleansing in this Jordan, i.e., Calvary.

Men are ever asking, "What can I do to earn salvation?" Most of the world is trying to earn its salvation by good works, but, in reality, all one has to do as it regards Calvary is to "wash, and be clean."

Why seven? There was nothing magical about the number, only that it denoted God's total and complete redemption, in other words, a finished work. Salvation makes a man whole. How many millions have dipped into the waters of Calvary and have seen all of their sins washed away? Man is spiritually dirty. This dirt cannot be cleansed by the soap of this world, but only by the precious blood of Jesus Christ.

PRIDE

It is very difficult for men or women of means to admit that they need a Saviour, especially on the same basis as the lowliest beggar.

That's the reason the Holy Spirit through Paul said:

> For you see your calling, brethren (refers to the nature and method of their heavenly calling), how that not many wise men after the flesh, not many mighty, not many noble, are called (are called and accept): But God has chosen the foolish things of the world to confound the wise (the preaching of the Cross confounds the wise because it falls out to changed lives, which nothing

man has can do); *and God has chosen the weak things of the world to confound the things which are mighty* (the Cross is looked at as weakness, but it brings about great strength and power regarding those who accept the finished work of Christ); *And base things of the world, and things which are despised, has God chosen* (it is God working in the base things and the despised things which brings about miraculous things), *yes, and things which are not, to bring to nought things that are* (God can use that which is nothing within itself, but with Him all things become possible): *That no flesh* (human effort) *should glory in His presence* (I Cor. 1:26-29) (The Expositor's Study Bible)

NAAMAN

Due to his station and position in life as the commander-in-chief of the armies of Syria, Naaman expected much ado to be made over him when he arrived at the home of the prophet. He wasn't happy at all that Elisha didn't even bother to come out and greet him, but rather *"sent a messenger unto him, saying, Go and wash in Jordan seven times, and your flesh shall come again to you, and you shall be clean."*

Everything that Elisha did here, the Lord told him to do it. Of course, the Lord knew that Naaman's problem, among other things, was pride. He was to learn that God honors no man, at least not in the fashion that Naaman expected.

So, when this lowly messenger delivered the message, the Scripture says, *"Naaman was wroth."*

The word *wroth* in the Hebrew is *quatsaph* and means "to burst out in a rage." In other words, Naaman was fighting mad. The idea that he would be treated in this fashion set him off, and did so severely. His real anger was that Elisha treated him in this fashion, a fashion that he concluded to be beneath him. There was no ceremony, no ritual, no nothing. There was just the word: *"Go and wash in Jordan seven times."*

Pride is a deadly thing. In fact, it is the crowning sin of all sins. In essence, pride says that I am better than what God says I am. Pride says that I must be treated in a way that corresponds with who I am. The upshot of all is that we refuse to admit *who* God says we are and *what* God says we are.

THE FOLLY OF PRIDE

A cure would not content Naaman unless he was cured with ceremony, with a great deal of pomp and parade. He scorned to be healed unless he was honored.

He took it hard that he must be sent to wash in Jordan, a river of Israel, which, in fact, was a muddy stream, when he thought Abana and Pharpar—rivers of Damascus—were better than all the waters of Israel. How slightly did he speak of the prophet's direction! He might wash in them and be clean from dirt but not wash in them and be clean from leprosy—that was the difference. He was angry that the prophet bid him wash and be clean. He thought it too plain or too common a thing for so great a man as he, or maybe he did not at all believe it would effect the cure.

Evidently he did not consider that Jordan was the river appointed, and if he expected a cure from the Divine Power, he ought to acquiesce to the divine will.

PRIDE AND THE SINNER

The way of a sinner's acceptance and sanctification through the blood, by the Spirit of Christ, and through faith alone in His name, does not sufficiently humor or employ self to please the sinner's heart. Human wisdom thinks it can supply more rational and preferable methods of cleansing. Too many laborious devices of superstition seem preferable to the fountain open for sin, while the proposals of the gospel affront the sins of pride and self-sufficiency.

On the other hand, some would hope to be saved, though they refuse self-denial, the mortification of the flesh, or attending to the appointed means of grace. However, the sinner, burdened with the sense of guilt and desirous to flee from the wrath to come, is ready to do great things, if required, to obtain forgiveness of sins and eternal life. Finding that none of these, or use of them, can avail, he rejoices in the fountain open and will wash and be clean as the Lord appointed.

Naaman turned away from the prophet's door in a rage. Proud men are the worst enemies to themselves. His own servants came to him, trying to reason with him. It certainly would not hurt to try what the prophet had suggested, they proclaimed. To be cured of leprosy, would he not do anything? If, in fact, he could be healed by obeying the prophet, would not it be a simple thing to do?

When diseased sinners are content to do anything, to submit to anything, or to part with anything for a cure, it is then, and not until then, that we begin to indulge some hopes for them. They will take Christ on His own terms when they are made willing to have Christ on any terms.

THE JORDAN RIVER, A TYPE OF CALVARY

Naaman, functioning from reason, surmised that the two main rivers in Syria, Abana and Pharpar, were much cleaner, much clearer, and much more desirable than this muddy stream of Jordan. So, why Jordan?

It is true that the two rivers spoken of by Naaman in Syria were some of the most beautiful rivers in the Middle East. Yet, the prophet didn't say those rivers, but rather Jordan.

Why?

The truth is that it was not the waters of Jordan that healed anything, and neither could it be the waters of the rivers in Syria that would heal anything. None of these rivers had any healing properties whatsoever.

THREE THINGS ARE INVOLVED HERE

1. The Lord was dealing with Naaman's pride. Man must be humbled before he will come to Christ.

2. Obedience was involved. Would he do what the Lord spoke through the prophet?

3. Most importantly, at least in this case, the river Jordan was a type of Calvary's Cross, what Jesus would there do when He would come. Yes, Jordan was muddy, was not at all enticing or desirable, and was much less attractive than the rivers of Syria. Likewise, Calvary is not a pretty picture. In fact, it is ugly, bloody, and speaks of a price that was paid that was beyond imagination. Due to the total depravity of mankind, such a price had to be paid. So, Calvary is not at all enticing, and to be brief and blunt, about the only positive thing that can be said about it is, it works. In fact, it is the only thing in this world that does work. It alone cures! It alone cleanses! It alone makes anew! It alone breaks the bondages of sin and darkness! So, mankind has the prerogative of accepting the ways of the world, although attractive, but which will heal no one, or accepting Calvary, although unattractive, which will cleanse the worst sinner!

WASH AND BE CLEAN

It was such a simple thing to do—stop at the river Jordan, wade out into that body of water, dip seven times, and be clean.

Likewise, as it regards salvation, it is believe and be saved, repent and be pardoned, and wash and be clean. The cure is effective in the use of the means prescribed. This can be attained by any and all by yielding to the will of God and by attending to His institutions. God will magnify His Word above all His name. The believing sinner applies for salvation by not neglecting, altering, or adding to the Saviour's direction. He is thus made clean from guilt and pollution, while others, neglecting His great salvation, live and die in the leprosy of sin. It is so easy, so simple, so plain, and so clear that even a child can understand the directions.

COME UNTO ME

The quotation is given by Christ:

Come unto Me (is meant by Jesus to reveal Himself as the giver of salvation), *all you who labor and are heavy laden* (trying to earn salvation by works), *and I will give you rest* (this 'rest' can only be found by placing one's faith in Christ and what He has done for us at the Cross [Gal. 5:1-6]). *Take My yoke upon you* (the 'yoke' of the 'Cross' [Lk. 9:23]), *and learn of Me* (learn of His sacrifice [Rom. 6:3-5]); *for I am meek and lowly in heart* (the only thing that our Lord personally said of Himself): *and you shall find rest unto your souls* (the soul can find rest only in the Cross). *For My yoke is easy, and My burden is light* (what He requires of us is very little, just to have faith in Him and His sacrificial atoning work) (Mat. 11:28-30) (The Expositor's Study Bible).

The Lord through the great prophet Isaiah also said:

Come now, and let us reason together, says the LORD: *though your sins be as scarlet, they shall be as white as snow; though they be red like crimson, they shall be as wool.* (There is no greater invitation found in the Bible than this one given by the Holy Spirit through the prophet Isaiah. In this passage, sins are spoken of as 'scarlet.' Such has a reference to blood-guiltiness. All sin is murder in some form, hence, the blood-guiltiness. This glorious passage illustrates to us the eternal truth that irrespective of the evil, wickedness, deception, and weight of sin, the Lord stands ready, upon proper confession and repentance, to forgive all and, therefore, to cleanse all. As stated, this is done exclusively by faith in Christ and His shed blood [Eph. 2:13-18]) (Isa. 1:18) (The Expositor's Study Bible).

Closing out the canon of Scripture, the Holy Spirit said:

And the Spirit and the bride say, Come. (This presents the cry of the Holy Spirit to a hurting, lost, and dying world. What the Holy Spirit says should also be said by all believers.) *And let him who hears say, Come.* (It means if one can 'hear,' then one can 'come.') *And let him who is athirst come* (speaks of spiritual thirst, the cry for God in the soul of man). *And whosoever will, let him take the Water of Life freely* (this opens the door to every single individual in the world; Jesus died for all and, therefore, all can be saved if they will only come) (Rev. 22:17) (The Expositor's Study Bible).

ACCORDING TO THE SAYING
OF THE MAN OF GOD

The question was, would he obey or would he not obey?

Ironically enough, there were many lepers in Israel at this time, but not a single one of them was healed, only Naaman the Syrian.

Why?

Jesus said concerning this very thing:

> *But I tell you of a truth* (will proclaim in no uncertain terms Israel's problem of self-righteousness resulting from pride), *many widows were in Israel in the days of Elijah, when the heaven was shut up three years and six months, when great famine was throughout all the land* (proclaims the time of Ahab and the great wickedness concerning the northern kingdom of Israel); *but unto none of them was Elijah sent, save unto Sarepta, a city of Sidon, unto a woman who was a widow* (she was a Gentile as well).

> *And many lepers were in Israel in the time of Elisha the prophet; and none of them was cleansed, saving Naaman the Syrian* (another Gentile). *And all they in the synagogue, when they heard these words, were filled with wrath* (the Jews at Nazareth that day were incensed that Jesus would hold up two Gentiles as examples of receiving from the Lord, while the Jews were shut out; He, in effect, was telling them that this is what would happen

to Israel; the Gentiles would receive Him, but Israel would refuse Him; 'wrath' is generally the response of unbelief) (Lk. 4:25-28) (The Expositor's Study Bible).

THEY WOULD NOT COME

The truth is, if any leper had come to Elisha asking for help and healing, it would have instantly been given by the Lord, but they would not come.

Jesus also said of Israel, *"And you will not come to Me, that you might have life"* (Jn. 5:40).

Why would not the lepers of Israel come to Elisha, the prophet of God?

Why would not Israel come to Christ?

The problem then was unbelief, and the problem now is unbelief! Despite the miracles that the Lord worked through Elisha, in fact, more so than any other prophet, and despite the miracles worked through Christ, which were beyond comprehension, still, they would not believe.

UNBELIEF

Unbelief is a want of faith and trust. It is, as well, a state of mind. In fact, unbelief toward Him was the prime sin of which Christ said that the Spirit would convict the world (Jn. 16:9). Unbelief in all its forms is a direct affront to the divine veracity (I Jn. 5:10), which is why it is so heinous a sin. The children of Israel did not enter into God's rest for two reasons:

1. They lacked faith (Heb. 3:19).
2. They disobeyed; unbelief finds its practical issue in disobedience (Heb. 4:6).

Listen again to what Jesus said:

And when He (the Holy Spirit) *is come, He will reprove* (convict) *the world of sin (the supreme sin of rejecting* Christ), *and of righteousness* (Jesus is righteousness and declared so by the resurrection), *and of judgment* (Satan was judged at Calvary, and all who follow Him are likewise judged): *of sin, because they believe not on Me* (to reject Christ and the Cross is to reject salvation); *of righteousness, because I go to My Father* (Jesus presented a spotless righteousness to the Father, namely Himself, which pertained to His sacrifice at Cavalry, that was accepted by God; consequently, that righteousness is imputed to all who will believe in Him and His work on the Cross), *and you see Me no more* (meaning that His work was finished); *of judgment, because the prince of this world is judged* (Satan and all of his fallen angels and demon spirits were completely defeated at Calvary and, thereby, judged as eternally condemned; all who follow him will suffer his fate, the lake of fire, and that fate will be forever and forever [Rev. 20:15]) (Jn. 16:8-11) (The Expositor's Study Bible).

JESUS CHRIST ALONE IS THE WAY OF SALVATION

Jesus Himself said, *"I am the way, the truth, and the life* (proclaims in no uncertain terms exactly who and what Jesus is): *no man comes unto the Father, but by Me* (He declares positively that this idea of God as Father, this approach to God for every man is through Him, the Lord Jesus Christ—through what He is and what He has done)" (Jn. 14:6) (The Expositor's Study Bible).

As someone has aptly said, "Now, what is it about this that Jesus has said that you don't understand?"

The crowning sin of the human race is unbelief as it regards Christ. Most of the world doesn't believe that He is the Son of God. They may accept Him as a prophet, a good man, and a miracle worker, but definitely not God manifest in the flesh. Therefore, they link Him with other men down through the ages, most of the time, at a lower level than others that might be named. Most of the world doesn't believe that Jesus' death on the Cross was the offering of Himself in sacrifice, which was necessary in order that the terrible sin debt of mankind be paid. Man owed a debt he could not pay, so God became man and paid the debt for man. That's what makes the rejection of Christ so awful. When men reject Him and what He did at the Cross, they are rejecting pure love!

TWO PROBLEMS

So, as it regards Christ, we have two problems:

1. Most do not believe that He is the Son of God.
2. Most do not believe that the sacrifice of Calvary was necessary in order that man might be saved.

That is the problem! It is the problem of unbelief!

This problem latched itself onto Naaman, and it almost caused him to die eternally lost and, as well, to die as a leper. However, after a little bit, he cooled down and reasoned that it certainly wouldn't hurt to try what the prophet said!

Considering that we are speaking here of eternal life or eternal damnation, considering that it's heaven or hell, and considering that man has an eternal soul, and that soul will spend eternity somewhere, "reason" would say, "Why not try Christ?"

That's exactly what Naaman did.

The Scripture says, "*Then went he down, and dipped himself seven times in Jordan, according to the saying of the man of God: and his flesh came again like unto the flesh of a little child, and he was clean*" (II Ki. 5:14).

Untold millions have dipped spiritually into that Jordan of Calvary, and every last one of them has come up clean.

The song says:

Millions have come,
There's still room for one,
There's room at the Cross for you.

GRACE

> *And He returned to the man of God, he and all his*
> *company, and came, and stood before him: and he said,*
> *Behold, now I know that there is no God in all the earth,*
> *but in Israel: now therefore, I pray you, take a blessing*
> *of your servant. But he said, As the* LORD *lives, before*
> *whom I stand, I will receive none. And he urged him to*
> *take it; but he refused. And Naaman said, Shall there*
> *not then, I pray you, be given to your servant two mules'*
> *burden of earth? for your servant will henceforth offer*
> *neither burnt offering nor sacrifice unto other gods, but*
> *unto the* LORD. *In this thing the* LORD *pardon your*
> *servant, that when my master goes into the house of*
> *Rimmon to worship there, and he leans on my hand,*
> *and I bow myself in the house of Rimmon: when I*
> *bow down myself in the house of Rimmon, the* LORD
> *pardon your servant in this thing. And he said unto*
> *him, Go in peace. So he departed from him a little way*
> (II Ki. 5:15-19).

There is some evidence that Elisha did receive offerings at other times. So, why not this time?

This entire episode was a picture portrayed by God of His grace. One cannot purchase grace; it is always a free gift from God. Money or good works are not the coin of this realm. If Elisha had taken money, it would instantly have nullified this work of grace.

It would have made a mockery of the blood of Jesus Christ.

Naaman now knew that the Lord of Israel was truly God and not the heathen idols he had been worshipping in Syria. He desired to offer burnt offerings to the Lord of Israel and felt that the soil of Syria was improper. Inasmuch as Israel was God's land, Naaman was far more theologically sound, at least at that time, than we might at first realize.

JEHOVAH

Instantly, this man who had known nothing but idol worship all of his life—having been born and raised in Syria and knowing precious little about the God of Israel—now and immediately after his healing said, *"Now I know that there is no God in all the earth, but in Israel."*

Pulpit said, "This is an acknowledgment of the sole supremacy of Jehovah on the part of a heathen, such as we scarcely find elsewhere."

Among the nations at that time, it was generally believed that every country had its own god. For instance, Baal was the god of Phoenicia. Chemosh was the god of Moab, with Moloch the god of Ammon. Babylon had Bel, and Syria had Rimmon, about which little is known. As well, whenever Jehovah was acknowledged by a heathen country, he was placed in a position of being one among many (Ex. 10:16-17; II Chron. 2:11; Dan. 2:47; etc.)

However, here, Naaman recognized Jehovah alone as the God of not only Israel but the entirety of the earth.

When a person truly gives his heart to God, the Scripture says, *"Therefore if any man be in Christ* (saved by the blood), *he is a new creature* (a new creation): *old things are passed away* (what we were before salvation); *behold, all things are become new.* (The old is no longer useable, with everything given to us now by Christ as 'new')" (II Cor. 5:17) (The Expositor's Study Bible).

BORN AGAIN

Jesus said, *"Except a man be born again* (the term 'born again' means that man has already had a natural birth but now must have a spiritual birth, which comes by faith in Christ and what He has done for us at the Cross, and is available to all), *he cannot see the kingdom of God* (actually means that without the new birth, one cannot understand or comprehend the 'kingdom of God')" (Jn. 3:3) (The Expositor's Study Bible).

The idea is that once one is truly born again, instantly everything changes. In fact, before one is saved, no matter how intellectual or educated a person might be, he simply cannot understand God or anything about His Word.

Concerning that, the Scripture also says, *"But the natural man receives not the things of the Spirit of God* (speaks of the individual who is not born again): *for they are foolishness unto him* (a lack of understanding): *neither can he know them* (fallen man cannot understand spiritual truths), *because they are spiritually discerned* (only the regenerated spirit of man can understand the things of the

Holy Spirit)" (I Cor. 2:14). (The Expositor's Study Bible).

I'm going to make a statement that at first glance may seem to be somewhat off balance; however, it is correct: Show me a 6-year-old little girl who has given her heart to Jesus Christ, and I'll show you someone who knows more about the Lord than the brightest Ph.D. in the world who doesn't know Christ.

Concerning the leprosy Naaman once had, not only was his physical body now changed, but, as well, his heart was also made anew. As a result, Jehovah was no longer just one god among many, but rather *the* God of the whole earth.

Whenever somebody claims to be a believer, and he is promoting evolution, I know that person has never truly been saved. Whenever a person who claims to be saved denies the miracles of Christ, His virgin birth, or His resurrection and ascension, I know that person is a professor of religion only and is not truly saved. There are certain fundamentals of the faith that quickly become obvious when a person truly knows the Lord.

GIVING TO THE WORK OF GOD

Naaman was very grateful for the tremendous miracle that had been accomplished in his physical body and, as well, in his heart and life. As a result, he wanted to give something in the form of money to the prophet. Now, while Elisha did not accept it or receive it, which we will comment on in a moment, this portrays the fact that when a person truly comes to the

Lord, there is an inbred desire to give to the work of God. I firmly believe that if that desire is not there, the person is not truly saved. Instantly, the new believer understands what the Lord has done for him, and he wants others to have what he has received. So he wants to give to the work of God in order that this great thing may be accomplished, and we speak of the spreading of the gospel.

Paul said, *"I am debtor* (true of every believer) *both to the Greeks, and to the barbarians; both to the wise, and to the unwise* (to all people, whomever they might be, and wherever they might be). *So, as much as in me is, I am ready to preach the gospel to you who are at Rome also"* (Rom. 1:14-15) (The Expositor's Study Bible).

A DEBTOR

In fact, every believer is a debtor, so to speak, and I speak of being a debtor to the entirety of the world.

How is that so?

As we've already stated, when one comes to Christ, one instantly realizes the tremendous salvation that he now possesses. He realizes what God has done for him. He realizes the price that Jesus paid at Calvary's Cross. Knowing how valuable all of this is, he instantly knows or realizes, as well, that every person who is not saved must have the opportunity that he has had. They may or may not accept the offering of redemption, but they must be given the opportunity. The Holy Spirit is insistent on that (Mk. 16:15).

We are debtors to every unsaved person in the world and due to that fact, they must be given the opportunity to accept the gospel. It's our responsibility that the gospel be presented to them. The idea is: Somebody gave, somebody prayed, somebody witnessed, and someone brought the message to me. In turn, I must take it to others.

HOW SHOULD THE WORK OF GOD BE SUPPORTED?

Tragically, most of the giving for that which claims to be the work of God is anything but!

Going back to Paul's day, the land was filled with the Judaizers, who were individuals claiming that Jesus was the Son of God and that He had really been raised from the dead and, thereby, Israel's Messiah. All of this was correct, but still, they claimed that all people must keep the law of Moses, as well, in order to be saved, which nullified the great gospel of grace. The law was finished with Christ in that He kept it perfectly and in every respect. As well, He addressed the broken law, which demanded spiritual death, by giving Himself as a sacrifice on the Cross, which solved the problem of the law (Acts 15:1-2; Gal. 2:21; Rom. 10:4).

Also, even as Paul stated, there were "grievous wolves" in the church, who were not truly preaching the gospel (Acts 20:29).

Paul also spoke of false apostles and deceitful workers in the church who were not truly preaching the gospel.

As well, Paul spoke of false apostles and deceitful workers, whom he referred to as Satan's ministers (II Cor. 11:13-15).

Now, I think common sense would tell one that such preachers, whomever they may have been, should not have been supported. When money is given to individuals of that nature, one, in effect, is helping to support Satan's efforts to pollute and corrupt the gospel.

The tragedy is that the far greater majority of so-called preachers presently fall into the category of those we have mentioned.

SEEK THE LORD

If the believer, whomever he or she might be, will ardently seek the Lord and ask what he should support and whom he should support, to be sure, the Lord will most definitely answer such a prayer.

Please remember the following: Believers support what they are!

If they support a crook, it is because they are crooked themselves in some way. If they support preachers who are greedy for filthy lucre, this means that they are greedy themselves. If they support con artists, so to speak, this means that they have deviousness within their own hearts. Let us say it again: believers support what they truly are.

If they support a man or a woman who is truly of God, which means that the proper fruit accompanies such a ministry, this means that they are truly of God as well.

CAN A TRUE BELIEVER BE DECEIVED?

It means to be deceived into supporting something that looks like God, acts like God, and purports to be of God but really isn't!

If a believer fails to follow the words of Christ as it regards false apostles and false prophets, yes, they can be deceived, but let me tell you how.

Very often, preachers are supported for all the wrong reasons.

The believer should first of all look at what is being preached, in other words, what type of doctrine is being proclaimed, rather than looking at the individual personally. While who and what the preacher is on a personal basis is, of necessity, extremely important, still, it is what such a preacher is preaching and proclaiming that is the real test.

Listen to what our Lord said:

> *Beware of false prophets, which come to you in sheep's clothing, but inwardly they are ravening wolves* ('beware of false prophets' is said in the sternest of measures! there will be and are false prophets and are some of Satan's greatest weapons).

THE FRUIT

> *You shall know them by their fruits* (this is the test as given by Christ as it regards identification of false prophets and

false apostles). *Do men gather grapes of thorns, or figs of thistles?* (It is impossible for false doctrine, generated by false prophets, to bring forth good fruit.) *Even so every good tree brings forth good fruit; but a corrupt tree brings forth evil fruit* (the good fruit is Christlikeness, while the evil fruit is self-likeness).

A good tree cannot bring forth evil fruit, neither can a corrupt tree bring forth good fruit (the 'good tree' is the Cross, while the 'corrupt tree' pertains to all of that which is other than the Cross). *Every tree that brings not forth good fruit is hewn down, and cast into the fire* (judgment will ultimately come on all so-called gospel, other than the Cross [Rom. 1:18]). *Wherefore by their fruits you shall know them* (the acid test). *Not everyone who says unto Me, Lord, Lord, shall enter into the kingdom of heaven* (the repetition of the word 'Lord' expresses astonishment, as if to say: 'Are we to be disowned?'); *but he who does the will of My Father which is in heaven* (what is the will of the Father? Verse 24 tells us).

I NEVER KNEW THEM

Many will say to Me in that day, Lord, Lord, have we not prophesied in Your name? and in Your name have cast out devils (demons)? *and in Your name done many wonderful works?* (These things are not the criteria, but rather faith in Christ and what Christ has done for us at the Cross [Eph. 2:8-9, 13-18]. The Word of God alone is to be the judge of doctrine.) *And then will I profess unto them, I never knew you* (again we say, the criteria alone is Christ and Him crucified [I Cor. 1:23]): *depart from Me, you who work iniquity* (we have access to God only through Christ, and access to Christ only through the Cross, and access to the Cross only through a denial of self [Lk. 9:23]; any other message is judged by God as 'iniquity' and cannot be a part of Christ [I Cor. 1:17]) (Mat. 7:15-23) (The Expositor's Study Bible).

To bring it down to the bottom line, if the preacher is not preaching the Cross of Christ, then actually, he's not really preaching the gospel (I Cor. 1:17). This means that he should not be supported.

Please remember that not only will we be held accountable for our support of the gospel, or the lack thereof, but, as well, we will be accountable for what we support.

Undoubtedly, there were many false prophets in the northern kingdom of Israel during the time of Elisha. Above all, those individuals, whomever they may have been, should not, under any circumstances, have been supported.

THE CROSS AND OUR SUPPORT

While Paul was in prison in Rome, the church at Philippi sent him a very generous offering, which he, no doubt, greatly needed. In fact, the entirety of the epistle to the Philippians is, in essence, a thank-you note for that gift.

He closed it by saying:

But I have all, and abound: I am full (proclaims the fact that the Philippian gift must have been generous), *having received of Epaphroditus the things which were sent from you* (Epaphroditus had brought the gift from Philippi to Rome, a distance of about a thousand miles), *an odor of a sweet smell* (presents the Old Testament odors of the Levitical sacrifices, all typifying Christ), *a sacrifice acceptable, well-pleasing to God.* (For those who gave to Paul, enabling him to take the Message of the Cross to others, their gift, and such gifts presently, are looked at by God as a part of the sacrificial atoning work of Christ on the Cross. Nothing could be higher than that!) (Phil. 4:18) (The Expositor's Study Bible).

TWO THINGS ARE SAID HERE

1. The Holy Spirit through Paul likens our giving to that, which is the Message of the Cross, as a part of the great sacrifice of Christ. That is so unbelievable as to be almost mind-boggling. There is nothing in the world greater than the sacrifice of Christ. For the Lord to place our gifts for His work on a par with that sacrifice, it tells us how important the sacrifice really is and our support of that which Christ has done.

2. All of this also tells us that unless we support the Message of the Cross, then we really aren't supporting the work of God.

SALVATION CANNOT BE BOUGHT

On the other hand, even though Naaman strongly desired to give money to the work of God, namely to Elisha, still, the prophet wouldn't receive it.

Why?

There is evidence that he received offerings at other times, so why not now?

This entire episode with Naaman was meant by the Holy Spirit to be a type of the sacrifice of Christ and the salvation that is afforded by that sacrifice.

Man receives this salvation by faith, meaning it cannot be earned. So, if Elisha had taken money for this healing, the "type" would have been greatly corrupted, as should be obvious.

Concerning salvation, Paul said:

For by grace (the goodness of God) *are you saved through faith* (faith in Christ, with the Cross ever as its object); *and that not of yourselves* (none of this is of us, but all is of Him): *it is the gift of God* (anytime the word 'gift' is used, God is speaking of His Son and His substitutionary work on the Cross, which makes all of this possible): *Not of works* (man cannot merit salvation, irrespective of what he does), *lest any man should boast* (boast in his own ability and strength; we are allowed to boast only in the Cross [Gal. 6:14]) (Eph. 2:8-9) (The Expositor's Study Bible).

PURCHASING FROM GOD?

Men have ever tried to purchase things from God, either with money or good works of some nature. Let it always be understood that God has nothing for sale. Everything He has is freely given to us upon simple faith in Him, which refers to having faith in Christ and what Christ did at the Cross.

The healing of Naaman is one of the greatest miracles recorded in the Word of God. It is a type of the sinner being cleansed by the precious shed blood of the Lord Jesus Christ. It was and is a free gift from the Lord, as it always will be a free gift from the Lord.

Whenever preachers put a price tag on that for which the Lord has paid such a price at Calvary's Cross, and we speak of a price tag for healing, or whatever, the sin that is being committed by such action borders on the edge of blasphemy.

Let us state it again that everything that comes from the Lord to anyone is always, and without exception, a gift. To obtain it, all we have to do is exercise faith in Christ and what Christ did for us at the Cross.

TWO MULES' BURDEN OF EARTH

In this short time, Naaman knew that Jehovah was the God not only of Israel but, as well, of the entirety of the earth, which meant that the idol god of Syria was nothing at all. He also knew that the land of Israel was God's land, meaning it was totally unlike any other part of the world. He recognized that, hence, his asking for this bit of earth that he could take back with him to Syria.

Why did he want these containers of dirt from Israel?

He probably intended to place the dirt near his home, where he possibly may have intended to offer a sacrifice at times. He made the statement, *"For your servant will henceforth offer neither burnt offering nor sacrifice to other gods, but unto the LORD."* That was probably what he had in mind.

ALL BASED ON WHAT CHRIST DID AT THE CROSS

And yet, instructions had been given by the Lord in the law of Moses that no sacrifice be offered anywhere except on the great altar before the temple in Jerusalem. Yet, as well, the great law of God was for Israel exclusively.

Considering that Elisha did not reprimand him in any way, quite possibly the Lord accepted his sacrifices, even though they were not offered strictly according to God's Word.

This we must remember: Naaman was a Gentile. In fact, this entire scenario was meant to portray the gospel going to the Gentiles, even as Jesus later stated (Lk. 4:25-27). Of course, with Calvary a fact, which it would be when Jesus came, the gospel would go out to the entirety of the world. This, it has done, with any and all believers everywhere allowed to worship the Lord in Spirit and truth wherever we may be—all based on what Christ did at the Cross.

GEHAZI

But Gehazi, the servant of Elisha the man of God, said, Behold, my master has spared Naaman this Syrian, in not receiving at his hands that which he brought: but, as the LORD lives, I will run after him, and take somewhat of him. So Gehazi followed after Naaman. And when Naaman saw him running after him, he lighted down from the chariot to meet him, and said, Is all well? And he said, All is well. My master has sent me, saying, Behold, even now there be come to me from Mount Ephraim two young men of the sons of the prophets: give them, I pray you, a talent of silver, and two changes of garments. And Naaman said, Be content, take two talents. And he urged him, and bound two talents of silver in two bags, with two changes of garments, and laid them upon two of his servants; and they bore them before him. And when he came to the tower, he took them from their hand, and bestowed them in the house: and he let the men go, and they departed. But he went in, and stood before his master. And Elisha said unto him, From where do you come, Gehazi? And he said, Your servant went nowhere. And he said unto him, Went not my heart with you, when the man turned again from his chariot to meet you? Is it a time to receive money, and to receive garments, and oliveyards, and vineyards, and sheep, and oxen, and menservants, and maidservants? The leprosy therefore of Naaman shall cleave unto you, and unto your seed for ever. And he went out from his presence a leper as white as snow (II Ki. 5:20-27).

This episode proclaims the efforts of Gehazi to change the great plan of salvation from the grace of God to salvation by works. It was met, as we shall see, with severe and stern judgment.

This story concocted by Gehazi was altogether most plausible and his demand prudently moderate, at least as far as Naaman was concerned.

The question asked by Elisha in Verse 26 is the same question that could be asked presently! The world is dying without God, and so many modern preachers are proclaiming a message of money. To be sure, their sin is no different than that of Gehazi.

Gehazi's sin and his incurring of Naaman's leprosy is a type of man voiding the grace of God by works salvation. Gehazi's acceptance of money was, in effect, saying that salvation could be purchased. He had made the grace of God of none effect, at least as it involved himself (Gal. 5:4).

MONEY AND THE LIE

Gehazi, the servant of Elisha, was so close to the power and presence of God but, at the same time, so very far away. This shows us that participation, association, and environment cannot save a soul. He, as Judas, had an excellent environment, was privileged to participate, and had the most excellent association in helping one of the greatest prophets who ever lived, but all was to no avail.

In fact, in the coming kingdom age when Christ will be ruling personally from Jerusalem, and the world will experience the greatest peace and prosperity by far that it has ever known in its history, still, there will be millions on earth at that time who, while obeying the law, at the same time will have a heart that is not after God. At that time, Satan and all of his demon spirits and fallen angels will be locked away in the bottomless pit. So, there is no temptation at that time. Yet, despite the almost perfect environment, still, millions will obey outwardly but disobey inwardly. When Satan is loosed for a little season at the end of the kingdom age, they will throw in their lot with him.

DECEPTION

The Scripture says concerning that time:

And when the thousand years are expired (should have been translated 'finished'), *Satan shall be loosed out of his prison* (is not meant to infer a mere arbitrary act on the part of God; He has a very valid reason for doing this), *and shall go out to deceive the nations which are in the four quarters of the earth, Gog and Magog* (the main reason the Lord allows Satan this latitude is, it seems, to rid the earth of all who oppose Christ; George Williams says: 'The creation Sabbath witnessed the first seduction, and the millennial Sabbath will witness the last'; the 'Gog and Magog' spoken of by John is a Hebrew term expressive of multitude and magnitude; here it embraces all nations, 'the four quarters of the earth'), *to gather them together to battle: the number of whom is as the sand of the sea* (proclaims the fact that virtually all of the population at that particular time, which did not accept Christ during the kingdom age, will throw in their lot with Satan).

THE LAKE OF FIRE

And they went up on the breadth of the earth, and compassed the camp of the saints about, and the beloved city (pictures Satan coming against Jerusalem with his army, which will be the last attack against that city): *and fire came down from God out of heaven, and devoured them.* (Stipulates that the Lord will make short work of this insurrection. In fact, very little information is given regarding this event, as is obvious.) *And the Devil who deceived them was cast into the lake of fire and brimstone* (marks the end of Satan regarding his influence in the world and, in fact, in any part of the creation of God), *where the Beast and the false prophet are* (proclaims the fact that these two were placed in 'the lake of fire and brimstone' some 1,000 years earlier [Rev. 19:20]), *and shall be tormented day and night forever and ever.* (This signifies the eternity of this place. It is a matter of interest to note that Satan's first act is recorded in Genesis, Chapter 3 [the third chapter from the beginning], whereas his last act on a worldwide scale is mentioned in Revelation, Chapter 20 [the third chapter from the end]) (Rev. 20:7-10) (The Expositor's Study Bible).

THE LOVE OF MONEY, THE ROOT OF ALL EVIL

Gehazi, Elisha's servant, ran after Naaman and requested of him money and garments. He was given more than that for which he asked.

However, he lied to Naaman about the entire episode:

- Elisha did not send him on this mission.
- There were not two young men of the sons of the prophets. This was a made-up story.
- The money and garments for which he asked were not for the supposed prophets, but rather for himself.

Far too many preachers presently have succumbed to the "greed gospel." Everything in the Bible—every message and every testimony—is turned toward money.

MAN'S PROBLEM IS NOT A LACK OF MONEY; MAN'S PROBLEM IS SIN

While it is definitely true that money is needed for the spread of the gospel, which means that churches and ministers must have money, still, whenever the entirety of the message is steered in that direction, something is wrong, very wrong!

Man's problem, as stated, is not a lack of money. Man's problem is sin. If the sin problem is eradicated, which it can only be by the shed blood of the Lord Jesus Christ, then the other problems will take care of themselves.

If one turns on presently that which purports to be Christian television, most of the preachers, sad to say, are little more than con artists. People are told that if they will give so much money, certain great things will happen. All too often, the people believe it, but the end result is never what they are told.

While the Lord definitely blesses those giving to His work, and does so abundantly, still, money must always be put in its proper perspective.

We must remember that if the things of God are handled wrongly, spiritual leprosy will always be the result.

LEPROSY

Gehazi told another lie, this time to Elisha. When the great prophet asked him, *"From where do you come, Gehazi?"* Gehazi answered, saying, *"Your servant went nowhere."*

He lied!

Then the prophet told him, in essence, that the Lord had revealed to him exactly what he had done.

He then went on to state, in essence, that the northern kingdom of Israel was in such a sad spiritual state that if the nation didn't turn to God, money wouldn't matter; everything was going to be destroyed, and so it ultimately was!

He then said to his servant, *"The leprosy therefore of Naaman shall cleave unto you, and unto your seed forever"* (II Ki. 5:27).

That which happened to Gehazi will also happen to all who misuse the Word of God. Such must be ever understood!

Since Gehazi is heard from again (II Ki. 8:3-6), this could mean one of two things: either the Lord healed Gehazi, or else the account given of his leprosy is not in chronological order, which is probably the case.

Must Jesus bear the Cross alone,
And all the world go free?
No, there's a Cross for everyone,
There's a Cross for me.

The consecrated Cross I'll bear,
Till death shall set me free,
And then go home to wear a crown,
For there's a crown for me.

Oh precious Cross! Oh glorious crown!
Oh resurrection day!
You angels from the stars come down,
And bear my soul away.

ELISHA

CHAPTER 7

MORE WITH US
THAN BE WITH THEM

MORE WITH US
THAN BE WITH THEM

"AND THE SONS OF *the prophets said unto Elisha, Behold now, the place where we dwell with you is too strait for us. Let us go, we pray you, unto Jordan, and take thence every man a beam, and let us make us a place there, where we may dwell. And he answered, Go you. And one said, Be content, I pray you, and go with your servants. And he answered, I will go. So he went with them. And when they came to Jordan, they cut down wood. But as one was felling a beam, the axe head fell into the water: and he cried, and said, Alas, Master! for it was borrowed. And the man of God said, Where fell it? And he showed him the place. And he cut down a stick, and cast it in thither; and the iron did swim. Therefore said he, Take it up to you. And he put out his hand, and took it"* (II Ki. 6:1-7).

SYMBOLIC OF THE CROSS

It seems that the unbelief registered in Chapter 2

(concerning the sons of the prophets) had at least given way to some faith. Prayerfully, their association with Elisha had done much to direct them toward the Lord; however, there is little record that God used these individuals in much capacity.

Of all the things that the sons of the prophets studied in this school, their association with Elisha was by far their greatest instruction.

One of the sons of the prophets was not satisfied with the prophet's mere approval of the enterprise but wished for his actual presence. Elisha acquiesced to the request.

The "stick," no matter how crude, was symbolic of the Cross of Jesus Christ. We learn from this the tremendous lesson of the power of Calvary. Every single blessing received by the child of God comes through Calvary. Elisha applied the Cross to the problem. Regrettably, most in the modern church have set the Cross aside and resorted to other things, which only bring death.

The Cross is a finished work; consequently, all the believer has to do is simply stretch out his hand and take it, which Verse 7 proclaims. All that the Cross represents is ours for the asking.

THE SONS OF THE PROPHETS

Verse 1 says, *"And the sons of the prophets said unto Elisha."* It seems here that Elisha had some connection with the sons of the prophets (school of the prophets).

Their unbelief of Chapter 2 seems to at least have given

way to some faith. Prayerfully, their association had done much to direct them toward the Lord. It is interesting that the Holy Spirit refers to them as *"sons of the prophets."* One can only be a prophet, an apostle, an evangelist, a pastor, or a teacher if he is called by the Holy Spirit as such. If, in fact, the calling is there, then a measurable benefit is awarded if he can associate with an Elisha. However, there is little record that God used these individuals in much capacity.

They proposed larger quarters for their school.

One requested of Elisha that he *"go with your servants,"* and he answered, as recorded in Verse 2, *"I will go."* They were most blessed to have this association. As to how much they allowed it to benefit them, we aren't told.

As we see with the ministry of Elisha and, in fact, every other man and woman of God who has ever lived, such constitutes the strength of a nation, especially the church. Unfortunately, most so-called religious leaders little see that, if at all.

THE AX HEAD—A TYPE OF STUBBORN, HARDENED MAN

II Kings 6:5 says, *"But as one was felling a beam, the axe head fell into the water: and he cried, and said, Alas, master! for it was borrowed."*

As the ax head was separated from the ax handle, due to the fall, man was separated from God and sank into the murky waters of trouble, sorrow, and discontent. As it was, man could not retrieve that which was lost. It was buried too deep and covered by the murky depth.

So is sin upon the soul. It literally covers man in every capacity and presses him down like a weight. As that ax head on its own could not swim to the surface, likewise, man is hopelessly entombed in the bondage of sin, at least as it regards his inability to save himself.

SIN

Of course, the world doesn't really understand sin as such, but the tragedy is, the modern church little understands it either. How do I know that?

To understand how bad, how awful, how terrible, and how murderous that sin actually is, one has to understand the price that was paid in order to deliver man from this monster. When man fell in the garden of Eden, he fell from the high and lofty position of total God-consciousness down to the far lower level of total self-consciousness. As such, his very nature became that of sin. In other words, sin was not merely something that attached itself to man, but it literally became a part of man—a part of his character, a part of his being, and a part of his very nature. In fact, the sin nature rules and controls the unconverted man 24 hours a day, seven days a week. This is the reason for man's inhumanity to man, the reason for all the crime and murder, the reason for all war and, in fact, the reason for all sickness, suffering, loneliness, heartache, and despair. Sin is the culprit!

The reason that I know the modern church little understands what sin actually is, is because of the manner or cavalier fashion that it is treated.

In the modern church growth movements, it is said that if sin is mentioned, in other words, if the preacher deals with sin, this will be offensive to the hearers. It's called "seeker sensitive." So, the truth is that such a person is never convicted of sin because the Holy Spirit is given no opportunity to register conviction. Consequently, the church is being filled with people who have never really been born again, and despite all the religious activity, are still in spiritual darkness, which means they are still in spiritual bondage (Jn. 3:3).

HUMANISTIC PSYCHOLOGY

Without a doubt, the greatest hindrance to the work of God in the last 50 years or so is humanistic psychology. Regrettably, basically the entirety of the church world has bought into this nefarious system and, in fact, embraced it in totality.

Let it be understood that humanistic psychology holds no answers for the ills, the perversions, and the sins of man. The great prophet Jeremiah said concerning this very thing: *"For My people have committed two evils; they have forsaken Me the fountain of living waters, and hewed them out cisterns, broken cisterns, that can hold no water"* (Jer. 2:13).

So there will be no misunderstanding, let me say it again: Humanistic psychology holds absolutely no answers whatsoever for mankind. In fact, psychology is the religion of humanism. Man without God has to have something, therefore, he has invented his own religion. Unfortunately, the church has bought into it in totality.

SLAVES

As such, believers are slaves without even really knowing that they are.

Jeremiah also said:

Is Israel a servant? is he a homeborn slave? why is he spoiled? (Israel was a son, not a slave, yet they were about to become slaves! In fact, Israel had become a 'servant,' i.e., slave, to the heathenistic gods. As a result, they would soon become a slave to a foreign power. The question, 'Is he a homeborn slave?' is interesting indeed! It has reference to an animal in a zoo. An animal was made by God to be free and unfettered. However, if born in a zoo and knowing nothing but the confines of such, it is a slave without really knowing it. Such was Israel, and such are so many modern believers.

WHY IS HE SPOILED?

The question, *'Why is he spoiled?'* refers to Judah, which had sinned so long with impunity that there was no fear of divine retribution) (Jer. 2:14) (The Expositor's Bible).

Let us say it again: Most modern Christians, born in spiritual slavery (as are all human beings), come into the world of religion without really being born again and continue being a slave to sin. It's what Jeremiah referred to as *"a homeborn slave."*

As animals born and raised in a zoo, likewise, most so-called modern Christians have no idea of what it is like to be free. They've never been free, they aren't free now, and they don't even really know what freedom actually means.

Why?

It's because they don't understand the Cross, through which all freedom comes, and only through which all freedom comes.

The ax head was buried beneath tons of water, and there was no way that it could come to the surface, at least not by its own power.

THE CROSS

II Kings 6:6 says, *"And he cut down a stick, and cast it in thither; and the iron did swim."*

That stick was the Cross, so to speak.

In fact, the verb *cut* in this verse is not the same as in Verse 4. It actually means "to neatly fashion something." In this case, it could be translated, "He neatly fashioned a handle."

This handle neatly fashioned was done so by the heavenly Father and typified the Cross of Christ, which alone meets man's condition. That should be understood!

Man's condition of sin and bondage is such that the Cross of Christ alone can meet the need. That's the reason that man's efforts as such are hopeless! There is nothing that man can do, no scheme that he can concoct, and no effort that he can make that will help. In fact, there is absolutely nothing that can break the bondage of sin and darkness. The Cross alone can accomplish this task. It was fashioned neatly for this very purpose.

When Elisha put this stick in the water, there is a possibility that he had in mind the experience of Moses in the wilderness, which the Holy Spirit, no doubt, brought to his mind.

The Scripture says concerning that incident:

And when they came to Marah, they could not drink of the waters of Marah, for they were bitter: therefore the name of it was called Marah (Marah means 'bitter.' Pink says, 'While the wilderness may and will make manifest the weakness of God's saints and, as well, our failures, this is only to magnify the power and mercy of Him who brought us into the place of testing. Further, and we must understand, God always has in view our ultimate good.' The bitter waters of Marah typify life and its disappointments.)

WHAT SHALL WE DRINK?

And the people murmured against Moses, saying, What

shall we drink? (Three days before, the children of Israel were rejoicing on the shores of the Red Sea. Now, some 72 hours later, they are 'murmuring against Moses.' Such presents a lack of faith. 'Tests' brought upon us by the Lord portray what is in us. Regrettably, it doesn't take much to bring out the unbelief.) *And he cried unto the* LORD (Moses set the example; there is no help outside of the Lord, but man, even the church, seems to find difficulty in believing this); *and the* LORD *showed him a tree* (the 'tree' is a type of the Cross [Acts 5:30; 10:39; 13:29; Gal. 3:13; I Pet. 2:24]), *which when he had cast into the waters, the waters were made sweet* (we must put the Cross into every difficulty and problem of life, which alone holds the answer; only by this means can the bitter waters be made 'sweet'): *there He* (God) *made for them a statute and an ordinance, and there He proved them* (tested them! We must understand that God doesn't give victory to men, only to Christ; His victory becomes ours as we are properly in Him [Jn. 14:20; Rom. 6:3-5]) (Ex. 15:23-25) (The Expositor's Study Bible).

The stick cast into the river by Elisha was a type of the Cross. The Scripture then says, *"The iron did swim."*

The power of God reached down into that murky depth and brought that iron ax head to the surface, with the implication being that the newly fashioned ax handle fit neatly into the ax head.

The Cross of Christ alone can join man with God.

USE YOUR HAND AND TAKE IT

The Scripture says in II Kings 6:7, "*Therefore said he, Take it up to you. And he put out his hand, and took it.*" The Cross is a finished work; consequently, all the believer has to do is simply stretch out his hand and take it. All that the Cross represents is ours for the asking.

What an invitation!

If it were something difficult, most of us could not accomplish the task; however, all the believing sinner has to do, and all the believing Christian has to do is to just simply put out his hand and take it. That's how easy, and that's how simple it is! Just put out your hand and take it.

Every evidence is that the young man did not question the miracle, as stupendous as it was, that took place before his very eyes. He accepted it, believed it, and did exactly as the prophet said to do—he put out his hand and took it.

Let the reader understand that the same invitation is extended to you and me. Right now, by faith, reach out your hand and take the promises of God and believe Him for great and mighty things. It has all been made possible by the Cross.

Let us say it again: Christ is the *source* of all things we receive from God, while the Cross is the *means* by which we receive those things.

THE SPIRIT WORLD

Then the king of Syria warred against Israel, and took

counsel with his servants, saying, In such and such a place shall be my camp. And the man of God sent unto the king of Israel, saying, Beware that you pass not such a place; for thither the Syrians are come down. And the king of Israel sent to the place which the man of God told him and warned him of, and saved himself there, not once nor twice. Therefore the heart of the king of Syria was sore troubled for this thing; and he called his servants, and said unto them, Will you not show me which of us is for the king of Israel? And one of his servants said, None, my lord, O king: But Elisha, the prophet that is in Israel, tells the king of Israel the words that you speak in your bedchamber. And he said, Go and spy where he is, that I may send and fetch him. And it was told him, saying, Behold, he is in Dothan. Therefore sent he thither horses, and chariots, and a great host: and they came by night, and compassed the city about. And when the servant of the man of God was risen early, and gone forth, behold, an host compassed the city both with horses and chariots. And his servant said unto him, Alas, my master! how shall we do? And he answered, Fear not: for they who be with us are more than they who be with them. And Elisha prayed, and said, LORD, I pray You, open his eyes, that he may see. And the LORD opened the eyes of the young man; and he saw: and, behold, the mountain was full of horses and chariots of fire round about Elisha. And when they came down to him, Elisha prayed unto the LORD, and

said, Smite this people, I pray you, with blindness. And
He smote them with blindness according to the word of
Elisha. And Elisha said unto them, This is not the way,
neither is this the city: follow me, and I will bring you
to the man whom you seek. But he led them to Samaria.
And it came to pass, when they were come into Samaria,
that Elisha said, LORD, open the eyes of these men, that
they may see. And the LORD opened their eyes, and they
saw; and, behold, they were in the midst of Samaria.
And the king of Israel said unto Elisha, when he saw
them, My father, shall I smite them? shall I smite them?
And he answered, You shall not smite them: would you
smite those whom you have taken captive with your
sword and with your bow? set bread and water before
them, that they may eat and drink, and go to their
master. And he prepared great provision for them: and
when they had eaten and drunk, he sent them away, and
they went to their master. So the bands of Syria came
no more into the land of Israel (II Ki. 6:8-23).

WALKING AFTER THE SPIRIT

The time frame of this occasion was possibly several years
after the healing of Naaman.

Despite Israel's spiritual degeneracy, the Lord helped
them through Elisha. He disclosed three or more times the
plans of the king of Syria.

For the man to have this information means that Elisha

evidently made no secret of the instructions that he was giving to the king of Israel concerning the king of Syria. It seems from this that the king of Syria should have been convicted in his heart for his misdeeds, but he was not. Man's ability to resist God is simply amazing! In his stupidity, he sent his army to take Elisha.

In this episode, the Holy Spirit is telling us here not to be daunted by that which appears on the surface. The believer is not to walk after the flesh, but rather after the Spirit (Rom. 8:1). The trouble with most Christians is that they know what is happening, but they don't know what's going on.

We should ever remember the statement given by Elisha, *"For they who be with us are more than they who be with them."* The promise applicable then is most assuredly applicable now!

THE HOLY SPIRIT

The Holy Spirit allowed this to happen that you and I may understand by faith that we are surrounded by horses and chariots of fire, at least when the need is there, even though not seen by the natural eye. What an encouragement! In this passage, we are given a glimpse into the spirit world of righteousness. The same gospel that softens also hardens. As well, that which opens blinded eyes can close open eyes. The gospel always has a powerful effect on anyone, whether it be positive or negative. The effect is according to the response of the individual.

No, the action of Elisha in Verse 19 was not a lie. The intention of the Syrians was to stop Elisha because he was hindering them from getting to the king of Israel. The king of Israel was the one whom they were really seeking. Verse 22 pictures a great work of grace. The king of Israel would kill them; however, Elisha proclaimed the love of God to them.

THE WORD OF KNOWLEDGE

It is believed that peace reigned for some time between Syria and Israel after the healing of Naaman; however, it is also believed that several years had now passed from that particular time. Evidently, Naaman had now passed on. It is doubtful that the king of Syria would have engaged in such activity against Israel had this man, who had experienced such grace from Jehovah in cleansing him from his leprosy, been alive.

At any rate, Syria now *"warred against Israel."* Evidently, the king of Syria sent into Israel his military leader with a number of soldiers, intending to ambush the king of Israel. Through a word of knowledge, Elisha told the king of Israel what was taking place.

Evidently, he did this several times as the king of Syria attempted his ambush. In fact, the situation became so bad that the king of Syria called in his staff and demanded to know whom the traitor was.

In other words, he thought that someone on his staff was giving information to the king of Israel.

"One of his servants said, None, my lord, O king: but Elisha, the prophet that is in Israel, tells the king of Israel the words that you speak in your bedchamber."

How did this servant know this?

It seems that Elisha did not keep it a secret at all as he told the king of Israel of the plans of the king of Syria. Undoubtedly, many people knew what Elisha was doing, and evidently, the word reached this particular servant, whomever he may have been.

WHAT IS THE WORD OF KNOWLEDGE?

The word of knowledge is a word from the Holy Spirit that is given to someone, regarding people, places, or things, as it regards the past or the present. Since the advent of the Holy Spirit after the Cross, which took place on the day of Pentecost, the word of knowledge is one of the nine gifts of the Spirit. As it regards the nine gifts (I Cor. 12:8-10), any person who has been baptized with the Holy Spirit, which is always accompanied by the speaking with other tongues (Acts 2:4), can have one or more of these gifts. All of this has been made possible by the Cross.

Before the Cross, the Holy Spirit was greatly limited as to what He could do because the blood of bulls and goats could not remove the sin debt. With certain ones, such as Elisha, the Holy Spirit moved and operated, but all of this was very limited as far as the number of people was concerned. As stated, the Cross of Christ, which atoned for all sin—making it possible for the Holy Spirit to abide permanently in the heart and life of the believer—changed all of that.

Also, it must be remembered that this which the Holy Spirit gives is just a "word," meaning an abbreviated account. The Holy Spirit does not give to someone who has this gift the full information on a particular subject, only that which is necessary at the time. That's why it is referred to as a "word of knowledge."

A PERSONAL EXPERIENCE

I could give several little illustrations as to how the word of knowledge has worked through this evangelist, but I think the following will suffice.

If I remember correctly, it was 1987. Two Baptist preachers had been put in jail in the state of Nebraska because they would not comply with the demands of the state regarding their private Christian school. The news was in all the papers. Everyone was wondering how such a thing could be—two preachers put in jail because of some rules, with which they felt, in all good conscience, they could not comply.

Somebody in Washington sent for three preachers to come to that city, hoping that a means could be devised so that the preachers in Nebraska could be released from jail. I was one of those preachers.

If my memory serves me correctly, we met in one of the large rooms in the Old Executive Office Building that is very near the White House.

THE PRESIDENT'S CABINET

The room was filled with lawyers. In fact, there were so many there that they were standing against the wall. Almost all of the president's cabinet was present, and I speak of President Reagan. Ed Meese, attorney general of the United States, was there. In fact, he was seated right next to me on my right. As well, the national security advisor and Secretary of Treasury James Baker, were also present.

Members of the president's cabinet spoke, stating that they would do anything that was legal to get these men released from jail, as long as it would not embarrass the president. Constitutional lawyers tried to figure out something from a legal viewpoint.

The other two preachers spoke, and I honestly don't remember what they said.

Attorney General Meese, who was seated right next to me, began to speak. While he was speaking, the Holy Spirit began to deal with my heart, giving me a word of knowledge as it regarded the situation. I'll be frank with you, I thought, Lord, if this isn't You, then I'll look like a fool.

The Lord gently spoke to my heart, telling me that as soon as the attorney general finished speaking, I should speak up and give to this group of men what the Lord had told me.

GO AHEAD

I waited for the attorney general to finish. No, I did not

mention to these men that it was the Lord who gave me this, and for all the obvious reasons.

When the attorney general finished, there was a silence for a moment, then the Lord said, "Go ahead."

I cleared my throat and began to speak, and, of course, all eyes were upon me. To say I was nervous would be an understatement.

I asked those present there, and I speak of the president's cabinet, "Isn't the president going to address the nation tonight?"

One of the cabinet members spoke up and said, "Yes, he is."

I stated, "Why not have the president mention this situation in Nebraska? That will draw a lot of attention to that which is happening and might cause the officials there to think twice and release these men."

When I finished, a silence gripped the entire room.

All of a sudden, the leading constitutional lawyer in the room, who was seated at the head of the table, jumped to his feet and slammed his fist down on the table and said, "Why didn't I think of that?"

The national security advisor to the president spoke up and said, "I'm writing the president's speech. I will make mention of this thing, and I know exactly what to say."

That night, President Reagan addressed the nation, mentioned the situation at hand, and the next morning, the two preachers were released from jail.

That was a word of knowledge that the Holy Spirit

revealed to me.

No, the Lord does not reveal such to me every time. In fact, He has only done such a few times in all of my life and living. This tells us that we as believers do not order the Holy Spirit around, but we rather wait on Him that He may give us in due time that which He wishes us to have.

THEY WHO BE WITH US ARE MORE
THAN THEY WHO BE WITH THEM

Upon hearing that it was Elisha who was relating to the king of Israel the plans of the enemy, the king of Syria determined to take out Elisha.

One observes all of this and is startled as it regards obstinacy and the hardness of man toward God. This heathen king had it revealed to him how that the God of Israel had related to Elisha the very plans of the enemy, but despite that, the king of Syria did not seem to be impressed. Did he not realize that God, who could do this thing, could do anything?

Despite incontrovertible proof and despite overwhelming evidence, still, recalcitrant man rebels against God! Man tries to make some excuse in his heart as to why certain things happen, refusing to give God the glory.

How stupid was the king of Syria, thinking he could stop Elisha! How stupid he was in failing to recognize what was taking place! However, such is man!

So, the king of Syria *"sent thither horses, and chariots, and a great host: and they came by night, and compassed the city about."*

When the servant of Elisha arose the next morning and observed this great host of the enemy that had surrounded them, he immediately asked Elisha, *"Alas, my master! how* (what) *shall we do?"*

Elisha's answer is very revealing. He said, *"Fear not: for they who be with us are more than they who be with them."*

Then the great prophet asked the Lord to open the eyes of his servant that he may see into the spirit world. What he saw, no doubt, was the most startling thing he had ever seen.

The Scripture says, *"And the LORD opened the eyes of the young man; and he saw: and, behold, the mountain was full of horses and chariots of fire round about Elisha."*

Truly, there was more with Elisha than there was with the Syrians.

THE SPIRIT WORLD

The spirit world of righteousness or unrighteousness is concealed from human beings, unless, of course, the Lord would deem it desirable for our eyes to be open to see what is really there. However, although invisible, these things are even more real than what we can see with our eyes.

While the king of Syria surrounded Elisha, no doubt, with hundreds, if not thousands, of soldiers and chariots, he thought he had a formidable force. He didn't realize at all what he was facing.

In answer to his evil effort, the Lord sent *"horses and*

chariots of fire round about Elisha," which possessed unlimited power.

Does this happen presently?

To be sure, such happens now on a greater scale; again, all made possible by the Cross.

It is for certain that Satan would kill every single child of God in this world if he could! Barring that, he would cripple every believer and make us bedfast to where we could be of little service to the work of God. In other words, anything that he could physically do to us, or any other way for that matter, to be sure, if he could do so, it would be done.

WHY DOESN'T HE DO THESE THINGS?

Satan and his minions of darkness—and we speak of demon spirits and fallen angels—do not do these things simply because they cannot do these things. To be sure and, as stated, if they could, they would!

The child of God is protected by the Lord in many and varied ways according to the need of the moment.

And then there are times that the Lord will not afford protection, and it is for His own purposes and reasons. Let's go to the Bible for examples.

James, the brother of John, was the first disciple chosen by Christ to die. He was executed by Herod.

The Scripture says:

"Now about that time (pertains to the time Paul and Barnabas went to Jerusalem) *Herod the king* (speaks of

Herod Agrippa, the son of Aristobulus, grandson of Herod the Great, who murdered the babies of Bethlehem) *stretched forth his hands to vex certain of the church* (was probably done to ingratiate himself with the Jewish leadership). *And he killed James the brother of John with the sword* (the first of the apostles to die; no successor for James was ever chosen; in fact, with the exception of Judas who was replaced by Matthias, no others ever followed any of the Twelve in office, so to speak; in other words, there is no such thing as apostolic succession as taught by some)" (Acts 12:1-2) (The Expositor's Study Bible).

WHY DIDN'T THE LORD DELIVER JAMES?

The time frame of this incident was approximately nine years after the crucifixion, resurrection, and ascension of Christ. Why didn't the Lord deliver James?

We aren't given that information. Evidently, the Lord was through with him and, thereby, took him home. James was probably about 30 years old at this time, actually, in the very prime of life.

Then immediately following this, Peter was arrested, with Herod determined to do to him what he had done to James. Peter was arrested and put in prison, with 16 soldiers, four to the watch, guarding him (Acts 12:4). He was to be executed on a certain day. Now, keep in mind that he was in prison, guarded by 16 soldiers, four to the watch, *"sleeping between two soldiers, bound with two chains."*

Then the Scripture says:

And, behold, the angel of the Lord came upon him (should have been translated, 'An angel of the Lord'), *and a light shined in the prison* (meaning there was no doubt this being was 'from the Lord'): *and he smote Peter on the side, and raised him up, saying, Arise up quickly* (simply means that the angel awakened him). *And his chains fell off from his hands* (great power!).

THE ANGEL

And the angel said unto him, Gird yourself, and bind on your sandals. And so he did. And he said unto him, Cast your garment about you, and follow me (speaks of the outer garment, with Peter now being fully dressed). *And he went out, and followed him* (presents Peter doing something, which at the moment he is not certain is real); *and wist not that it was true which was done by the angel; but thought he saw a vision* (he had difficulty making the transition to the supernatural; he kept thinking that he was seeing a vision). *When they were past the first and the second ward* (probably means that Herod had placed Peter in the inner prison; as well, they went through the doors and passed the guards without them knowing what was happening; in some way, the angel made all of this invisible to these individuals), *they came unto the iron gate that leads unto the city* (pertained to the gate of the prison); which opened to them of his own accord (means that it opened automatically): *and they went out, and passed on through one street; and forthwith the angel departed from him* (so miraculous that it actually defies description).

PETER

And when Peter was come to himself (meaning he now knows that this had not been a vision or a dream, but that he had been truly delivered by an angel), *he said, Now I know of a surety, that the Lord has sent His angel, and has delivered me out of the hand of Herod* (proclaims Peter giving God all the glory), *and from all the expectation of the people of the Jews* (Herod would be deprived of his show, and all who were expecting to see the bloodletting) (Acts 12:7-11) (The Expositor's Study Bible).

Now, why didn't the Lord deliver James as he delivered Peter? It certainly wasn't a lack of power on the part of the Lord, as should be obvious.

CAUSED OR ALLOWED BY THE LORD?

As stated, we cannot give the answer to that question, except to say that the Lord was through with James and was not yet through with Simon Peter.

Nothing happens to a child of God, and I mean nothing, unless it is caused or allowed by the Lord. To be sure, the Lord does not cause believers to sin, to fail, etc., but He does allow such, that is, if we are so foolish as to do that which is wrong. However, even then, He watches over us and uses means to bring us back to the right way, that is, if we will but obey.

Again, we state, the spirit world is real, in fact, more real than this present world in which we live. This present world is temporal, but the spirit world is eternal. The soul and spirit of human beings are eternal as well.

That's why Jesus said, *"For what is a man profited, if he shall gain the whole world, and lose his own soul?"* (Mat. 16:26).

Most of the world prepares for this life, which is so temporal, and prepares not at all for the life to come, which is eternal—whether in heaven or hell!

THE GRACE OF GOD

Every evidence is that had the king of Syria been able to do so, he would have killed Elisha. In Elisha's actions, however, we see the grace of God in action.

First of all, Elisha prayed that the Lord would smite this heathen army with blindness, which is exactly what happened.

The great prophet then approached them and stated, *"Follow me, and I will bring you to the man whom you seek."*

While they were there to stop Elisha, in essence, they really wanted to get at the king of Israel. So, Elisha was not relating something that was untrue.

He led this heathen army to Samaria. When they arrived there, not really knowing where they were, the prophet prayed, *"LORD, open the eyes of these men, that they may see. And the LORD opened their eyes, and they saw; and, behold, they were in the midst of Samaria."*

Evidently, they were then surrounded by the army of Israel, with the king of Israel then saying to Elisha, *"My father, shall I smite them? shall I smite them?"*

Elisha answered, saying, *"You shall not smite them."*

He then told the king to prepare for them an excellent meal and then let them go back to Syria. This was grace in action!

If self-will had had its way, untold thousands of homes would have been seriously affected by the death of a husband, a brother, a son, or a grandson. As it was, the grace of God extended to this heathen army brought about the very opposite effect.

WHAT IS GRACE?

Grace is simply the goodness of God extended to undeserving people. It's the Lord doing things to us and for us that we do not at all deserve, and, of course, we speak of good things, for that's all that the Lord does. The grace of God has all been made possible by the Cross of Christ. The

Holy Spirit superintends this tremendous quality of our Lord. God doesn't have any more grace today than He did thousands of years ago. In fact, God is grace, one might say!

Before the Cross, the blood of bulls and goats was woefully insufficient as it regarded paying the sin debt; therefore, the grace of God could be extended not nearly as much as it is presently.

The Cross of Christ settled the sin debt, thereby, making it possible for God to do wonderful and good things for those who love Him and seek to please Him.

As we see here during the time of Elisha, the grace of God was extended to these undeserving soldiers, but it was extended because of Elisha. We must never forget that.

Whenever God extends His goodness to people who do not know Him, do not serve Him, and do not regard Him, it is because of believers somewhere who are requesting such.

AFTER THIS

And it came to pass after this, that Ben-hadad king of Syria gathered all his host, and went up, and besieged Samaria. And there was a great famine in Samaria: and, behold, they besieged it, until a mule's head was sold for fourscore pieces of silver, and the fourth part of a cab of dove's dung for five pieces of silver. And as the king of Israel was passing by upon the wall, there cried a woman unto him, saying, Help, my lord, O king. And he said, If the Lord does not help you, how shall I help you? out of the barnfloor, or out of the winepress? And the king said unto her, What ails you? And she answered, This woman said unto me, Give your son, that we may eat him today, and we will eat my son tomorrow. So we boiled my son, and did eat him: and I said unto her on the next day, Give your son, that we may eat him: and she has hid her son (II Ki. 6:24-29).

Several years had now passed since the action of Elisha regarding Syria and the invasion now of Israel by Ben-hadad, king of Syria.

This invasion would never have taken place had Ahab put Ben-hadad to death when he was in his power. The sufferings recorded in this passage would have been avoided. This siege and its horrors fulfilled the prophecy then made to Ahab by the rebuking prophet (I Ki. 20:31-34).

The siege had become so severe that the people of Israel, God's chosen people, had resorted to cannibalism. Moses had predicted that this would happen if the people turned their backs upon God (Deut. 28:53-57).

THE WAGES OF SIN

Here we see God's people, God's chosen people at that, in dire straits, to say the least!

Ben-hadad, king of Syria, had laid siege to Samaria, the capital city of the northern kingdom of Israel. This means that his soldiers surrounded the city to such an extent that nothing could come in or go out. Evidently, the army of Israel was not strong enough to resist the Syrians, so the city was shut up, which means it shortly ran out of food.

How could God's chosen people come to this place? They did so because of sin!

A long time before, Moses had said to Israel:

> *All these curses shall come upon you, and shall pursue you, and overtake you, till you be destroyed; because you hearkened not unto the voice of the* LORD *your God, to keep His commandments and His statutes which He commanded you. And you shall eat the fruit of your own body, the flesh of your sons and of your daughters, which the* LORD *your God has given you, in the siege, and in the straitness, wherewith your enemies shall distress you* (Deut. 28:45, 53).

THREE EXAMPLES

This happened three times, at least that is recorded. They were:

1. In Samaria on the present occasion.
2. In Jerusalem during the last siege by Nebuchadnezzar (Lam. 4:10).
3. In Jerusalem during the last siege by Titus, which was recorded by Josephus.

Israel had forsaken the Lord and was worshipping idols.

Despite the ministry of Elisha, and despite repeated warnings, now, due to the fact that they had sown to the wind, they were now reaping the whirlwind.

About seven years earlier, due to the power of God manifested on behalf of Israel, a great victory was won over the Syrians.

Ahab at that time spared the life of Ben-hadad, the king of Syria, even though the Lord had demanded that he be executed.

The Scripture says, *"Thus says the LORD, Because you have let go out of your hand a man whom I appointed to utter destruction, therefore your life shall go for his life, and your people for his people"* (I Ki. 20:42).

BEN-HADAD

It happened exactly as the prophet said. Ahab was killed in battle a short time later, and by the Syrians at that.

And now, this same Ben-hadad besieged Samaria, all because Ahab did not do what the Lord instructed him to do. He spared Ben-hadad's life, and now his son was faced by the same Ben-hadad.

Why will men disobey the Lord, especially when the direction is so clear?

Disobedience always results in a very negative conclusion.

Everything that God does is right, not merely because He is the one who does such, but because it, in fact, is right!

Regrettably, virtually everything that man does, at least

without the leading and guidance of the Holy Spirit, is wrong!

Now, the people of Samaria, God's chosen people, had been reduced to the level of cannibalism. And yet, the entire episode, with all of its sordid happenings and with all of its pain and suffering, all and without exception, was totally unnecessary. How much sorrow and heartache we bring on ourselves simply because we fail to obey the Lord!

NO TRUE REPENTANCE

And it came to pass, when the king heard the words of the woman, that he rent his clothes; and he passed by upon the wall, and the people looked, and, behold, he had sackcloth within upon his flesh. Then he said, God do so and more also to me, if the head of Elisha the son of Shaphat shall stand on him this day. But Elisha sat in his house, and the elders sat with him; and the king sent a man from before him: but before the messenger came to him, he said to the elders, You see how this son of a murderer has sent to take away my head? look, when the messenger comes, shut the door, and hold him fast at the door: is not the sound of his master's feet behind him? And while he yet talked with them, behold, the messenger came down unto him: and he said, Behold, this evil is of the LORD; what should I wait for the LORD any longer? (II Ki. 6:30-33).

Despite Jehoram, the king of Israel, wearing sackcloth,

there was no true repentance on his part; the sackcloth was only a ceremony. While it was definitely a sign of his tremendous problems, it did not point to the cause of those problems, which was his terrible sin. In fact, the church presently is loaded with similar ceremonies. However, the ceremonies are not based on the Cross and, therefore, aren't valid.

OPPOSITION TO THE MAN OF GOD

The opposition tendered by Jehoram against Elisha shows his spiritual condition. As well, law will always attack grace. Instead of the modern church realizing the cause of its problems and, thereby, repenting, it attacks the ones who are preaching the answer, namely the Cross.

Elisha was supernaturally warned of what was about to take place—that an executioner was coming almost immediately to take his life, and that the king himself would arrive shortly after.

Jehoram had, apparently, to some extent, repented of his hasty message and had hurried after his messenger to give Elisha one further chance at life. We must understand that they had been in communication previously on the subject of the siege, and that Elisha had encouraged the king to wait for an interposition of Jehovah. The king now urged that the time for waiting was over. In effect, he said, "What use is there in waiting any longer? Why should he not break with Jehovah, behead the lying prophet, and surrender the town?

What has Elisha to say in reply?"

The next chapter tells us.

BLAME GOD!

Evidently, when Ben-hadad laid siege to Samaria, Jehoram, the king of Israel, and Elisha had discussed the matter. The great prophet had told the king, as it regarded the situation, *"Wait on the LORD."* As is evident, the king was now tired of waiting!

He blamed God for his predicament and did so by blaming Elisha.

Man's patience with himself is infinite, but man's patience with God is very short-lived. In other words, if the Lord doesn't move instantly, most jump ship, so to speak.

Evidently, Jehoram sent a messenger to the house of Elisha with instructions given him to take the life of the prophet, but the Lord told Elisha what the king was doing.

ELISHA

Elisha and the elders of the city were discussing the situation when Elisha said, *"See you how this son of a murderer has sent to take away my head? look, when the messenger comes, shut the door, and hold him fast at the door: is not the sound of his master's feet behind him?"*

Obviously, Jehoram had had second thoughts as it regarded taking the life of Elisha, so he hurried to the prophet's home in order to stop the messenger.

When he arrived, he surmised, and rightly so, that what was happening to them was caused by the Lord. In that, he was correct! He also surmised that due to that fact, it was useless to wait for the Lord any longer, meaning that the Lord was not going to do anything.

But now, Elisha had a message for this *"son of a murderer,"* and it would be very positive. In fact, it would be so positive as to be unbelievable!

Alas! And did my Saviour bleed?
And did my Sovereign die?
Would He devote that sacred head,
For such a worm as I?

Was it for crimes that I had done,
He groaned upon the tree?
Amazing pity! Grace unknown!
And love beyond degree!

Well might the sun in darkness hide,
And shut His glories in;
When Christ, the mighty maker died,
For man the creature's sin.

Thus might I hide my blushing face,
While His dear Cross appears;
Dissolve my heart in thankfulness,
And melt my eyes to tears.

But drops of grief can never repay,
The debt of love I owe;
Here, Lord, I give myself away;
'Tis all I can do.

ELISHA

CHAPTER 8

WHY SIT WE HERE
UNTIL WE DIE?

WHY SIT WE HERE UNTIL WE DIE?

"THEN ELISHA SAID, Hear you the word of the LORD; Thus says the LORD, Tomorrow about this time shall a measure of fine flour be sold for a shekel, and two measures of barley for a shekel, in the gate of Samaria. Then a lord on whose hand the king leaned answered the man of God, and said, Behold, if the LORD would make windows in heaven, might this thing be? And he said, Behold, you shall see it with your eyes, but shall not eat thereof" (II Ki. 7:1-2).

How amazing is grace! In response to the murderous unbelief of the king's heart and the scornful unbelief of the messenger, an abundance of food was promised, and it was soon to be had for almost nothing!

This was a word of wisdom that was given to Elisha by the Lord as it regarded the abundance of food that would be available the next day.

The reward of unbelief would be death, as the reward of unbelief is always death.

THE WORD OF WISDOM

As it regarded the pronouncement given by Elisha concerning the abundance of food that would be available on the next day, this was a word of wisdom, as it is referred to presently.

Like the word of knowledge, the word of wisdom is one of the nine gifts of the Spirit.

Seven of the nine gifts (minus tongues and interpretation of tongues) were available in Old Testament times. These gifts, however, were not nearly as pronounced then as they are now. Basically, with some few exceptions, only those such as Elisha would have these gifts available to them. As we said previously, the Cross of Christ made it possible for the Holy Spirit to come in a new dimension, which began on the day of Pentecost. Paul outlines these gifts in Chapter 12 of I Corinthians.

The word of wisdom is a word concerning people, places, or things as it relates to the future. (As stated, the word of knowledge pertains to people, places, or things as it regards the present or the past.)

INSTRUCTION

This chapter provides much instruction regarding the circumstances of even the most afflicted child of God.

Verse 1 says, *"Then Elisha said, Hear you the word of the* LORD; *Thus says the* LORD, *Tomorrow about this time shall*

a measure of fine flour be sold for a shekel." How amazing
is the grace that in response to the murderous unbelief of
the king's heart and the scornful unbelief of the courteous
promise, such an abundance of food was so soon to be had for
almost nothing. A righteous judgment, however, forbids its
enjoyment to the unbelieving captain.

Did the Lord tell Elisha how the abundance of food would
come about?

There is no evidence that He did!

Obviously, the king and the elders believed Elisha, or
thought it was worth waiting until the next day to see if it
would really happen.

Elisha saw more miracles performed than any of the
prophets of the Old Testament. In fact, he saw more miracles
than anyone else, other than our Lord Himself. Strangely
enough, most of these miracles were performed in the
northern kingdom of Israel, which had totally lost her way
with God. Not one single king that graced the throne of the
northern kingdom was righteous. All were ungodly, some
more than others, but all nevertheless!

UNBELIEF

In the midst of the faith of Elisha and the great promise
given, we find unbelief.

Upon hearing this word as given by the great prophet
(and to be sure, it was quite a word), the Scripture says, *"Then
a lord on whose hand the king leaned answered the man of*

God, and said, Behold, if the LORD would make windows in heaven, might this thing be?"

We hear in these words scorn, sarcasm, and rank, raw unbelief! Sadly and regrettably, this man, whose life was now limited to a few hours, was not totally unlike the majority of the present world.

There are millions presently who scoff at the promises of God, with many in the so-called church doing the same. In fact, most in the modern church simply do not believe in miracles. When a miracle occurs, even the miracles of the Bible, they try to explain them away in natural terms, which, of course, is impossible. In other words, they make God out to be a liar!

Let it be understood that God is a worker of miracles, and He does such constantly. The Bible opens with miracles, continues with miracles, and closes out with miracles.

No, the Lord doesn't perform miracles on cue; however, at times and according to His will, He most definitely does. He is still in the miracle-working business!

UNBELIEF AND DEATH

Faith looks upward, while unbelief looks downward. Faith believes, while unbelief doesn't believe. Faith springs toward life, while unbelief springs toward death.

In response to his answer of unbelief, the prophet said to this man, *"Behold, you shall see it with your eyes, but shall not eat thereof."* Even though the statement was not made here, in effect, the sentence of death was now pronounced upon this man of unbelief. The next day, as the food was made available, he was killed exactly as the prophet predicted—he did not eat thereof. Let it ever be understood that unbelief will never eat thereof!

LEPROSY

> *And there were four leprous men at the entering in of the gate: and they said one to another, Why sit we here until we die? If we say, We will enter into the city, then the famine is in the city, and we shall die there: and if we sit still here, we die also. Now therefore come, and let us fall unto the host of the Syrians: if they save us alive, we shall live; and if they kill us, we shall but die. And they rose up in the twilight, to go unto the camp of the Syrians: and when they were come to the uttermost part of the camp of Syria, behold, there was no man there* (II Ki. 7:3-5).

Leprosy in the Old Testament was a type of sin. Its horrid desperation was such that in the eyes of Israel, a leper was hopeless.

How many Christians find themselves presently in such a perilous condition—a condition, we might add, so disastrous that there is no help from any quarter except God. Nevertheless, no condition is such that God cannot change it.

"Why sit we here until we die?" This is the beginning of

an adventure. Little did these lepers know what the results would be. Little did they realize how God would use them. So, these four lepers acted.

WHY SIT WE HERE UNTIL WE DIE?

The manner in which God answers prayer (that which He uses) is sometimes beyond the pale of understanding. Man is very limited as to what he can use, but God is unlimited!

As previously stated, even though one can sense faith in the question, *"Why sit we here until we die?"* still, I doubt very seriously that these lepers were thinking of faith in God whatsoever. They were just four men who were hungry and, in fact, dying. If they had had real faith themselves, I think that they would have long since gone to Elisha and requested healing, as did Naaman. There is no record that they did such, but irrespective, God would use them to bring about a miracle of unprecedented proportions.

There was no food in the city of Samaria, so no help could come from that source. So, these four men reasoned within themselves that quite possibly, the Syrians, who were camped nearby the city, might give them some food. They reasoned that they had nothing to lose. If they stayed where they were, they were going to die!

A VALUABLE LESSON

Many Christians are caught in the same place and position

as those lepers of old. Sin is in their lives, which is typified by leprosy. The situation around them has grown dire, and if the situation continues (whatever the situation is), it will spell disaster.

Such a believer needs to do two things:

First of all, if God has been wronged in any way, repentance must be forthcoming, and that repentance must be totally sincere, which means it is from the heart. The individual must take the blame because God certainly isn't to blame.

Second, the believer must place his faith exclusively in Christ and the Cross and realize that this is the only way to victory. In fact, any believer who's in a negative position is there because his faith has been placed in something other than Christ and the Cross. Fulfillment and development are all in the Message of the Cross. No believer can be what he ought to be, can defeat self, or can rise above emotional problems until such a believer understands where his victory is.

WHERE IS YOUR VICTORY?

I think that is probably one of the most important questions that could be asked—where is your victory?

I'm really referring to the source of victory—how one lives for God, how one believes God, etc. The tragedy is that the source of most proposed victory is anything but the right thing. There is only one place where the believer's faith can be registered that will guarantee victory, and that is the Cross of

Christ. It doesn't matter what a believer does, how dedicated he might be in that pursuit, or the effort made. Victory will not be forthcoming unless one's faith is exclusively in Christ and the Cross.

Paul said: *"But God forbid that I should glory* (boast), *save in the Cross of our Lord Jesus Christ* (what the opponents of Paul sought to escape at the price of insincerity is the apostle's only basis of exultation), *by whom the world is crucified unto me, and I unto the world.* (The only way we can overcome the world, and I mean the only way, is by placing our faith exclusively in the Cross of Christ and keeping it there)" (Gal. 6:14) (The Expositor's Study Bible).

As simple as that is and as blatantly exposed as it is in the Word of God, still, it is the place of victory that is little known.

Please understand that the veracity of the Cross is the same now as it was when our Lord gave this great truth to the apostle Paul (Gal. 1:12).

It is a fountain of blessing, of grace, and of power, which will change one's life and, in fact, is the only thing that will change one's life.

THINGS WHICH GOD USES

As previously stated, I don't think these lepers were evidencing faith when they went toward the camp of the Syrians. They were just desperate men, knowing that if they didn't obtain some food shortly, they would die. So, they felt they had nothing to lose by what they were doing.

And yet, the Lord would use what they did, and do so in a miraculous way.

God used a whale to bring Jonah into line. He used Joshua and the children of Israel marching around the walls of Jericho to topple that fortress. He used a staff in the hand of Moses to open the Red Sea. Here he used four lepers to bring about one of the greatest miracles found in the history of man. As we have already stated, man is very much limited, but God is unlimited! We should remember that when we have problems. As someone has well said, "If we seek the help of men, we will get the help that men provide, which is precious little, if any. If we seek the help we need from God, we will get the help that He can give, which is unlimited."

When the lepers came to the camp of the Syrians, everything was in place, but the Scripture says, *"Behold, there was no man there."*

HOW EASY IT IS FOR THE LORD TO DO ANYTHING!

For the LORD had made the host of the Syrians to hear a noise of chariots, and a noise of horses, even the noise of a great host: and they said one to another, Lo, the king of Israel has hired against us the kings of the Hittites, and the kings of the Egyptians, to come upon us. Wherefore they arose and fled in the twilight, and left their tents, and their horses, and their asses, even the camp as it was, and fled for their life. And when these lepers came to the uttermost part of the camp, they went into one tent, and did eat and drink, and carried thence silver, and gold, and raiment, and went and hid it; and came again, and entered into another tent, and carried thence also, and went and hid it. Then they said one to another, We do not well: this day is a day of good tidings, and we hold our peace: if we tarry till the morning light, some mischief will come upon us: now therefore come, that we may go and tell the king's household. So they came and called unto the porter of the city: and they told them, saying, We came to the camp of the Syrians, and, behold, there was no man there, neither voice of man, but horses tied, and asses tied, and the tents as they were. And he called the porters; and they told it to the king's house within. And the king arose in the night, and said unto his servants, I will now show you what the Syrians have done to us. They know that we be hungry; therefore are they gone out of the camp to hide themselves in the field, saying, When they come out of the city, we shall catch them alive, and get into the city. And one of his servants answered and said, Let some take, I pray you, five of the horses that remain, which are left in the city, (behold, they are as all the multitude of Israel who are left in it: behold, I say, they are even as all the multitude of the Israelites who are consumed:) and let us send and see. They took therefore two chariot horses; and the king sent after the host of the Syrians, saying, Go and see. And they went after them unto Jordan: and, lo, all the way was full of garments *and vessels, which the Syrians had cast away in their haste. And the messengers returned, and told the king* (II Ki. 7:6-15).

LOOK WHAT THE LORD HAS DONE

The Syrians thought some powerful army from a higher nation was coming upon them, and they fled. How easy it is for the Lord to do anything. How so important it is for the Christian not to limit God, but sadly, we do limit Him.

Quite possibly, when these four lepers began to walk toward the camp of the Syrians, the Lord magnified their footsteps until they sounded like the march of a mighty army. We exhibit faith, and God does the rest, but what we do must be in the will of God.

The sun had set the day before on a day of disaster for Samaria, but the sun would now rise on one of the greatest days of blessing in her history. Faith in God would do this thing.

In type, Samaria is a picture of the world with its hunger, starvation, pain, and agony. The lepers, as pitiful as they were, are a type of preachers of the gospel of good news. The abundance that we have found is a product of the gospel of Jesus Christ, which alone can satisfy the hunger and the craving of a starving world.

Just as the lepers, we must not hold our peace. We have good news to bring, in fact, the greatest news that man has ever known: Jesus saves, Jesus baptizes with the Holy Spirit,

Jesus delivers, and Jesus is coming again.

THIS IS A DAY OF GOOD TIDINGS

That's exactly what it was. This day that began with such foreboding would close with such victory as to defy all description. Only God could do such a thing!

Someone has well said that when these four lepers started toward the camp of the Syrians, the Lord magnified their footsteps, making them sound like a mighty army.

However, whatever it was that the Lord did, the Syrians evidently thought that Israel had hired the Egyptians or another mighty army to come against them.

Whatever they heard, it was so dramatic and so powerful in its presentation that they felt that if they didn't flee immediately, in fact, leave everything in its place (even the gold and the silver), they would be dead in a few moments.

As these four lepers came close to the encampment, everything seemed in place, but there seemed to be no one there. That's exactly the way it was. It was completely empty of all soldiers, yet, everything had been left, which included the food, the gold and silver, and the costly garments, in fact, everything.

After these lepers had feasted, and they realized that there was enough food there for the entirety of the city, and much more, one of them stated, *"This day is a day of good tidings ... We may go and tell the king's household."*

LOOK WHAT THE LORD HAS DONE

When they brought the news, it was not readily believed. The king of Israel thought it was a ruse on the part of the Syrians. They would come out toward the camp and then be set upon by the Syrians. They were to find that that was not the case at all. The prophecy given by Elisha would come true in totality exactly as the Lord had spoken through the prophet.

Samaria stands for this world in all of its privation and want. The people in the city were starving to death. The Syrians had encompassed them for many days, and there was no food left in the city; likewise, Satan has stolen, killed, and destroyed until many places in this world are in serious peril. In fact, if the truth be known, all who do not know the Lord—no matter the outward trappings they may have—still function from the realm of a wasted life and a broken heart. Outside of Jesus Christ, there is no development, no fulfillment, no prosperity, and no freedom—only slavery to the powers of darkness.

BELIEVE IT AND PROSPER!

In a sense, these four lepers are types of preachers of the gospel, as poor as that type might be. As lepers, they were not looked at too favorably during the time of Elisha. Likewise, true preachers of the gospel are not looked at too favorably at the present time. However, it was the lepers who knew where to find the food; it was the lepers who knew where the gold and the silver was; and it was the lepers who knew where there was an answer to the terrible dilemma in which Samaria found itself.

True preachers of the gospel are the only ones in the world at this time, and, in fact, ever have been, who have the answer for hurting and dying humanity.

With the Lord, no matter what the circumstances might be, it must be understood, *"This day is a day of good tidings."* Believe it and prosper!

FOOD, GOLD, SILVER, AND
BEAUTIFUL GARMENTS

> *And the people went out, and spoiled the tents of the Syrians. So a measure of fine flour was sold for a shekel, and two measures of barley for a shekel, according to the word of the LORD. And the king appointed the lord on whose hand he leaned to have the charge of the gate: and the people trode upon him in the gate, and he died, as the man of God had said, who spoke when the king came down to him. And it came to pass as the man of God had spoken to the king, saying, Two measures of barley for a shekel, and a measure of fine flour for a shekel, shall be tomorrow about this time at the gate of Samaria: And that lord answered the man of God, and said, Now, behold, if the LORD should make windows in heaven, might such a thing be? And he said, Behold,*

you shall see it with your eyes, but shall not eat thereof.
And so it fell out unto him: for the people trode upon
him in the gate, and he died (II Ki. 7:16-20).

The city would find that exactly as Elisha had spoken, so it
would be. Food would be had in abundance, along with gold
and silver, beautiful garments, etc.

The fate of the mocker, the one who, in essence, laughed
at the prophecy of Elisha when it was given a day before,
would fall out exactly as Elisha had said. He would see this
prophecy fulfilled before his eyes but would not eat thereof.
Because of unbelief, the man died, and because of unbelief,
untold millions are dying presently.

ACCORDING TO THE WORD OF THE LORD

When Elisha had prophesied the day before, *"Tomorrow*
about this time shall a measure of fine flour be sold for a
shekel, and two measures of barley for a shekel," such a
word seemed to be totally preposterous. How could such a
thing be? How could it happen?

The city of Samaria was shut up tight, and food had long
since run out. In fact, as previously stated, this situation had
become so bad that certain ones in the city had resorted to
cannibalism, as horrible as that was!

Having laid siege to the capital of the northern kingdom
of Israel, the Syrians were camped all around the city, waiting
now for it to fall any day. So, how in the world could a

prophecy such as given by Elisha come to pass?

Let it be understood that it doesn't matter what is said, if it is the Lord who is saying it, irrespective as to how preposterous it may sound, it is going to come to pass. That's the reason the Bible is so very, very important. It is the Word of the Lord, and, as such, every prediction in it is going to ultimately come to pass.

THE BIBLE, THE ULTIMATE AUTHORITY

Jesus said as it regards the Bible:

For verily I say unto you (proclaims the ultimate authority!), *Till heaven and earth pass* (means to be changed or pass from one condition to another, which will take place in the coming perfect age [Rev., Chpts. 21-22]), *one jot* (smallest letter in the Hebrew alphabet) *or one tittle* (a minute ornamental finish to ancient Hebrew letters) *shall in no wise pass from the law, till all be fulfilled* (the law was meant to be fulfilled in Christ and was, in fact, totally fulfilled by Christ in His life, death, and resurrection, with a New Testament, or new covenant being brought about [Acts 15:5-29; Rom. 10:4; II Cor. 3:6-15; Gal. 3:19-25; 4:21-31; 5:1-5, 18; Eph. 2:15; Col. 2:14-17]). *Whosoever therefore shall break one of these least commandments, and shall teach men so, he shall be called the least in the kingdom of heaven* (those who are disloyal to the authority of the Word of

God shall be judged; 'He shall be called the least,' means that he will not be in the kingdom at all): *but whosoever shall do and teach them, the same shall be called great in the kingdom of heaven* (the Lord sets the Bible as the standard of all righteousness, and He recognizes no other) (Mat. 5:18-19) (The Expositor's Study Bible)

The Lord recognizes nothing but the Bible simply because the Bible, at least a word-for-word translation, is the Word of God. This means that it is the embodiment of truth, and is the only embodiment of truth. This means that the Bible is by far the single most important work on the face of the earth. It is the only revealed truth in the world and, in fact, ever has been. As someone has well said:

- No Bible, no freedom!
- A little Bible, a little freedom!
- Much Bible, much freedom!

THE DEATH OF UNBELIEF

Exactly as the Lord had spoken through Elisha, the fate of the government official who scoffed at Elisha's prediction concerning the abundance of food would fall out exactly as the prophet had said. He would see what God did but would not eat thereof.

Evidently, when the people of the city heard that the Syrians had fled and had left all of their provisions in the camp, by the thousands they bolted through the gate to get to the food. The scoffer happened to be in their path. It would not be a good place. They trampled him down, and the Scripture says he died. It doesn't pay to scoff at the promises of the Lord.

Let the reader understand that God doesn't change. He is the same in character, in nature, and in His very being as He was when this incident took place some 2,900 years ago.

The Lord wants His people to believe Him, and that is an understatement.

In fact, I think the proof is in the Scriptures that God demands that His people believe Him. To fail to do so brings spiritual death, if not physical death.

STUDY THE WORD

As stated, this is the reason that believers should pore over the pages of the Bible. In essence, the Word of God should be made a lifelong study for every single believer. The Bible is the Word of God. It contains the promises, and what promises they are!

We should understand that the God of miracles in the Bible is the God of miracles presently. We should ask Him for great and mighty things and believe Him for great and mighty things.

Above all, we should believe the Lord to bless us spiritually and in every capacity. We must grow in the grace and knowledge of the Lord, which we can do by placing our faith exclusively in Christ and what He did for us at the Cross.

We must believe Him to bless us physically. Jesus Christ is still the same yesterday, today, and forever. He is the Saviour, and He is the healer.

We should believe Him to bless us financially, not that we may heap up money for our own satisfaction, but that we may bless the work of God. In fact, in a very concise manner, the Holy Spirit through John the Beloved said the very thing I have just stated.

He said:

Beloved, I wish above all things that you may prosper (refers to financial prosperity and should be the case for every believer) *and be in health* (speaks of physical prosperity), *even as your soul prospers* (this speaks of spiritual prosperity; so we have here the whole gospel for the whole man) (III Jn., Vs. 2) (The Expositor's Study Bible).

A PERSONAL EXPERIENCE

To use a page from the beginning days of my ministry, I go back in my mind's eye to 1957, that is, if I remember the year correctly.

The Lord had called me to be an evangelist, so that's what I set out to do. However, to get started seemed to be an impossibility.

We lived in a little backwater town, actually, a small village with a population of about 200 or 300 people.

My dad had built a church in that community several years before.

Actually, this is where I met Frances, which was the greatest thing that ever happened to me outside of the salvation of my soul.

I knew the Lord had called me, and I knew what I must do, but I did not know how that it could be brought about. The denomination with which we were then associated looked at me (even as they should have), as they did with most every other young preacher getting started, with a sort of wait-and-see attitude.

At any rate, those things were actually incidental. It was the Lord who had to make a way for me, or else, no way would be made. He began early teaching me that He was my source and not anything or anyone else.

One particular day, I was greatly perturbed about the situation, and as I was taught to do, I went before the Lord in prayer.

THE LORD WOULD ANSWER

At that time, Frances and I lived in a little tiny house trailer, 32 feet long and 8 feet wide. Donnie was then about 3 years old. Frances had gone somewhere, and during her absence, I went to prayer.

I began to importune the Lord, laying these matters before Him, which to me were gigantic, but to Him, of course, were insignificant.

At any rate, at a point in time, the Lord brought to my mind a little chorus that we had learned a few weeks earlier. The words were used by the Holy Spirit to minister grandly to my soul and to give me encouragement for what the Lord had called me to do.

Those words are:

My Lord is able, He is able,
I know that He is able,
I know my Lord is able to carry me through.

My Lord is able, He is able,
I know that He is able,
I know my Lord is able to carry me through.

For He has healed the brokenhearted,
Made the blind to see,
Healed the sick, raised the dead,
And walked upon the sea.

My Lord is able, He is able,
I know that He is able,
I know my Lord is able to carry me through.

The Lord used that little chorus to buttress my soul. I will never forget it. I sat there on the floor, leaning up against the bed at the back of that little trailer as the tears flowed down my face, and the Lord spoke to me saying, "I am able!"

THE LORD SPOKE AGAIN THE OTHER DAY

The Lord that day so long ago was telling me that it didn't matter what the problems were, it didn't matter what the difficulties were, and it didn't matter what circumstances said. The Lord said, "I am able."

The other day in prayer, the Lord brought this incident to my thinking once again. I relived those moments for just awhile, and then the Lord spoke to my heart and said, "Back in 1957, you were asking Me for meetings wherever the door would open, no matter how small the church was, and now you are asking Me for the entirety of the world."

I sat there on the floor for a few moments, lost in that word the Lord had given me, for that's exactly what was happening. I was importuning the Lord to open doors all over the world for the Sonlife Broadcasting Network, which He most definitely was and is doing.

At this time, we are airing the network 24 hours a day, seven days a week in more than 80 million homes in America and in over 70 foreign countries. I am told that, if it is desired, some 2 billion people can now tune in to SBN. In other words, the programming covers a great majority of the entirety of the world, and the Lord held that up to me.

He said, "You were asking Me in those days of long ago for just a place to preach, wherever it was, and now you are asking Me for the whole world." He then said, "I was able then, and I am able now. Believe Me for great and mighty things, for I am the God of the impossible."

———————— ～ ————————

Have you been to Jesus for the cleansing power?
Are you washed in the blood of the Lamb?
Are you fully trusting in His grace this hour?
Are you washed in the blood of the Lamb?

Are you walking daily by the Saviour's side?
Are you washed in the blood of the Lamb?
Do you rest each moment in the crucified?
Are you washed in the blood of the Lamb?

When the bridegroom comes,
Will your robes be white?
Pure and white in the blood of the Lamb?
Will your soul be ready for the mansion bright,
And be washed in the blood of the Lamb?

Lay aside the garments that are stained with sin,
And be washed in the blood of the Lamb!
There is a fountain flowing for the soul unclean;
Oh, be washed in the blood of the Lamb!

ELISHA

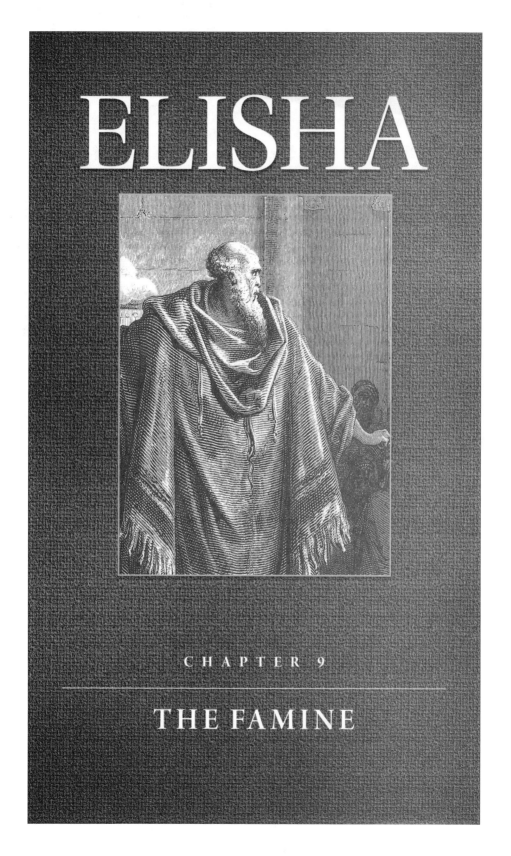

CHAPTER 9

THE FAMINE

THE FAMINE

"THEN SPOKE ELISHA UNTO the woman, whose son he had restored to life, saying, Arise, and go you and your household, and sojourn wheresoever you can sojourn: for the LORD has called for a famine; and it shall also come upon the land seven years. And the woman arose, and did after the saying of the man of God: and she went with her household, and sojourned in the land of the Philistines seven years" (II Ki. 8:1-2).

DOUBLE BLESSING, DOUBLE JUDGMENT

This is the same Shunammite woman whose son was raised from the dead.

Any connection with that of God, as proven here by this dear lady, proclaims continued protection. She would be given advance warning of the coming famine and actually would be told to move elsewhere. This shows that the famine was going to be very extensive.

Almost everything that happened to Elijah was doubled with Elisha, which pertained to the double portion received by Elisha. The famine in the days of Elijah was three and a half years, and this famine under Elisha was seven years. With the double blessing also came double judgment.

The Lord sent this famine on Israel because of her sin. The famine evidently did not include the land of the Philistines.

THE FAMINE

The previous chapter expressed a time of tremendous blessing, while this chapter expresses a time of tremendous judgment.

As it regarded Israel or Judah, famines in the Old Testament were called by God because of the sin of these nations. There is little record that God plagued the surrounding nations with such judgment.

Judah and Israel belonged to the Lord. They were His chosen people. He blessed them abundantly when they obeyed Him. Regrettably, the northern kingdom of Israel evidenced no obedience whatsoever. So, at times, the Lord would resort to judgment, extensively so, even as this famine. There is no hint in the Scripture that the famine came upon the southern kingdom of Judah or upon any of the other surrounding nations. It was Israel only, at least at this time.

DOES JUDGMENT GUARANTEE REPENTANCE?

No, it doesn't guarantee such at all. In fact, the record

shows that much of the time, judgment drives people further away from God. So, with that being the case, why would the Lord bring judgment?

The Lord is unalterably opposed to sin. When He warns repeatedly, and men repeatedly spurn that warning, the righteousness of God demands that at a point in time, judgment must come, despite the negative results. God cannot wink at sin. While He will deal with mercy, with grace, and with longsuffering, if it is repeatedly resisted, at some point in time, judgment will follow.

I believe that one can say with certainty that due to the fall of man (as is outlined at the beginning of Genesis) and Satan becoming the prince of the powers of the air and the god of this world, natural disasters are mostly his handiwork.

The storm that came up, as recorded in Matthew, Chapter 8, when Jesus was asleep in the boat, certainly was not caused by God. It was caused by Satan. Yet, as stated here, some so-called natural disasters are definitely ordained by the Lord because of great sin on the part of the people. As well, even though Satan brings about that which steals, kills, and destroys, and we speak of the elements, he can do nothing unless he receives permission from the Lord (Job, Chpts. 1-2).

THE COMING JUDGMENT

As well, when Israel rejected the kingdom when it was offered to them by Christ (and did so by rejecting Him, even crucifying Him), this submitted the world to a continued time of trouble, with the elements being greatly disturbed. This has now lasted for nearly 2,000 years.

Concerning this particular period of time, Jesus said, *"For nation shall rise against nation, and kingdom against kingdom: and there shall be famines, and pestilences, and earthquakes, in divers places"* (Mat. 24:7).

The fall at the beginning disrupted the entirety of creation. In fact, the Holy Spirit through the apostle Paul said concerning this very thing:

> *For the earnest expectation of the creature* (should have been translated, 'for the earnest expectation of the creation') *waits for the manifestation of the sons of God* (pertains to the coming resurrection of life).

SUBJECT TO VANITY

> *For the creature* (creation) *was made subject to vanity* (Adam's fall signaled the fall of creation), *not willingly* (the creation did not sin, even as such cannot sin, but became subject to the result of sin, which is death), *but by reason of Him who has subjected the same in hope* (speaks of God as the one who passed sentence because of Adam's fall but, at the same time, gave us a 'hope'; that 'hope' is Christ, who will rectify all things), *because the creature* (creation) *itself also shall be delivered* (presents this 'hope' as effecting that deliverance, which He did by the Cross) *from the bondage*

of corruption (speaks of mortality, i.e., 'death') *into the glorious liberty of the children of God* (when man fell, creation fell! when man shall be delivered, creation will be delivered, as well, and is expressed in the word 'also'). *For we know that the whole creation* (everything has been affected by Satan's rebellion and Adam's fall) *groans and travails in pain together until now* (this refers to the common longing of the elements of the creation to be brought back to their original perfection) (Rom. 8:19-22) (The Expositor's Study Bible).

When Jesus Christ comes back, tornadoes, famines, pestilences, hurricanes, tidal waves, earthquakes, etc., will end, but not until He comes back.

SEVEN YEARS

If it is to be noticed, Elisha saw twice what Elijah saw in both blessing and judgment because of the double portion. A seven-year famine is dire indeed!

Under Elijah, there had been a three and a half year famine, but now, that would be doubled, which would, no doubt, devastate the land, and do so in totality.

Why would the Lord be so severe at this time?

The northern confederation of Israel had witnessed the ministry of both Elijah and Elisha, but there was still no repentance on their part. While there were a few people in that land who served the Lord, the truth is, they were few indeed! As we have stated, as far as bringing individuals to God, judgment does not normally have a positive effect upon people. Still, the nature of God demands that sin be punished when pleadings for repentance are given over and over again and are met with a deaf ear. To be sure, Israel was more wicked now than ever, that is, if such were possible.

THE PROTECTING HAND OF GOD

When the Lord spoke to Elisha about the coming famine of seven years, He, no doubt, told the prophet to tell the dear lady who had been so kind to him to take her family to another land and sojourn there. In other words, if she had stayed in Israel for that period of time, the results could have been severe, even to the loss of her life and her family. So, she was told to leave.

As far as we know, the Holy Spirit through the prophet did not give this information to anyone else.

RIGHTEOUSNESS, TEMPERANCE, AND JUDGMENT TO COME?

And it came to pass at the seven years' end, that the woman returned out of the land of the Philistines: and she went forth to cry unto the king for her house and for her land. And the king talked with Gehazi the servant of the man of God, saying, Tell me, I pray you, all the great things that Elisha has done. And it came to pass, as he was telling the king how he had restored a dead body to life, that, behold, the woman, whose son he had restored to life, cried to the king for her house and for her land. And Gehazi said, My lord, O king, this is the woman, and this is her son, whom Elisha restored to life. And when the king asked the woman, she told him. So the king appointed unto her a certain officer, saying, Restore all that was hers, and all the fruits of the field since the day that she left the land, even until now (II Ki. 8:3-6).

Even though the king wanted to know all about Elisha and the miracles performed, still, all of these great things had not served the purpose to cause the king or Israel to repent. The king desired to hear the story of miracles, but nothing could be said of righteousness, temperance, or judgment to come. Regrettably, it is the same presently.

GOD'S WATCHFUL CARE

Chapter 5 of II Kings records Gehazi being stricken with leprosy. So, the account of the healing of Naaman may not have been given in chronological order. In other words, it is possible that the healing of Naaman happened after this incident. If that is incorrect, then possibly Gehazi had been healed. However, there is no scriptural record of such.

The Holy Spirit went to great lengths in relating this for the express purpose of showing God's watchful care over this woman. The Lord had her come to the palace at exactly the same time that Gehazi was telling her story. The Lord would continue to bless her for the good deeds she had done to the Lord's prophet in building him an apartment onto her house some 10 years earlier. Our gifts to Him are so fleeting while His blessings to us are everlasting.

THE LORD TIMED IT PERFECTLY

According to the Scriptures, the seven-year famine had now passed. The trials and hardships of that time are left silent. The scene opens with the woman, whom Elisha had greatly befriended, coming back from the land of the Philistines and finding that her property had been confiscated by others.

She happened to come to the palace to plead her case, in other words, for the return of her property, at the exact time that the king was asking Gehazi about Elisha and the miracles performed. The most notable of all was the raising of this woman's son from the dead, which Gehazi now related to the king.

Right in the midst of the illustration, the lady appeared before the king with her son. The Lord timed it perfectly.

As should be obvious, the hand of the Lord can be greatly seen watching over this dear lady, all because she had befriended the prophet some 10 years earlier.

As we shall see, sin has a way of continuing its evil results, even for many years to come. Thankfully, righteousness has a way of continuing its results also, even for many years to come. What we do, whether good or bad, is not something that passes away with the moment. Either one, righteousness or unrighteousness, has a life of its own. In effect, the evidence is that the Lord would watch over this woman all the days of her life simply because of her love for Him and her care for God's prophet, Elisha.

I think none of us properly know and understand how awful that sin is or, at the same time, how powerful that righteousness actually is.

THE LAW OF THE SPIRIT OF LIFE IN CHRIST JESUS AND THE LAW OF SIN AND DEATH

The two most powerful laws in the universe— the law of the Spirit of life in Christ Jesus and the law of sin and death— both deal with this subject. The law of sin and death is the second most powerful law in the universe, with the law of the Spirit of life in Christ Jesus the only law that is stronger.

Concerning these two laws, Paul said:

For the law (that which we are about to give is a law of God, devised by the Godhead in eternity past [I Pet. 1:18-20]; this law, in fact, is 'God's prescribed order of victory') *of the Spirit* (Holy Spirit, i.e., 'the way the Spirit works') *of life* (all life comes from Christ but through the Holy Spirit [Jn. 16:13-14]) *in Christ Jesus* (anytime Paul uses this term or one of its derivatives, he is, without fail, referring to what Christ did at the Cross, which makes this 'life' possible) *has made me free* (given me total victory) *from the law of sin and death* (these are the two most powerful laws in the universe; the 'law of the Spirit of life in Christ Jesus' alone is stronger than the 'law of sin and death'; this means that if the believer attempts to live for God by any manner other than faith in Christ and the Cross, he is doomed to failure) (Rom. 8:2) (The Expositor's Study Bible).

THE MOST POWERFUL LAW IN THE UNIVERSE

Even though the law of sin and death has been in existence ever since the fall in the garden of Eden, it was not until the Cross that the law of the Spirit of life in Christ Jesus made its debut. In other words, the Cross made this law possible.

As we've already stated, this law is the most powerful law in the universe, having been devised by the Godhead even before the foundation of the world (I Pet. 1:18-20).

If the believer attempts to live for God by any means other than by this law, the results will always be defeat. This means that our faith must be placed exclusively in Christ and what Christ has done for us at the Cross, and we must not allow our faith to be moved to other things.

With this being done and maintained, the Holy Spirit, who works within the parameters of the finished work of Christ—even as Romans 8:2 proclaims—will then begin to work mightily on our behalf.

THE HOLY SPIRIT

Let it be understood that whatever needs to be done in our hearts and lives, the Holy Spirit alone can carry out this work. If we try to do it any other way—by our own ability, talent, strength, or personal power—we will fail, and fail miserably.

If it is to be noticed, virtually the entirety of the Bible is given over to telling people how to live for God. Of all the instruction given, it can be summed up in Verse 2 of this great chapter of Romans (Rom. 8:2).

If the reader will notice, the Holy Spirit through Paul referred to this as a law, meaning that it is set in concrete, so to speak. In other words, it's not going to change.

This is God's way, and I'm speaking of the way that we live for Him and come out victorious over the world, the flesh, and the Devil.

Regrettably, most of the church world is attempting to live for God by means other than that which is given to us in the Word of God, in other words, without the Cross.

For a greater treatment on this all-important subject, I would strongly advise the reader to secure our study guide from the Cross of Christ series, *God's Prescribed Order of Victory (Rom., Chpt. 6)*. It is a dissertation on the first 14 verses of Romans, Chapter 6.

As well, the reader will definitely want to get for your own benefit the book, *The Message Of The Cross*. It is a hardback volume that goes into even greater detail.

RIGHTEOUSNESS, TEMPERANCE, AND JUDGMENT

The king was very interested in the miracles concerning Elisha and wished Gehazi to relate them to him.

However, he had little or no interest at all in the things that really counted, which were righteousness, temperance, and judgment. Unfortunately, he was not alone regarding such rejection.

An occasion from the ministry of Paul the apostle proclaims this truth.

The Scripture says:

And after certain days, when Felix came with his wife Drusilla, which was a Jewess (his wife was the young daughter of Herod Agrippa I, the Herod who killed James [the brother of John] with a sword [Acts 12:1-2]), *he sent for Paul, and heard him concerning the faith in Christ* (it seems to imply that his interest was sincere). *And as he* (Paul) *reasoned of righteousness* (righteousness can only come through Christ) *temperance* (the bondages and vices which affect humanity), *and judgment to come* (all must one day stand before God), *Felix trembled, and answered* (proclaims tremendous Holy Spirit conviction), *Go your way for this time; when I have a convenient season, I will call for you* (this presents the sinner's excuse when under conviction and refusing to surrender) (Acts 24:24-25) (The Expositor's Study Bible).

THE MESSAGE PREACHED BY THE APOSTLE PAUL

No doubt, Felix, the governor, would have been very interested in miracles, the same as Jehoram, king of Israel, but Paul's message cut straight through to the man's heart. It was either yield to Christ or resist the Holy Spirit. He chose the path of resistance and lost his eternal soul.

Unfortunately, in the modern church, this scene repeats itself all over again as it regards miracles. The church is very interested in such, or at least that which purports to be miracles, when, in reality, they aren't miracles at all. It is little interested, however, in righteousness, temperance, and judgment. In fact, according to modern marketing examples, the message preached by the apostle Paul finds no place in the modern church.

ELISHA AND THE KING OF SYRIA

And Elisha came to Damascus; and Ben-hadad the king of Syria was sick; and it was told him, saying, The man of God is come hither. And the king said unto Hazael, Take a present in your hand, and go, meet the man of God, and inquire of the LORD by Him, saying, Shall I recover of this disease? So Hazael went to meet him, and took a present with him, even of every good thing of Damascus, forty camels' burden, and came and stood before him, and said, Your son Ben-hadad king of Syria has sent me to you, saying, Shall I recover of this dis-

ease? And Elisha said unto him, Go, say unto him, You may certainly recover: howbeit the LORD has showed me that he shall surely die. And he settled his countenance steadfastly, until he was ashamed: and the man of God wept. And Hazael said, Why weeps my lord? And he answered, Because I know the evil that you will do unto the children of Israel: their strong holds will you set on fire, and their young men will you kill with the sword, and will dash their children, and rip up their women with child. And Hazael said, But what, is your servant a dog, that he should do this great thing? And Elisha answered, The LORD has showed me that you shall be king over Syria. So he departed from Elisha, and came to his master; who said to him, What said Elisha to you? And he answered, He told me that you should surely recover. And it came to pass on the morrow, that he took a thick cloth, and dipped it in water, and spread it on his face, so that he died: and Hazael reigned in his stead (II Ki. 8:7-15).

THE WORD OF THE LORD

It seems that respect for Elisha had grown considerably, even in the heathen country of Syria.

It's amazing how much faith a wicked king like Ben-ha-dad would have in Elisha and in the Lord but still not accept Jehovah as Lord of all.

Whether Elisha received or accepted this gift sent to him

by Ben-hadad is not known. To be sure, it was a gift of sizable proportions.

In other words, Ben-hadad most definitely could recover, but he wouldn't. The reason? Hazael would kill him.

Elisha fixed on Hazael a long and meaningful look until Hazael felt embarrassed, and his eyes fell. Elisha wept because of the long series of calamities that Israel would suffer at the hands of Syria during Hazael's reign.

INQUIRE OF THE LORD

The balance of this chapter portrays God's dealings with nations that did not particularly belong to Him, yet, they bordered Israel; therefore, God designed their direction. Anyone who comes in contact with God's children enters, at least in some measure, into God's dealings with them. The working of God with believers is so powerful that it affects all with whom they come in contact. As to how it affects them is dependent upon their actions toward the believer.

It is amazing how much faith that a wicked king like Ben-hadad, an idol worshipper, would have in Elisha, and in the Lord, as well, and still not repent of this woeful direction.

The evidence is clear that Ben-hadad knew Elisha and was well acquainted with Jehovah, at least enough to know and understand what God could do. Why didn't Ben-hadad go to his heathen idols? He didn't because it was pointless to do so.

Proverbially speaking, if push comes to shove, untold millions in this world know that Jesus Christ is the Son of

God. They know that He died on Calvary and rose from the dead, but, still, they will not serve Him.

WHY?

The reasons would vary with individuals; however, the major problem with all, I think, is that they really do not know what it means to live for God. They don't understand the spiritual welfare and the feeling of security, in other words, the blessedness of living for the Lord. They don't understand it, and to be frank, they cannot understand it until they are born again.

They do not realize that once a person comes to Christ, he becomes a new creation. Old things pass away, and all things become new (II Cor. 5:17). What they once hated, they now love, and what they once loved, they now hate.

Due to the fact that all unsaved people are *"dead in trespasses and sins,"* the truth is that unredeemed people can have no true thoughts of God.

Paul said:

And you has He quickened (made alive), *who were dead in trespasses and sins* (total depravity due to the fall and original sin); *wherein in time past you walked according to the course of this world* (refers to the fact that the unredeemed order their behavior and regulate their lives within this sphere of trespasses and sins), *according to the prince of the power of the air* (pertains to the fact that Satan heads up the system of this world), *the spirit that now works in the children of disobedience* (the spirit of Satan, which fills all unbelievers, thereby, working disobedience):

THE CHILDREN OF DISOBEDIENCE

Among whom (the children of disobedience) *also we all had our conversation* (manner of life) *in times past in the lusts of our flesh* (evil cravings), *fulfilling the desires of the flesh and of the mind* (the minds of the unredeemed are the laboratory of perverted thoughts, impressions, imaginations, etc.); *and were by nature the children of wrath, even as others.* (God's wrath is unalterably opposed to sin, and the only solution is the Cross) (Eph. 2:1-3) (The Expositor's Study Bible).

So, the unbeliever has to be dealt with by the Holy Spirit, who works on the premise of the Word of God that is delivered in some way to that person. The Holy Spirit convicts that individual of his lost condition and gives him faith to believe—that is, if he will—then that person can be saved.

In fact, unless the Holy Spirit draws an unbeliever, it is impossible for that unbeliever to come to Christ. Jesus said, *"No man can come to Me, except the Father who has sent Me draw him* (the idea is that all initiative toward salvation is on the part of God toward the sinner and not from the sinner himself; without this 'drawing of the Father,' which is done by the Holy Spirit, no one could come to God, or even have any desire to come to God" (Jn. 6:44) (The Expositor's Study Bible).

What Ben-hadad knew of God, he knew through Elisha. He knew that Elisha had performed any number of miracles, even to the raising of the dead. Consequently, he knew that Jehovah worked through Elisha, hence, his inquiring of the Lord through the great prophet.

MONEY

When Ben-hadad heard that Elisha was coming to Damascus, he hurriedly gathered together a tremendous gift to give to the prophet. Exactly what this was or how much it was, we aren't told. We do know that whatever it was, it took 40 camels to carry it. In doing something of this nature, the Orientals would at times make it seem bigger than it really was by putting a small portion on each beast of burden. Whatever happened here, however, the gift was substantial. It is not known whether Elisha accepted the gift or not, yet, there is some small indication that he did.

And yet, the gifts of God are just that—gifts. It means that God has nothing for sale. While the Lord loves a cheerful giver, and for all the right reasons, still, our giving must be in support of His work and not that it earns us anything from Him.

THE MESSAGE FROM THE LORD

The Lord revealed to the prophet that Ben-hadad could

definitely recover from his illness but, in fact, would not recover.

Why?

Although revealing that Ben-hadad would die, the Lord did not at this time state how he would die, but He did say that Hazael would become king. The truth is that Hazael would murder Ben-hadad. This is the same Hazael, who some 20 years earlier, the Lord had told Elijah would be king over Syria (I Ki. 19:15).

The Lord, of course, had nothing to do with Hazael's murderous action, but for His own reasons, He would allow Ben-hadad's death.

Verse 11 says, *"And the man of God wept,"* meaning Elisha, because of *"the evil that you will do unto the children of Israel."*

Because of Israel's great sin (sin, incidentally, that continued to increase), the Lord allowed depraved Hazael to become king. This should inform us that our consecration to God or our rebellion against God determines many things that will happen to us.

Hazael would prove to be exactly as Elisha had predicted—a great persecutor of Israel.

JUDAH

And in the fifth year of Joram the son of Ahab king of Israel, Jehoshaphat being then king of Judah, Jehoram the son of Jehoshaphat king of Judah began to reign.

Thirty and two years old was he when he began to reign;
and he reigned eight years in Jerusalem. And he walked
in the way of the kings of Israel, as did the house of
Ahab: for the daughter of Ahab was his wife: and he
did evil in the sight of the LORD. *Yet the* LORD *would*
not destroy Judah for David His servant's sake, as He
promised him to give him always a light, and to his chil-
dren. In his days Edom revolted from under the hand
of Judah, and made a king over themselves. So Joram
went over to Zair, and all the chariots with him: and
he rose by night, and smote the Edomites which com-
passed him about, and the captains of the chariots: and
the people fled into their tents. Yet Edom revolted from
under the hand of Judah unto this day. Then Libnah
revolted at the same time. And the rest of the acts of
Joram, and all that he did, are they not written in the
book of the chronicles of the kings of Judah? And Joram
slept with his fathers, and was buried with his fathers
in the city of David: and Ahaziah his son reigned in his
stead (II Ki. 8:16-24).

THE RESULT OF JEHOSHAPHAT'S SIN

At this point, the history of the kingdom of Judah is taken
up. Jehoram's reign was sometimes counted from the 17th
year of his father's when he was given the royal title; sometimes from his father's 23rd year, when he was associated; and
sometimes from his father's death in his 25th year when he

became sole king. In other words, Jehoram reigned jointly with his father Jehoshaphat for a period of time.

The verses quoted here proclaim the result of Jehoshaphat's sin regarding his union with Ahab and that wicked family. Regrettably, sin has a continued effect.

The light referred to in Verse 19 pertains to a kingdom according to the Davidic covenant of II Samuel, Chapter 7. A natural consequence of Jehoram's apostasy would have been the destruction of the house of David and the starting of another dynasty, as in the case of Jeroboam (I Ki. 14:10), but the promises to David prevented this, and Jehoram was punished in other ways.

Because this king of Judah did evil in the sight of the Lord, the Holy Spirit excised from his name the Jehovah–syllable, reducing from "Jehoram" to "Joram."

Joram died after an illness of an incurable disease of his bowels that lasted two years. There was no regret at his death.

THE WICKEDNESS OF JEHORAM, THE KING OF JUDAH

The account in the sacred text now switches from the northern kingdom of Israel to the southern kingdom of Judah. While the northern kingdom did not have a single godly king, the southern kingdom at times did, with Jehoshaphat being one of those godly kings. Regrettably, his son, Jehoram, was the opposite of his father. Yet, the sin of Jehoshaphat, in his constant union with Ahab and his family of the northern kingdom, would now bring forth bitter fruit.

Verse 18 says of *"Jehoram the son of Jehoshaphat"* that *"he walked in the way of the kings of Israel, as did the house of Ahab: for the daughter of Ahab was his wife."* Then the Holy Spirit says, *"He did evil in the sight of the* LORD.*"* In fact, his evil was so great that if the Lord had not promised David an eternal destiny, the southern kingdom of Judah would have been destroyed.

Jehoram walking *"in the way of the kings of Israel"* means that he introduced into Judah Baal and Astarte worship, both heathenistic idols. It seems that Jehoram was induced by his wife, Athaliah, the daughter of Ahab, to engage such idol worship in Judah. In fact, when Athaliah usurped the throne upon the death of her son Ahaziah, which we will see, she made Baal worship the state religion in the southern kingdom of Judah.

BAAL WORSHIP

The wicked actions of Jehoram are recorded at some length in II Chronicles, Chapter 21.

Shortly after he became king, he put to death his six brothers—Azariah, Jehiel, Zechariah, Ahaziah, Michael, and Shephatiah.

With Judah going the way of Baal worship, the Lord didn't have a single nation in the world at that time that worshipped Him. There were definitely some few people in Israel and others in Judah who loved and served the Lord, but the leadership, as is painfully obvious here, had pulled away from Jehovah in totality.

As stated, the situation was so bad that if the Lord had not made promises to David regarding the throne of Judah being occupied by the progeny of David, which would extend even unto Christ, He would have totally destroyed the southern kingdom and raised up another kingly dynasty. However, the Lord would not do this and, in fact, could not do this because of the promises that He had made to the sweet singer of Israel.

So, Jehoram was punished in other ways, which the next few verses proclaim.

JUDGMENT

II Kings 8:20 says, *"In his days Edom revolted from under the hand of Judah."* Verse 22 says, *"Libnah revolted at the same time."*

Disobedience to the Lord, and in this case gross disobedience, results in conquered territories being lost.

In the spiritual sense, such refers to Satan making inroads, meaning that victories previously won are now victories lost. In other words, Satan gains ascendancy in the individual's life by whatever means and matters.

We must ever understand that obedience to the Lord is absolutely required. We must also understand that such obedience cannot be rendered unless the believer places his faith exclusively in Christ and the Cross, which then gives the Holy Spirit latitude to work within his heart and life.

Unfortunately, the Cross of Christ is not the object of faith with most believers, but something else entirely. As such, the Holy Spirit is greatly limited as to what He can do for us simply because such a believer is functioning in a state of spiritual adultery (Rom. 7:1-4). Sadly, that is the state of most modern Christians.

WHAT IS SPIRITUAL ADULTERY

Even though we have addressed this problem previously, due to its seriousness, please allow us to briefly look at this subject again.

The believer is admonished to place his faith exclusively in Christ and the Cross, and to keep his faith in Christ and the Cross (Rom. 6:1-5; I Cor. 1:17-18, 23; 2:2; Gal., Chpt. 5; 6:15; Eph. 2:13-18; Col. 2:10-15).

If the believer places his faith in anything else, whether through ignorance or otherwise, such a direction is listed as unfaithfulness to Christ. As Paul stated (Rom. 7:4; II Cor. 11:1-4), we are married to Christ. He meets our every need and is perfectly capable of doing so, as should be overly obvious. While He is the source of all things that we receive from God, it is the Cross that is the means that makes it all possible. The Holy Spirit works exclusively within the parameters of the finished work of Christ. In fact, He will not work outside of those parameters, and that is a law.

"For the law of the Spirit of life in Christ Jesus has made me free from the law of sin and death" (Rom. 8:2).

This means that when Christians place their faith in anything except Christ and the Cross, no matter what it is and no matter how good it may be in its own right, such a believer is being unfaithful to Christ. That is, in fact, spiritual adultery. Let me list a few things that have been very big in the church in the last few decades, which constitutes spiritual adultery, or being unfaithful to Christ. To be sure, our list will by no means include every false direction but only a few. However, I think you, the reader, will get the point.

DEMON SPIRITS

The first one is casting demons out of Christians and claiming that this is the cause of the problem, whatever the problem might be. In the first place, while Christians can definitely be oppressed by demon spirits, we cannot be possessed by demon spirits. While demon spirits most definitely are involved in any type of sin and failure, that doesn't mean the person is demon possessed. The truth is that demon spirits have such latitude because our faith is improperly placed. Irrespective that this doctrine is believed by many, demon spirits are not the real cause of the problem, whatever the problem might be. Even though demon spirits most definitely are involved, the problem rather is that one's faith is improperly placed. So, if such a believer thinks that he can get a preacher to lay hands on him and cast out some demon, such as a demon of lust, etc., he will find to his dismay that the problem is unaffected. By him placing his faith in such, which is error, this constitutes spiritual adultery.

MANIFESTATIONS

By the use of the word *manifestations*, we speak of falling out in the Spirit, etc. To be sure, the Lord at times definitely can cause people to fall out under the power, so to speak. It's real, that is, if it truly is, and will be a blessing to the person. However, the answer to problems in one's life is not a manifestation, as helpful as that manifestation might be in other ways. You won't find such in the Bible.

The answer to the problem is, *"You shall know the truth, and the truth shall make you free"* (Jn. 8:32).

While some manifestations are definitely scriptural and real, still, those things aren't the solution.

LAUGHTER

The laughing phenomenon, which was big in the early 1990s, is another case in point. While the Lord at times most definitely does come upon a person in a spirit of joy, resulting in protracted laughter, still, that's not the solution for the problems of the church. The solution, and the only solution, is faith in Christ and what He has done for us at the Cross.

PROMISE KEEPERS

While this sounded good to the general public, still, it was little more than a law, which means that the end result was not to be what the people had hoped—and it wasn't! In the first place, men making promises in this fashion, as it regarded their wives and families, amounted to men making promises that could not be kept. It was all in the flesh and, as such, garnered no positive results. Once again, the answer and the solution, and the only answer and the only solution is Christ and the Cross and our faith in that finished work.

FAMILY CURSE

While there are definitely all types of curses on the human race because of the fall, when the individual comes to Christ, he instantly becomes a new creation, with old things passing away and all things becoming new (II Cor. 5:17). Most Christians, not understanding the Cross of Christ, will then incur difficulties and problems in their life and living. Unfortunately, at this stage, some preacher tells them that their problem is "the family curse." In other words, somewhere back in their family tree, a family member did some terrible thing, and now the curse of God has descended upon this individual several generations later. There is nothing in the Bible that substantiates such foolishness.

Such a believer most definitely may be having problems, and to be sure, if one looks long enough, one can find a family member somewhere back there that did some terrible thing. However, that's not the cause of the present difficulties.

Once again, the cause of the present difficulties, whatever they might be in the life of the Christian, is faith that is improperly placed. Our faith at all times must be in Christ and the Cross. With that being done, that means that our faith is now finally in the Word of God.

PURPOSE DRIVEN LIFE

The present craze is the Purpose Driven Life scheme. This is supposed to be the answer and solution for all problems. It isn't! How do I know it isn't? I know because whatever it is they are proclaiming, it's not the Cross of Christ, but rather something else. Please understand that it doesn't really matter what the something else is, no matter how good it may seem to be on the surface, and no matter how good it may actually be in its own right. The truth is, if it's not faith in Christ and the Cross, even as I have repeatedly stated, there will be no positive results. The facts are that anyone who engages in any of these things, plus a hundred and one other things that I haven't mentioned, has placed his faith in those efforts, with the end result being negative instead of positive. In fact, such a person, no matter his good intentions, is committing spiritual adultery, which, as one should understand, is not a good thing.

HUMANISTIC PSYCHOLOGY

In the 1940s, the denominational church world began its foray into humanistic psychology. Regrettably, in the 1960s, the Pentecostal denominations began to follow suit. At this time, virtually the entirety of the church world has opted for this nefarious system.

Humanistic psychology is from the wisdom of this world. The Holy Spirit through James said, *"This wisdom descends not from above, but is earthly, sensual, devilish"* (James 3:15). I think it should be obvious to the believer that anything that falls into this category is not scriptural, to say the least.

Humanistic psychology holds no solution and no answer for anyone, be it Christian or otherwise. In fact, such is the religion of humanism, meaning that it's the religion of the world. The world, having rejected Christ, has to have something, and humanistic psychology is that something. As someone has capably said, "Its proposed treatments are worthy of a Roman circus." Yet, the modern church has bought into this system, and the question must be asked, why?

WHY?

The church has abandoned Christ and the Cross and, as such, has abandoned the answer and the solution. It has done so through ignorance or rank unbelief. From years of studying this subject, I am persuaded that while ignorance abounds, still, unbelief is the true culprit. This means that the modern church simply doesn't believe that what Jesus did at the Cross answers every spiritual problem, irrespective of what it might be. Upon rejecting the Cross, they have turned to humanistic psychology. As stated, there is no help from that source, none whatsoever!

Every single victory over sin, perversion, transgression, and spiritual darkness has all come about through the Cross in totality. So, if the believer begins to opt for anything other than the Cross of Christ, he will find possessions that were gained in spiritual warfare now being lost exactly as Judah experienced.

JEHOSHAPHAT'S SIN OF UNITY WOULD TAKE ITS DEADLY TOLL FOR YEARS TO COME

In the twelfth year of Joram the son of Ahab king of Israel did Ahaziah the son of Jehoram king of Judah begin to reign. Two and twenty years old was Ahaziah when he began to reign; and he reigned one year in Jerusalem. And his mother's name was Athaliah, the daughter of Omri king of Israel. And he walked in the way of the house of Ahab, and did evil in the sight of the LORD, *as did the house of Ahab: for he was the son-in-law of the house of Ahab. And he went with Joram the son of Ahab to the war against Hazael king of Syria in Ramoth-gilead; and the Syrians wounded Joram. And King Joram went back to be healed in Jezreel of the wounds which the Syrians had given him at Ramah, when he fought against Hazael king of Syria. And Ahaziah the son of Jehoram king of Judah went down to see Joram the son of Ahab in Jezreel, because he was sick (II Ki. 8:25-29).*

It is conjectured that Ahaziah began to reign as viceroy to his father during his severe illness in Jehoram's 11th year and became sole king at his father's death the following year.

The Joram of Verse 29 is the king of Israel, while the Joram of Verse 21 was the king of Judah. They were two different men!

EVIL IN THE SIGHT OF THE LORD

Verses 25 through 29 record the continued evil of the sixth king of Judah. Verse 27 says, *"And he walked in the way of the house of Ahab."*

Then the Holy Spirit proclaims, *"For he was the son-in-law of the house of Ahab."* The bitter fruit of what Jehoshaphat did in attempting to wed Judah with Israel would take its deadly toll for years to come.

The believer must understand that while we are in the world, we must not be of the world. We do not march to its tune, we do not sing its songs, and we will have nothing to do with its spirit.

And yet, at the same time, we must have correspondence with the world in that we can witness to them about our Lord, who has saved us and can save them.

Our light is not to be hidden, but rather to be set on high to where it can be seen. As stated, there is a line drawn between the believer and the non-believer. Jehoshaphat did not recognize that line and crossed it.

He first of all joined with Ahab in attacking Syria.

Second, he brought in the daughter of Ahab to be the wife of his son Jehoram, and the result of that union is obvious to all. The evil spread until it was now at the stage of destruction.

My faith looks up to You,
Thou Lamb of Calvary,
Saviour divine;
Now hear me while I pray,
Take all my sins away,
Oh let me from this day
Be wholly Thine!

May Your rich grace impart
Strength to my fainting heart,
My zeal inspire;
As You have died for me,
Oh, may my love to Thee,
Pure, warm and changeless be,
A living fire!

While life's dark maze I tread,
And griefs around me spread,
Be Thou my guide;
Bid darkness turn to day,
Wipe sorrow's tears away,
Nor let me ever stray
From Your side.

ELISHA

CHAPTER 10

VENGEANCE IS MINE; I WILL REPAY, SAITH THE LORD

VENGEANCE IS MINE; I WILL REPAY, SAITH THE LORD

"AND ELISHA THE PROPHET called one of the children of the prophets, and said unto him, Gird up your loins, and take this box of oil in your hand, and go to Ramoth-gilead: And when you come thither, look out there Jehu the son of Jehoshaphat the son of Nimshi, and go in, and make him arise up from among his brethren, and carry him to an inner chamber; then take the box of oil, and pour it on his head, and say, Thus says the LORD, I have anointed you king over Israel. Then open the door, and flee, and tarry not. So the young man, even the young man the prophet, went to Ramoth-gilead. And when he came, behold, the captains of the host were sitting; and he said, I have an errand to you, O captain. And Jehu said, Unto which of all us? And he said, To you, O captain. And he arose, and went into the house; and he poured the oil on his head, and said unto him, Thus says the LORD God of Israel, I have anointed you king over the people of the LORD, even over Israel. And you shall smite the house of Ahab your master, that I may avenge the *blood of My servants the prophets, and the blood of all the servants of the LORD, at the hand of Jezebel. For the whole house of Ahab shall perish: and I will cut off from Ahab him who urinates against the wall, and him who is shut up and left in Israel: And I will make the house of Ahab like the house of Jeroboam the son of Nebat, and like the house of Baasha the son of Ahijah: And the dogs shall eat Jezebel in the portion of Jezreel, and there shall be none to bury her. And he opened the door, and fled. Then Jehu came forth to the servants of his lord: and one said unto him, Is all well? wherefore came this mad fellow to you? And he said unto them, You know the man, and his communication. And they said, It is false; tell us now. And he said, Thus and thus spoke he to me, saying, Thus says the LORD, I have anointed you king over Israel. Then they hasted, and took every man his garment, and put it under him on the top of the stairs, and blew with trumpets, saying, Jehu is king"* (II Ki. 9:1-13).

JUDGMENT

The judgment of the house of Ahab now commenced, and Jehu was the divine instrument chosen to execute that judgment. We will find that Jehu illustrates how zealous an unconverted man can be for God when it suits his personal interests and ambitions to attack national evils. What he did on behalf of righteousness, he did well and with energy, but his zeal was carnal. He utterly destroyed Baal but permitted the golden calves to remain. This fact alone shows that his heart was a stranger to divine faith. He was an instrument of God's wrath, carrying out God's will, at least in the destruction of Ahab and his family, but he never had a personal knowledge of God. So now, the second part of Elijah's prophecy that was given years earlier, concerning the anointing of Jehu as king over Israel, came to pass (I Ki. 19:16).

HIS PEOPLE?

Verse 2 of this passage proclaims the fact that secrecy was of extreme importance lest Joram should get knowledge of what was happening and prepare himself for resistance. Had he not been taken by surprise, the result might have been a long, bloody, civil war.

The conference with Jehu was to be inside closed doors so that no one would see or hear what took place. Then the messenger was to leave instantly. All of this was according to the directions of the Lord given to Elisha.

Even though Israel was in a sad state spiritually, the Lord still longingly referred to them as His people.

What Jehu was commissioned to do was plainly a command and not a prophecy. Jehu was expressly ordered by God to smite and to utterly destroy the whole house of Ahab. In fact, Elijah had prophesied many years before of the awful end of Jezebel (I Ki. 21:23).

The sudden appearance and disappearance then of the messenger who spoke to Jehu had evidently created an impression that all was not well.

Jehu then revealed to the others present what the young prophet had said to him.

THE WORD FROM THE LORD

Elisha the prophet is the central figure in this historical drama. He had received a word from the Lord that a new dynasty, that of Jehu, was to be raised up in the northern kingdom of Israel.

Jehu had been in a high position under Ahab and had been pointed out to Elijah by divine revelation as the future king of Israel (I Ki. 19:16).

Jehu served as a commander under Ahaziah and Jehoram, Ahab's sons, and according to Josephus, attained such distinction that he became one of the captains of the host.

Incidentally, the Jehoshaphat mentioned in II Kings 9:2 was not the Jehoshaphat, king of Judah.

The young man, *"one of the children of the prophets,"* delivered the message, which was threefold in its application:

1. *"Thus says the LORD God of Israel, I have anointed you king over the people of the LORD, even over Israel."* They were called the people of the Lord even though they were in deep sin. This did not mean that they were saved but only that God was still dealing with them, attempting to bring them to a place of repentance.

2. *"And you shall smite the house of Ahab your master."*

He meant the whole house of Ahab. He would cast the dead body of this ungodly king on the very piece of ground that the vineyard of Naboth formerly occupied, thereby, attesting the fulfillment of the prophecy.

3. *"And the dogs shall eat Jezebel in the portion of Jezreel."* As we shall see, it happened exactly as the Holy Spirit proclaimed.

VENGEANCE IS MINE; I WILL REPAY, SAYS THE LORD

Under Ahab, tremendous persecution had been leveled at all of the true prophets of the Lord, plus anyone who served Jehovah. There was evidently a general persecution, not merely a persecution of the prophets.

The record seems to indicate that Jezebel, the wife of Ahab, was at the bottom of all the persecutions. Concerning this, Pulpit says, "Sometimes she took matters into her own hands, gave her own orders, and saw them carried out (I Ki. 18:13; 21:8-14). At other times she was content to 'stir up her husband' (I Ki. 21:25) and incite him to evil courses."

As it regards all of this, the Lord said, *"That I may avenge the blood of My servants the prophets, and the blood of all the servants of the Lord."*

In respect to vengeance, Paul wrote, *"Dearly beloved, avenge not yourselves* (proclaims action respecting fellow human beings), *but rather give place unto wrath* (speaks of God's wrath and means to leave room for it and not take God's proper work out of His hands): *for it is written, Vengeance is Mine; I will repay, says the* LORD ([Lev. 19:18] the righting of wrong is to be committed to the Lord)" (Rom. 12:19) (The Expositor's Study Bible).

WRONGED BELIEVERS

When we as believers are wronged, especially by other believers, the temptation is great to take matters into our own hands. However, such is never correct and always will fall out to harm to us. We are to leave all vengeance in the hands of the Lord. There are reasons for this:

- Even though we are the ones who were wronged, we only have scant knowledge of all the players and the procedures. On the other hand, God knows everything.

- Even if we take vengeance into our hands, how much vengeance do we obtain? Of course, we do not have the answer to that.

The Lord knows when, what, where, and why. To be sure, He most definitely will address the situation just as He was doing in the matter of the house of Ahab. The young son of a prophet did exactly what Elisha told him to do. He anointed Jehu to be king, delivered the message he was told to deliver, and then fled, again as ordered.

When the elders of Israel understood what had transpired, they immediately began to accept Jehu as king. This was a death warrant for Joram, who was then king.

JORAM

So Jehu the son of Jehoshaphat the son of Nimshi conspired against Joram. (Now Joram had kept Ramoth-gilead, he and all Israel, because of Hazael king of Syria. But king Joram was returned to be healed in Jezreel of the wounds which the Syrians had given him, when he fought with Hazael king of Syria.) And Jehu said, If it be your minds, then let none go forth nor escape out of the city to go to tell it in Jezreel. So Jehu rode in a chariot, and went to Jezreel; for Joram lay there. And Ahaziah king of Judah was come down to see Joram. And there stood a watchman on the tower in Jezreel, and he spied the company of Jehu as he came, and said, I see a company. And Joram said, Take an horseman, and send to meet them, and let him say, Is it peace? So there went one on horseback to meet him, and said, Thus says the king, Is it peace? And Jehu said, What have you to do with peace? turn you behind me. And the watchman told, saying, The messenger came to them, but he comes not again. Then he sent out a second on horseback, which came to them, and said, Thus says the king, Is it peace? And Jehu answered, What have you to do with peace? turn you behind me. And the watchman told, saying,

He came even unto them, and comes not again: and the driving is like the driving of Jehu the son of Nimshi; for he drives furiously. And Joram said, Make ready. And his chariot was made ready. And Joram king of Israel and Ahaziah king of Judah went out, each in his chariot, and they went out against Jehu, and met him in the portion of Naboth the Jezreelite. And it came to pass, when Joram saw Jehu, that he said, Is it peace, Jehu? And he answered, What peace, so long as the whoredoms of your mother Jezebel and her witchcrafts are so many? And Joram turned his hands, and fled, and said to Ahaziah, There is treachery, O Ahaziah. And Jehu drew a bow with his full strength, and smote Jehoram between his arms, and the arrow went out at his heart, and he sunk down in his chariot. Then said Jehu to Bidkar his captain, Take up, and cast him in the portion of the field of Naboth the Jezreelite: for remember how that, when I and you rode together after Ahab his father, the LORD laid this burden upon him; Surely I have seen yesterday the blood of Naboth, and the blood of his sons, says the LORD; and I will requite you in this plat, says the LORD. Now therefore take and cast him into the plat of ground, according to the word of the LORD (II Ki. 9:14-26).

DIVINE PROVIDENCE

Again, the Jehoshaphat of Verse 14 is not the same Jehoshaphat who had been the king of Judah.

As soon as Jehu was proclaimed as king, he addressed himself to the captains, denoting that he had the military behind him and proposed a policy in which he swore everyone to secrecy.

The object of Jehu was to surprise Joram and to kill or capture him before he could take any steps to organize a defense.

The idea of Verse 18 is that the messenger was not allowed to take back any message whatsoever.

Divine providence had so ordered matters that vengeance for the sin of Ahab was exacted upon the very sin of his guilt regarding Naboth. The mills of God grind slowly, but they grind exceedingly fine. In other words, the Lord misses nothing.

Whoredoms mean "idolatries," as so frequently used in the Old Testament (Lev. 19:29; 20:5; Jer. 3:2, 9; 13:27; Ezek. 16:17, etc).

As Joram was king of Israel, Ahaziah was king of Judah. Jehu and Bidkar, who had personally ridden in the same chariot with Ahab, had heard the sentence of punishment addressed toward this evil king as spoken by Elijah the prophet (I Ki. 21:17-26).

Because of Ahab's repentance at one point, the evil prophesied against Ahab had been formally and expressly deferred to the future days of his son (I Ki. 21:29).

ACCORDING TO THE WORD OF THE LORD

When Jehu became king of the northern confederation of Israel, he set about to do what he should have done, that is, to eliminate the family of Ahab, which was to *"avenge the blood of My servants, the prophets, and the blood of all the servants of the LORD at the hand of Jezebel."* In other words, he was definitely commissioned by the Lord to do this thing because of the terrible sins of these people, even though Ahab had been dead for some time.

Of all the terrible sins of Ahab, who was greatly influenced by his evil wife Jezebel, who, incidentally, was a Zidonian (I Ki. 16:31), the murder of Naboth by Ahab seems to have been the worst. The Scripture says of him: *"But there was none like unto Ahab, who did sell himself to work wickedness in the sight of the LORD, whom Jezebel his wife stirred up"* (I Ki. 21:25).

Yet, this evil man sincerely and truly repented after he heard the pronouncement of Elijah concerning the judgment that was coming upon his house (I Ki. 21:17-26). The Scripture says, *"He rent his clothes, and put sackcloth upon his flesh, and fasted, and lay in sackcloth, and went softly"* (I Ki. 21:27).

In respect to that, the Lord told Elijah to tell Ahab, *"I will not bring the evil in his days: but in his son's days will I bring the evil upon his house"* (I Ki. 21:29).

THE BLOOD OF NABOTH

Ahab's son Jehoram, while wicked, still was not as wicked as his father Ahab (II Ki. 3:1-3). Yet, in a sense, because of his refusal to repent, the Lord through Jehu took his life, with his blood being poured out in the same place where Naboth died, who was killed by Ahab and Jezebel. As stated, the evil prophesied against Ahab had been formally and expressly deferred to his son's days because of Ahab's repentance. Incidentally, his repentance did not last.

Concerning this thing, the Lord said, *"Surely I have seen yesterday the blood of Naboth, and the blood of his sons* (evidently murdered along with their father), *says the LORD; and I will requite you in this plat, says the LORD. Now therefore take and cast him into the plat of ground, according to the word of the LORD"* (II Ki. 9:26).

So, the body of Jehoram was thrown into the vineyard that had once belonged to Naboth.

When hands of hurt are laid on those who belong to the Lord, it should be understood that the Lord does not look kindly on such.

Barring repentance, the end result of those who do such things will be what they have rendered to others and more.

THE MILLS OF GOD

But when Ahaziah the king of Judah saw this, he fled by the way of the garden house. And Jehu followed after him, and said, Smite him also in the chariot. And they did so at the going up to Gur, which is by Ibleam. And he fled to Megiddo, and died there. And his servants carried him in a chariot to Jerusalem, and buried him in his sepulchre with his fathers in the city of David.

And in the eleventh year of Joram the son of Ahab began Ahaziah to reign over Judah (II Ki. 9:27-29).

From a spiritual point of view, Jehu felt he could justify the act of killing Ahaziah, the king of Judah. The commission given to him was to smite all the house of Ahab, and Ahaziah, king of Judah, was Ahab's grandson.

In fact, Ahaziah had reigned but a year over the southern kingdom of Judah.

The mills of God may grind exceedingly slow, but, as stated, to be sure, they grind exceedingly fine, meaning that they miss nothing.

THE DEATH OF AHAZIAH

Ahaziah the king of Judah was also called Jehoahaz (II Chron. 21:17). He was the youngest son of Jehoram, king of Judah.

He was placed on the throne by the inhabitants of Jerusalem as the sole surviving heir. His reign of less than a year was characterized by a close association with his uncle, Jehoram, king of Israel, no doubt, under the influence of Athaliah. He was murdered, as stated here, during the purge of Jehu while visiting Jehoram, who was convalescing in Jezreel.

The Scripture says of him, *"And he walked in the way of the house of Ahab, and did evil in the sight of the LORD, as did the house of Ahab: for he was the son in law of the house of Ahab"* (II Ki. 8:27).

JEZEBEL

> *And when Jehu was come to Jezreel, Jezebel heard of it; and she painted her face, and tired her head, and looked out at a window. And as Jehu entered in at the gate, she said, Had Zimri peace, who killed his master? And he lifted up his face to the window, and said, Who is on my side? who? And there looked out to him two or three eunuchs. And he said, Throw her down. So they threw her down: and some of her blood was sprinkled on the wall, and on the horses: and he trode her under foot. And when he was come in, he did eat and drink, and said, Go, see now this cursed woman, and bury her: for she is a king's daughter. And they went to bury her: but they found no more of her than the skull, and the feet, and the palms of her hands. Wherefore they came again, and told him. And he said, This is the word of the* LORD, *which He spoke by His servant Elijah the Tishbite, saying, In the portion of Jezreel shall dogs eat the flesh of Jezebel: And the carcass of Jezebel shall be as dung upon the face of the field in the portion of Jezreel; so that they shall not say, This is Jezebel* (II Ki. 9:30-37).

Jezebel looked out to see, but more so, to be seen. It would not turn out well for her.

The eunuchs who *"looked out"* to Jehu were probably the chief eunuchs of the palace, who had authority over the others and, indeed, over the court officials generally.

A CURSED WOMAN

There appears to have been no hesitation on the part of these eunuchs. The boldness of Jehu communicated itself to those whom he addressed. Jehu had his chariot driven over the prostrate corpse so that the hoofs of his horses, and perhaps his own person, were sprinkled with her blood.

Jehu called Jezebel a *"cursed woman"* not inappropriately:

- She had brought a curse on her husband, her sons, and on her grandsons, as well as on the entirety of Israel and Judah.

- She had been the prime mover in a bloody persecution of the worshippers of Jehovah, so now, she must answer to the Lord, and that she did.

Evidently, her remains were eaten by wild dogs. The prophecy given by Elijah the Tishbite some years earlier, and here quoted by Jehu, is that which is recorded in I Kings 21:23.

The fragments of her body were so scattered that there could be no collective tomb, no place where admirers could congregate and say, "Here lies the great queen—here lies Jezebel."

To rest in no tomb was viewed in those days as a shame and a disgrace. So concludes the life of this woman who had wrought such evil in both Israel and Judah. In one way or the other, all who reject Jesus Christ have an ignoble end.

To die without God is a death of eternal darkness.

THE DEATH OF JEZEBEL

II Kings 9:36 proclaims the fulfillment of the awful prophecy by Elijah the Tishbite, saying, *"In the portion of Jezreel shall dogs eat the flesh of Jezebel."*

Jezebel was thrown down, and the horses were splashed with her blood.

The dogs were turned away from the skull, while the hands and feet that had once designed and executed such abominations were without a tomb, but infamy perpetuates her memory.

Without a doubt, this woman was one of the most wicked used by Satan to bring tremendous evil to both the northern kingdom of Israel and the southern kingdom of Judah.

Jehoshaphat, the king of Judah, who was otherwise a godly king, played into Satan's hands by having his son Jehoram marry one of Jezebel's daughters, Athaliah, which proved to be a terrible leaven to Judah (II Chron. 18:1; 21:6; II Ki. 8:18). Regrettably, Jehoram turned out to be like the kings of Israel instead of following in the footsteps of his father.

The Scripture says of him, *"And he walked in the way of the kings of Israel, as did the house of Ahab: for the daughter of Ahab was his wife: and he did evil in the sight of the* LORD*"* (II Ki. 8:18).

So, Jezebel's long shadow cast its evil over Judah, which did terrible harm.

Now she died, unlamented and unmourned.

WAS GOD JUST IN ORDERING
SUCH AN IGNOMINIOUS DEATH?

Of course, the answer to that is simple: God is always just in everything that He does. The reason that believers are not allowed to avenge themselves is because the godliest of us, whomever that might be, cannot function from a perfectly pure heart for the simple reason that the best of us are flawed. God alone can exact judgment and order the sentence.

It must be remembered, of any human being, Jezebel had witnessed the greatest array of miracles under the ministries of both Elijah and Elisha. However, despite all of that, she still would not repent. She had opportunities to do so but instead wreaked untold murderous action on anyone who claimed the name of the Lord. The truth is, the Lord showed amazing patience with this woman by allowing her to live as long as she did. The judgment carried out on her was justified in every respect, and is always justified when carried out by the Lord.

Let all know and understand that those who set themselves against God, and who set themselves against His work and His people, in one way or the other, will come to such an ignominious end, whether in this life or the one to come.

One should look long and hard at the passage that tells us that there was nothing left but her *"skull, and the feet, and the palms of her hands."* The dogs ate the rest! The Holy Spirit says that her very corpse was treated as dung because that's what she was.

The sacred text closes with the words, *"This is Jezebel."*

Careless soul, why will you linger,
Wandering from the fold of God?
Hear you not the invitation?
Oh prepare to meet thy God.

Why so thoughtless are you standing,
While the fleeting years go by,
And your life spent in folly?
Oh prepare to meet thy God.

Hear you not the earnest pleadings,
Of your friends who wish you well?
And perhaps before tomorrow,
You'll be called to meet your God.

If you spurn the invitation,
Till the spirit shall depart,
Then you'll see your sad condition,
Unprepared to meet your God.

ELISHA

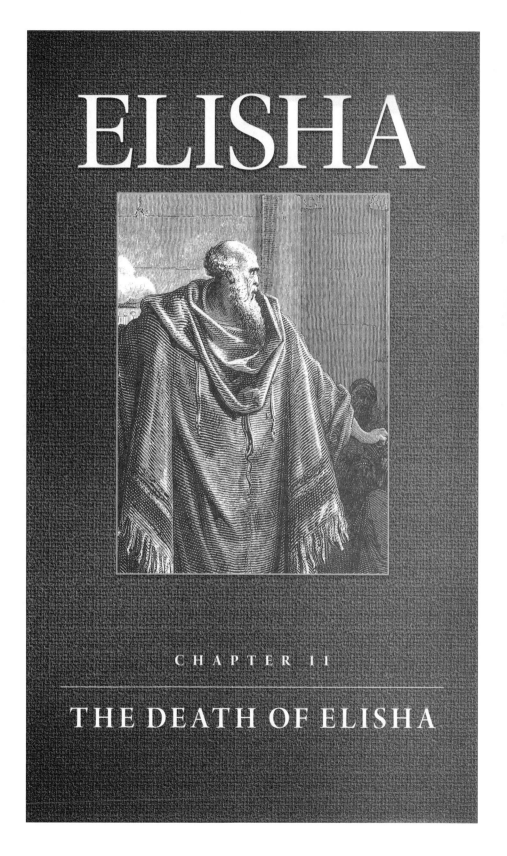

THE DEATH OF ELISHA

THE DEATH OF ELISHA

"NOW ELISHA WAS FALLEN sick of his sickness whereof he died. And Joash the king of Israel came down unto him, and wept over his face, and said, O my father, my father, the chariot of Israel, and the horsemen thereof. And Elisha said unto him, Take bow and arrows. And he took unto him bow and arrows. And he said to the king of Israel, Put your hand upon the bow. And he put his hand upon it: and Elisha put his hands upon the king's hands. And he said, Open the window eastward. And he opened it. Then Elisha said, Shoot. And he shot. And he said, The arrow of the LORD's deliverance, and the arrow of deliverance from Syria: for you shall smite the Syrians in Aphek, till you have consumed them. And he said, Take the arrows. And he took them. And he said unto the king of Israel, Smite upon the ground. And he smote thrice, and stayed. And the man of God was wroth with him, and said, You should have smitten five or six times; then had you smitten Syria till you had consumed it: whereas now you shall smite Syria but thrice" (II Ki. 13:14-19).

ELISHA PUT HIS HANDS ON THE KING'S HANDS

It is believed that Elisha was at least 80 years old at this time. His illness was probably the result of mere natural decay.

It is amazing how Joash, like the previous kings of Israel, knew of the worth of Elisha but still would not serve Elisha's God. Men love their sins!

Although not mentioned here, evidently, Joash at this time had sought direction from the Lord through Elisha concerning the threat of Syrian domination. The Holy Spirit evidently told Elisha what to do.

Regarding Elisha putting his hands on the king's hands, the intention, no doubt, was to show that the power that would be manifested was not the king's own power, but it came from the Lord, and came through the mediation of His prophet Elisha.

Why eastward?

The sun rose in the east, therefore, in this symbolism the Lord through Elisha was telling the king of Israel that if true repentance would be forthcoming, Israel's sun would not be setting, but rather rising.

The promise of total and complete victory over the Syrians had been given, but because of a lack of faith, Israel fell short. To the king of Israel, defeating the Syrians three times was big in his sight; however, the Lord was ready to give much more. How often do we fail to achieve God's best simply because we stop short of total victory?

ELISHA

Elisha's ministry lasted for about 66 years. The first 20 years appear to have been active years, closing with the anointing of Hazael. Then follows a long silence of about 45 years in which he once again appeared, but he was very sick and then died.

Some very dedicated Christians believe that true servants of God are never afflicted with sickness, nor can be, because all sickness comes from the Devil. While it is certainly true that all sickness comes from Satan as a result of the fall of man, still, due to the fact that we do not as of yet have glorified bodies, true servants of God, and even mighty prophets such as Elisha, ultimately fall sick and die of sickness.

Nevertheless, Elisha's sickness did not show a lack of faith on his part, just as sickness does not necessarily show a lack of faith on the part of modern prophets.

Elisha performed more miracles than any prophet in the Old Testament, so why could he not believe God for his own healing at the last?

THE ANOINTING

Many misunderstand the anointing of God upon one such as Elisha. The prophet did not use the anointing, but rather the anointing used the prophet. Men today make the mistake of trying to use God instead of God using them. To be frank, that is basically the mistake of the modern Charismatic movement.

Two truths should be noted here:

1. The few who truly have the anointing of the Holy Spirit can see this anointing used as God wills and not, as stated, of their own discretion. The Scripture says: *"But all these work that one and the self-same Spirit* (refers to the fact that all the abilities and powers of the gifts are produced and operated by the energy of the Spirit), *dividing to every man severally as He* (the Holy Spirit) *will.* (All the distribution is within the discretion of the Holy Spirit, which means that men or women cannot impart gifts to other individuals, or even use these gifts at will. This is the domain of the Spirit alone)" (I Cor. 12:11).

2. While the Lord most definitely heals, still, believers are not promised immunity from the decay of old age. That freedom will not come until the trump sounds, and every believer (with the sainted dead being raised) will be given a glorified body. Until then, regrettably, due to the fall and these physical bodies not yet being redeemed, we are subject to sickness and eventually to death—even great prophets like Elisha.

Some foolish preachers have made the statement that if Elisha, and even the apostle Paul, had had their faith, all sickness and problems could have been avoided. Such absurdity is not actually worthy of comment.

MY FATHER, MY FATHER, THE CHARIOT OF
ISRAEL, AND THE HORSEMEN THEREOF

The very fact of the visit of this king to Elisha constituted a very unusual occurrence. Normally, prophets waited upon kings, not kings upon prophets; therefore, Joash, the king of Israel, coming to Elisha portrays something quite out of the ordinary. Of course, Elisha was very sick and, no doubt, unable to go to the king, so the king would go to him.

At any rate, all of this proclaims the fact that this man knew and understood quite well the worth of Elisha. And yet, like his father before him, he wouldn't live for God.

When Joash came into the presence of Elisha, the Scripture says that he *"wept over his face."*

Why?

He also addressed the great prophet as *"my father, my father, the chariot of Israel, and the horsemen thereof."*

All of this shows that Joash knew of the worth and value, so to speak, of this great man of God. Knowing that, why didn't he serve the Lord? Most individuals who do not know redemption have no idea of the worth or value of believers in their midst, especially those who are greatly called of God; however, Joash did! Yet, he wouldn't serve Elisha's God, even though he knew Jehovah to be God.

No doubt, his place and position entered greatly into this. In other words, if he had turned to Jehovah exclusively and had done away with all of the idol worship in Israel, to be sure, there would have been a price to pay. Virtually all of his so-called friends would have turned against him; however, he didn't realize what he would gain by this move, which would be everything.

BORN-AGAIN BELIEVERS

At this moment, the power and strength of the nations of America and Canada are wrapped up in hundreds of thousands who are truly born again and Spirit-filled, who, in effect, are the salt of the earth and the light of the world.

However, I'm afraid that many in the modern church are presently losing the preservatives of the salt, so to speak, and the illumination of the light.

Jesus said:

You are the salt (preservative) *of the earth: but if the salt have lost his savour, wherewith shall it be salted? it is thenceforth good for nothing, but to be cast out, and to be trodden under foot of men* ('salt' is a type of the Word of God; the professing believer who no longer holds to the Word is of no use to God or man). *You are the light of the world* (we are a reflector of the light that comes from Christ). A city that is set on an hill cannot be hid (proper light will not and, in fact, cannot be hidden). *Neither do men light a candle, and put it under a bushel, but on a candlestick* (the light is not to be hidden); *and it gives light unto all who are in the house* (that is the purpose of the light). *Let your light so shine before men, that they may see your good works* (proper faith will always produce proper works, but proper works will never produce proper faith), *and glorify your Father which is in heaven* (proper works will glorify our heavenly Father, while improper works glorify man) (Mat. 5:13-16) (The Expositor's Study Bible).

THE STATE OF THE MODERN CHURCH

If so-called Christian television is to be a barometer of the church, and it most definitely is, then the situation is acute indeed!

I think one can say that there have always been three types of ministries in the world, at least since the inception of Christianity, beginning on the day of Pentecost. However, I think that the three types are more visibly portrayed presently than ever. They are:

1. Ministry without the Holy Spirit. These of which I speak do not even believe in the baptism with the Holy Spirit with the evidence of speaking with other tongues. In fact, they oppose it stringently. As a result, their appeal is mostly an intellectual appeal, and the truth is, precious little is actually being done for the Lord in those circles. Their churches are filled with people who have never truly been born again, and what few who have, they never really grow at all because of a denial of the Holy Spirit.

2. Hucksters. I speak now of the shysters and the
   hucksters who claim to be filled with the Spirit and,
   no doubt, once were. Satan has been very successful at
   polluting the true message of the Spirit by using these
   hucksters and shysters. In these circles, in whatever
   direction is taken, money is the object. Consequently,
   the gospel, at least that which is referred to as gospel,
   is for sale.

3. Those who truly love God. Then there are the few who
   truly love God and are trying to present the gospel, at
   least as they know it, to a hurting and dying world.
   Regrettably, this number is infinitesimally small, even
   as it always has been. Yet, in this small number, there
   are actually only a few who preach the Cross and who
   truly see the results that should be seen. If the overall
   number of this particular group is infinitesimally
   small, then the number that truly preaches the Cross
   is even smaller!

Yet, ever how small this group might be, it carries tremendous weight in heaven, so to speak. It is truly *"the chariot of
this nation, and the horsemen thereof,"* to use the phrase as
was used of Elisha.

THE HANDS OF GODLINESS

Even though the Scripture does not go into any detail, it
must be that Joash spoke to Elisha and related to him the dan-

ger from Syria. In fact, Hazael, the king of Syria, had made a number of incursions into Israel, with great loss to the latter country (II Ki. 10:32-33).

In response to this, Elisha told the king of Israel to take bow and arrows, and then to put his hand upon the bow. The Scripture then says, *"And he put his hand upon it: and Elisha put his hands upon the king's hands."*

By Elisha telling Joash to take bow and arrows, this let Joash know that the differences with Syria would not be reconciled—there would be war.

By Elisha telling the king to put his hand upon the bow, this was telling the king of Israel that he would be the one who led the conflict against Syria. Then *"Elisha put his hands upon the king's hands."*

THE CHARIOT OF ISRAEL, AND
THE HORSEMEN THEREOF

What a beautiful picture it must have been for the ancient and gnarled hands of the aged prophet to be placed on the hands of the king of Israel. He placed his hands upon the king's hands to make it clear that the victory would be wholly of grace and from God, and that it would be absolutely certain.

The faith, however, in the heart of the king, divided as it was between Jehovah and the golden calf, was necessarily feeble and moved the grief and indignation of the mighty heart of Elisha, who loved the people and thirsted for their complete deliverance.

As well, Elisha's hands upon the hands of the king verified the fact that the people of God in Israel (headed up by Elisha), as few as they were, were truly *"the chariot of Israel, and the horsemen thereof."* Regrettably, the king saw this only in part.

The truth is that when Elisha died, there seems to have been no one to take his place. Consequently, the downward slide of Israel continued until a little over 100 years later, they were destroyed as a nation by Assyria and actually ceased to exist.

OPEN THE WINDOW EASTWARD

Why eastward?

Actually, Syria was not really east of Israel, but rather northeast, and in reality, more north than anything else. However, Gilead and Bashan, both districts in Israel, which had been the scene of Hazael's (the king of Syria) victories, was eastward, but now the scene would be reversed. There was, I think, a greater object lesson than even that of the direction of eastward being specified by the Holy Spirit.

As is obvious, the sun rises in the east, which signals the beginning of the day. I believe the Lord was telling Israel through Elisha that day that if Israel would turn toward Him, their sun would not be setting, but rather rising. In other words, this scene before us here, with the king of Israel before the aged prophet Elisha, presents the destiny of the nation. Everything rode upon the decision of Joash at this time.

There are times of faith, which come to the hearts of every believer, that decide the future in one way or the other. Will it be one of victory or one of defeat?

I firmly believe that the Message of the Cross is that deciding factor in any life. Whenever the believer is privileged to hear this, everything is at stake. In reality, it is not something new but that which was given to the apostle Paul nearly 2,000 years ago.

THE CROSS OF CHRIST, THE DIVIDING LINE

In truth, the Cross of Christ has always been the dividing line between the true church and the apostate church. One can go to Chapter 4 of Genesis, which presents the first page of human history, and see that line that is drawn in the sand, so to speak. It has always been that way. The Cross of Christ is the deciding factor.

Martin Luther stated, and rightly so, "As one viewed the Cross, so one viewed the Reformation. If they opposed the Cross, they opposed the Reformation. If they accepted the Message of the Cross, then they were in the favor of the Reformation."

It has not changed from then until now.

I know in my heart that as the Message of the Cross goes out, if the major church denominations reject it, irrespective of how strong they may be numerically or financially, spiritually, the slide downward will accelerate. That goes for the Pentecostal denominations, as well, and especially for the

Pentecostal denominations. The Cross of Christ is the dividing line. It is the window that has opened eastward, that is, if accepted.

PERSONAL

Not only does it pertain to religious denominations, but it pertains to each individual as well. As the Message of the Cross goes out, our acceptance of it means life, while our rejection means death.

That's why Paul said: *"Examine yourselves, whether you be in the faith* (the words, 'the faith,' refer to 'Christ and Him crucified,' with the Cross ever being the object of our faith); *prove your own selves.* (Make certain your faith is actually in the Cross and not other things.) *Know you not your own selves, how that Jesus Christ is in you* (which He can only be by our faith expressed in His sacrifice), *except you be reprobates?* (Rejected)" (II Cor. 13:5) (The Expositor's Study Bible).

The prophet told the king to shoot, and the Scripture says, *"And he shot."* The Lord then said through the prophet, *"The arrow of the LORD's deliverance, and the arrow of deliverance from Syria: for you shall smite the Syrians in Aphek, till you have consumed them."* So far, the king had complied with the word of the Lord, but the Holy Spirit through the prophet demanded one more thing.

THE WAYS OF THE LORD

"And he said, Take the arrows. And he took them. And he said unto the king of Israel, Smite upon the ground.

And he smote thrice, and stayed" (II Ki. 13:18).

Why didn't the king of Israel smite the arrows many more times? Why would the Lord ask such a thing?

The ways of the Lord are not always understandable. In the natural and in reality, smiting arrows on the ground had nothing to do with anything. It was a test of faith. Above all of that, the entirety of the nation of Israel was at stake as it regarded what the king would do.

If he had smitten many times, this would have meant the total destruction of Syria and, no doubt, every other foe, even the Assyrians who would later come against them. However, that would be predicated on Joash giving his heart to God, thereby, doing away with all idols in the land and serving the Lord exclusively. Again I state the fact that the destiny of the nation was at stake. While Joash rendered a partial obedience, it was only partial. Consequently, the victory would be only partial. Ultimately, Israel would be totally lost and taken over by the Assyrians, which would come about in a little over 100 years into the future.

PARTIAL VICTORY

Most Christians, and possibly it can be said for all of us, have only a partial victory, at least at particular times in our lives.

Let me make this statement: It is impossible, and I mean impossible, for the believer to have total victory within one's life unless one's faith is exclusively in Christ and the Cross. It doesn't matter how consecrated or how dedicated to the Lord that one might be. I don't care who the person is, whether he pastors the largest church in the world, or whether he is the evangelist drawing the largest crowds. If his faith is not exclusively in Christ and the Cross, the very best that can be done in his life is a partial victory.

In some way, the individual will be taken over by works of the flesh (Gal. 5:19-21). With some, it will be the vices, and with others, it will be something far worse, such as self-righteousness or heresies. While all are wicked, and extensively so, still, the latter is most wicked simply because it is covered under a cloak of religion.

Everyone knows that the vices are wicked and evil. However, the others mentioned, plus many we have not mentioned, come from the good part of the Tree of Life and, thereby, deceive many.

It must be remembered that it was not the drunks, the libertines, etc., as wicked as they were, who crucified Christ, but rather the religious leaders of that day. In other words, self-righteousness crucified Christ.

ESTABLISHING THEIR OWN RIGHTEOUSNESS

Listen again to Paul:

For they being ignorant of God's righteousness (spells the story not only of ancient Israel, but almost the entirety of the world, and for all time; 'God's righteousness' is that which is afforded by Christ and received by exercising faith in Him and what He did for us at the Cross. It was all on our behalf; Israel's ignorance was willful!), *and going about to establish their own righteousness* (the case of anyone who attempts to establish righteousness by any method other than faith in Christ and the Cross), *have not submitted themselves unto the righteousness of God* (God's righteousness is ensconced in Christ and what He did for us at the Cross) (Rom. 10:3) (The Expositor's Study Bible).

JESUS ADDRESSED THIS PERSONALLY

"Verily I say unto you, That the publicans and the harlots go into the kingdom of God before you (He said this to their faces and before the people; He could not have insulted them more, putting them beneath publicans, whom they considered to be traitors, and harlots)" (Mat. 21:31).

To be sure, Jesus was definitely not condoning harlotry or fraud, but He was merely stating that these individuals knew that what they were doing was wrong, and some of them would repent. However, as it regarded the religious leaders of Israel, in their self-righteousness, they would not repent. In fact, they crucified the Lord of glory, which was the most dastardly crime ever perpetrated by any person or group of people.

Without one's faith exclusively in the Cross of Christ, at least according to the light the person has, such a believer (if one is to refer to himself as such) will fall into one of two categories—either vice or unbelief.

Total victory in Christ, and we speak of victory over the world, the flesh, and the Devil, can be brought about only by the believer placing his faith exclusively in Christ and what Christ has done for us at the Cross (Rom. 6:1-14; I Cor. 1:17-18, 21, 23; 2:2; Gal., Chpt. 5; 6:14; Col. 2:10-15).

THE ANGER OF THE LORD?

The Scripture says that Elisha was angry with the king because he said to him, *"You should have smitten five or six times; then had you smitten Syria till you had consumed it: whereas now you shall smite Syria but thrice."*

I think one can say without fear of contradiction, at least in the setting described here, that when the man of God grows angry because of the faithlessness of someone else, God does the same.

Only the Lord knows what hinged on the action of the king at this time.

Had he smitten the ground any number of times, at least double or triple what he did, there is a possibility that it could have changed the entirety of the future for the nation of Israel.

In other words, they may not have been taken captive by the Assyrians a little over 100 years from this particular time. Of course, that is only speculation, but we do know that the Holy Spirit was not pleased at all with the action of the king, which played out to faithlessness.

One cannot say that this king did not have any faith at all. He knew of the power of God through Elisha, but as far as him having faith in God, as an unbeliever, that was not possible.

So, what he did was simply at the behest of the prophet, in whom he did have some confidence. However, not understanding spiritual things, it seems that his patience had worn a little thin with the strange things that Elisha had told him to do.

THE REASONING OF THE MIND

He, no doubt, reasoned in his mind as to what good it would do to open the window eastward and shoot an arrow at nothing.

Then, the request by the prophet that he should smite the ground with the arrows, no doubt, seemed nonsensical to Joash. So, he smote only three times.

There is no evidence that Elisha told him the significance of these things before they were done. It just seems that he simply told him what to do without any explanation.

Once again, we come back to the partial victory. Due to the faithlessness of this king, Israel would not defeat Syria as the Lord desired that they be defeated and, in fact, could have been defeated. Joash went away with the promise that Syria would be defeated three times, and so they were.

However, the truth is, they could have been defeated to such an extent that they would not have been a problem to Israel for many, many years, and possibly forever, but Joash lacked the faith.

We can understand this king doing what he did—he did not know the Lord, did not serve the Lord, and, thereby, did not trust the Lord. However, believers have no excuse.

How many of us settle for a partial victory? The Lord, I think, is put out with half measures. He desires that His children walk in total victory—victory over the world, the flesh, and the Devil—and without reservation.

That is what the Holy Spirit intends and desires, and that should be what we intend and desire. Half measures are not sufficient as it regards this walk before the Lord.

THE CROSS OF CHRIST

Once again, allow me to state the truth. It is impossible for the believer to walk in victory, and we mean perpetual victory, without his faith being exclusively in Christ and the Cross and nothing else.

It is not so much what we do, but rather what we believe. To be sure, what we believe must be Christ and Him crucified (I Cor. 1:23).

The whole Christian experience is wrapped up in Christ and His work on the Cross. While anything and everything that Christ did was of utmost significance, still, it was the Cross that brought victory to the child of God, and it was the Cross alone.

Paul said, *"For the preaching of the Cross is to them who perish foolishness; but unto us who are saved it is the power of God"* (I Cor. 1:18).

HOW IS THE PREACHING OF THE
CROSS THE POWER OF GOD?

To be sure, there was no power in that wooden beam, which should be obvious. As well, there was no power in death. So, where is the power?

The power is ensconced totally and completely in the Holy Spirit (Acts 1:8; Rom. 8:1-11). The idea is that the Holy Spirit works entirely within the framework of the finished work of Christ.

In other words, it is the Cross of Christ that has given and does give the Holy Spirit the legal right to do all the things that He does. Before the Cross, the Holy Spirit was limited as to what He could do for and with believers.

The reason was that animal blood was woefully insufficient. It simply could not take away the sin debt of mankind (Heb. 10:4). However, when Jesus died on the Cross, thereby, atoning for all sin, this opened the door for the Holy Spirit to come into the hearts and lives of all believers. This is done immediately at conversion, and He abides there permanently, one might say forever (Jn. 14:16-17).

Therefore, if the believer wants the power of the Holy Spirit operative within his heart and life on a perpetual basis, his faith must be entirely within the finished work of Christ, i.e., the Cross of Christ.

THE LAW OF THE SPIRIT OF LIFE IN CHRIST JESUS

Listen to Paul:

For the law (that which we are about to give is a law of God devised by the Godhead in eternity past [I Pet. 1:18-20]; this law, in fact, is 'God's prescribed order of victory') *of the Spirit* (Holy Spirit, i.e., 'the way the Spirit works') of life (all life comes from Christ but through the Holy Spirit [Jn. 16:13-14]) *in Christ Jesus* (anytime Paul uses this term or one of its derivatives, he is, without fail, referring to what Christ did at the Cross, which makes this 'life' possible) *has made me free* (given me total victory) *from the law of sin and death* (these are the two most powerful laws in the universe; the 'law of the Spirit of life in Christ Jesus' alone is stronger than the 'law of sin and death'; this means that if the believer attempts to live for God by any manner other than faith in Christ and the Cross, he is doomed to failure) (Rom. 8:2) (The Expositor's Study Bible).

The sad truth is that most of the church has no idea how the Holy Spirit works. In fact, most Christians simply take the Holy Spirit for granted. Consequently, they see precious few results of His work and action within their hearts and lives.

As a result, most Christians live a life of defeat in one way or the other.

While the Bible does not teach sinless perfection, it most definitely does teach, however, that sin shall not have dominion over us (Rom. 6:14).

THE DOMINION OF SIN

What did Paul mean when he said, *"For sin shall not have dominion over you: for you are not under the law, but under grace?"* (Rom. 6:14). First of all, he was speaking of the sin nature. He was telling us that if our faith is exclusively in Christ and the Cross, even as he explains to us in Romans 6:3-5, then the sin nature will not have dominion over us.

Due to the fact that most Christians little understand the Cross of Christ as it refers to our sanctification, in other words, how we live for God on a daily basis, the sin nature, in fact, rules in one way or the other in most Christians.

This means that there is something in one's life, such as an uncontrollable temper, lust, jealousy, envy, etc., that actually rules that person. It may not be one of these particular things, but it very well could be heresy, meaning that a believer has accepted false doctrine in one way or the other. At any rate, it is the sin nature dominating the individual.

There is only one answer for this, as we have stated, and that is faith in Christ and what Christ has done for us at the Cross (Rom. 6:1-14).

THE LAST GREAT MIRACLE

"And Elisha died, and they buried him. And the bands of the Moabites invaded the land at the coming in of the year. And it came to pass, as they were burying a man, that, behold, they spied a band of men; and they cast the

man into the sepulchre of Elisha: and when the man was let down, and touched the bones of Elisha, he revived, and stood up on his feet" (II Ki. 13:20-21).

Jerome says that the place of Elisha's sepulchre was near Samaria. According to Josephus, his funeral was magnificent.

This was the final miracle attributed to Elisha, even though he was now dead.

This last miracle fulfilled the promise of God in that his ministry numbered twice as many miracles as Elijah's, and some were twice as great. So, the double portion held true, even to the very end (II Ki. 2:9-10).

The Word of God cannot fail.

THE DOUBLE PORTION

When Elisha died, he was actually one miracle short of having exactly double the miracles that the Lord had given to Elijah.

Perhaps Israel, in her disconcerted spiritual state, did not think of this, and probably didn't even care, but to be sure, the Lord did not forget.

The numbers have varied, but some have claimed that the Holy Spirit performed 16 miracles through Elijah. When Elisha died, they say that he had only seen 31 miracles, one short of the double portion; however, God's Word cannot fall to the ground, even as we shall see.

When Elisha asked for a double portion of Elijah's power and anointing, it is doubtful that he actually himself knew that for which he had asked (II Ki. 2:9), but the Lord, of course, knew exactly what he meant.

That's exactly what happened. Elisha's ministry, in every respect, functioned on the premise of this double portion. As there was a double portion of the miracles, there was also a double portion of judgment, etc.

Undoubtedly, there were some who were close to Elisha, who knew of the number of miracles performed by the great prophet.

As well, they very well must have wondered about the one miracle they were lacking, but now, Elisha was dead, and how could it be fulfilled?

AND ELISHA DIED

The Scripture says, *"And Elisha died, and they buried him."* Thus died one of the greatest men of God who ever lived.

One day every child of God who has ever lived will ultimately have the pleasure in the portals of glory of discussing these events contained in the Word of God as it concerns this great prophet. However, with the body of Elisha being placed into the tomb, his great faith must record one more miracle.

It was possibly some months later, perhaps even a year or two. The Scripture says, *"And the bands of the Moabites invaded the land at the coming in of the year."*

One of their party had been killed, and they were in the process of burying him.

They then were surprised by a band of men, which meant they couldn't finish the task.

One of them spied the sepulchre of Elisha. No doubt, they did not know it was the sepulchre of Elisha and possibly had scant knowledge of the great prophet, if any at all.

At any rate, when they hurriedly rolled back the stone that covered the mouth of the tomb and let down this man, his corpse *"touched the bones of Elisha."*

When this happened, the power of God, which was still resident within the remains of Elisha, flowed into the body of that Moabite, and the Scripture says he *"stood up on his feet."* Thus finished out the double portion and the ministry of Elisha exactly as the Lord had promised.

I wonder what impact all of this had upon this heathen Moabite?

He leads me, O blessed thought!
O words with heavenly comfort fraught!
Whatever I do, wherever I be,
Still 'tis God's hand that leads me.

Sometimes 'mid scenes of deepest gloom,
Sometimes where Eden's bowers bloom,
By waters still, over troubled sea,
Still 'tis His hand that leads me!

Lord, I would clasp Your hand in mine,
Nor ever murmur nor repine,
Content, whatever lot I see,
Since 'tis my God who leads me!

And when my task on earth is done,
When by Your grace, the victory's won,
Even death's cold wave I will not flee,
Since God ever leads me.

REFERENCES

CHAPTER 3

H.D.M. Spence, The Pulpit Commentary: II Kings 3:20, Eerdmans Publishing Company, Grand Rapids, 1978.

CHAPTER 5

Kenneth S. Wuest, Wuest's Word Studies in the Greek New Testament: II Timothy 4:5, Eerdmans Publishing Company, Grand Rapids, 1942.

CHAPTER 6

H.D.M. Spence, The Pulpit Commentary: II Kings 5:15, Eerdmans Publishing Company, Grand Rapids, 1978.

George Williams, William's Complete Bible Commentary, Kregel Publications, Grand Rapids, 1994 , Pg. 1054.

CHAPTER 7

Arthur W. Pink, Gleanings in Exodus, Sovereign Grace Publishers, Lafayette, 2002, Pg. 118.

CHAPTER 10

H.D.M. Spence, The Pulpit Commentary: II Kings 9:7, Eerdmans Publishing Company, Grand Rapids, 1978.

CHAPTER 11

H.D.M. Spence, The Pulpit Commentary: II Kings 13:20, Eerdmans Publishing Company, Grand Rapids, 1978.

ABOUT EVANGELIST JIMMY SWAGGART

The Rev. Jimmy Swaggart is a Pentecostal evangelist whose anointed preaching and teaching has drawn multitudes to the Cross of Christ since 1955.

As an author, he has written more than 50 books, commentaries, study guides, and The Expositor's Study Bible, which has sold more than 2.5 million copies.

As an award-winning musician and singer, Brother Swaggart has recorded more than 50 gospel albums and sold nearly 16 million recordings worldwide.

For more than six decades, Brother Swaggart has channeled his preaching and music ministry through multiple media venues including print, radio, television and the Internet.

In 2010, Jimmy Swaggart Ministries launched its own cable channel, SonLife Broadcasting Network, which airs 24 hours a day to a potential viewing audience of more than 1 billion people around the globe.

Brother Swaggart also pastors Family Worship Center in Baton Rouge, Louisiana, the church home and headquarters of Jimmy Swaggart Ministries.

Jimmy Swaggart Ministries materials can be found at **www.jsm.org**.

CHARACTERS OF THE BIBLE
A COLLECTION BY JIMMY SWAGGART

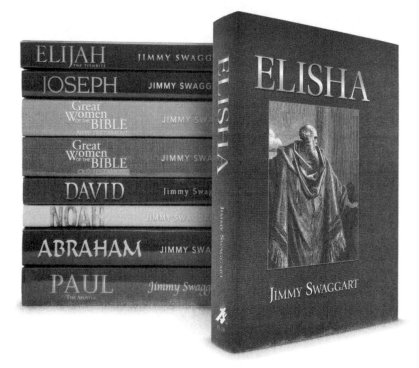

(09-119)	ABRAHAM	(09-121)	GREAT WOMEN OF THE BIBLE: NEW TESTAMENT
(09-117)	DAVID	(09-120)	GREAT WOMEN OF THE BIBLE: OLD TESTAMENT
(09-128)	ELIJAH	(09-124)	JOSEPH
(09-134)	ELISHA	(09-118)	NOAH
		(09-108)	PAUL, THE APOSTLE

START YOUR COLLECTION TODAY
FIND THEM AT SHOPJSM.ORG